T0067201

THE MYSTIC'S MAP

A GUIDE TO THE SPIRITUAL JOURNEY

Rev. Carol Bodeau, PhD

BALBOA
PRESS

A DIVISION OF HAY HOUSE

Balboa Press books may be ordered through booksellers or by contacting:

Balboa Press
A Division of Hay House
1663 Liberty Drive
Bloomington, IN 47403
www.balboapress.com
1 (877) 407-4847

Print information available on the last page.

ISBN: 978-1-5043-7558-0 (sc)
ISBN: 978-1-5043-7559-7 (e)

Balboa Press rev. date: 03/21/2017

With deep appreciation to all the teachers, companions, and guides who have shared my own journey.

Table of Contents

Introduction

Welcome to a new world! As the 21st century dawns, the "new age" is truly upon us. As spiritual beings, we are waking up to a much greater sense of who we are. The experience of going on a "mystical journey" is becoming more and more commonplace, even mainstream. Once the purview of saints and hermits, the mystical journey has become a staple of popular culture. There is a wealth of information available—in bookstores, on cable TV, on the internet—about a wide range of mystical subjects. You can easily delve into topics such as angels, aliens, telepathy, mediumship, past lives, and any number of other psychic, spiritual, and metaphysical subjects. More and more people now feel called to live their lives, and commit their personal relationships and work time, to spiritual purposes that are part of this greater movement. It is exciting, engaging, and inspiring.

And it can also be intimidating, and overwhelming. The tidal wave of mystical information that has flooded the marketplace brings both blessings and challenges. And many of us were trained by a previous, less mystical era, so we have to search for the right guidance, the right helpers, the right traditions, to match our unique personality, gifts, and interests. How do you know whom to ask for answers to the innumerable questions that are coming up for you, and for us all? How do we know which traditions suit us best, or which paths to take in pursuing our dream of being part of the transformation of the world?

For many of us, right alongside the excitement, the curiosity, and the enthusiasm of the spiritual journey, we can find uncertainty, frustration, impatience and even fear. It is an enticing, liberating path to be sure, but also fraught with confusing twists and turns. The spiritual path, as the mystics and sages of all the ages have made clear, is not a straight one. Instead, it is circuitous, curving back upon itself over and over again, inviting us to spiral deeper and deeper with each new curving, winding way. Somewhere along the path to what has been called "awakening" or "enlightenment," chances are good that you have encountered or will yet encounter parts of the road, or of your own inner landscape, that are misty or dark. It's also likely that, at least once or twice, you will feel lost. Perhaps you are at the beginning of the path, and wondering what is coming just around the next bend. Or perhaps you've been on this journey awhile, and have come to a resting place, or maybe even what seems to be a dead end. Just when we think we have the path figured out, it offers us yet another opportunity to expand our minds and hearts, by presenting us with something unexpected, something we may or may not want to experience.

If you have come to a comfortable place on your journey, you may be feeling curious and ready to explore next steps. You may have made peace with the uncertainty, or developed a willingness to just wait and see what happens. But still, even from this easier, more comfortable place, it's nice to know there are companions, and perhaps some familiar landmarks, along the way. And if you are in a place of discomfort or pain, you may be grasping for support and help to get through the next roadblock.

Of all the resources out there to assist you on your journey, how are you to know which books to read, which teachers to follow, which workshops to take, or which traditions to study? How do you figure out which path is right for you, at any given moment in time? One of the great mystical answers to this question, of course, is that *there is no 'right' path*, nor any 'wrong' path, either. In the world of mystical awareness, many teachers—including me—see dualistic evaluations like 'right' and 'wrong,' or 'good' and 'bad' as illusions. There is no path that is truly 'bad' for an eternal soul that is here to experience its own creativity. We can learn from anything, if we choose to. You are just exactly where you need to be, right now, on the path meant just for you. And you are creating it as you go.

And yet, some paths are easier than others, and it doesn't hurt to have a little guidance and companionship along the way, to help you avoid the really big pitfalls and potholes in the road. Hopefully, this book offers some of that guidance.

As an alternative healer, ordained minister, life coach and spiritual teacher, I have spent a lot of time thinking about the questions that come up on the spiritual journey. In addition to spending my entire life on this winding, wonderful road, I have worked with many people who are at various stages along the way. Some are new to the mystic's path, just considering for the first time that any of this amazing, magical information might be true. They are exploring possibilities they never considered before, but which now make perfect sense to them. They are asking if any of their own experiences match the stories and teachings they are hearing from friends, or from books, movies and websites.

Others come to me after years of exploring and expanding their own spiritual abilities. Some of them are simply seeking friends for the journey, while others have hit a major roadblock and are wondering if they've "lost it"— lost their ability, or their muse, or their inspiration. Others have realized that the pace of their seeking has slowed, and that the mundane world is encroaching on their magical path. From group retreats, to private client sessions, to conversations with whole congregations, I've learned that the mystical journey is never the same for any two people. It does, however, have some common landmarks that help us get our bearings, assess our progress, and inspire us to move on.

This book is about those landmarks. It's about some of the most common stages or segments of the mystical journey that I and my friends, colleagues, and students have experienced. Many of these stages happen in a somewhat predictable order, especially for westerners born in the mid-to-late 20th century. But, because the path is not linear, and because each of us brings our own unique genius to the journey, the variations are infinite, much like our souls. So while we can share some basic experiences, some common abilities or stages of development and growth, we must each find our own way. So this book is more like a map than an itinerary. It can show you some basic features of the landscape, and help you see how they might figure in relationship to one another. But it cannot plot your course. Only you, with the spirits of your highest self, your guidance and angelic help, can do that.

When I work one-to-one with people on the spiritual path, I am able to listen carefully to where they have already been, where they are now, and where they hope to go. In a book (which by its very nature requires a linear format), that sort of organic listening and weaving is not possible. Instead, I must offer these stages as if they come in a line. Each stage is characterized by certain qualities, or experiences, that may be familiar to you. And each stage contains within it the seeds of essential spiritual wisdom and truth. Though these (and perhaps many more) basic ideals are central to the spiritual path, and though they are often cumulative, building upon one another, there is no one right order in which to experience or claim them. You, the reader, must decide what the progression from place to place and truth to truth has been, and will be, for your own journey.

And, just as I cannot help you chart your specific journey by mapping it one-to-one with you here, I also cannot be the audience for your personal stories, which are so essential to you understanding your own unique path. In an office or retreat center, a teacher listens closely to the stories that may be making you feel stuck or confused, stories that might hold the key to hidden powers or inspiration you haven't yet uncovered. Because reading is a solitary endeavor, here you will have to be your own good audience. You have to open your own ears and heart to the stories that play in your head and body as you read. I encourage you to take plenty of time to process the questions, the exercises, and the meditations I have included. These are designed to mimic the experience of being guided by an in-person, third-dimensional, physical teacher. Your voice is as important as mine in the experience we are sharing on the pages of this book. This is not a "how to" book. It is a "how are you?" book. The point is for you to use the words, the ideas, and the stories I tell to explore and understand your own stories and experiences more fully.

There are some basic assumptions I am making here, and they provide the underpinnings of my explanation of the spiritual journey. They are interwoven in the text, but it's worthwhile to take a moment and name them right at the start.

1) I believe that we are eternal beings, that we have spirits or souls that transcend the physical body and this one life.

2) I believe that time is an illusion. Like our perception that the earth is flat (even though we know it is round), our perception of time being linear is just a function of the way we move through it.

3) There is a transcendent reality—called by many names (e.g. God, the Life Force, Love, Unified Field, Collective Unconscious)—which is in and of all things, and of which we are a part. We are all one within this transcendent reality.

4) We are made of energy, as is everything we experience and perceive.

5) Because of our energetic nature, we have access to the transcendent reality through the energetic part of ourselves.

6) Because we are made of energy, we have the ability to alter events and circumstances by using our minds, bodies, and emotions to change energy patterns.

7) Most of life—all the parts of it that are not direct contact with the transcendent mystery—is illusory and yet inherently beautiful, rich and valuable.

8) We have incredible agency in this life, and all events have transcendent value and worth, even the ones that from a human perspective are seen as 'tragic.' While pain is real, and must be honored, suffering is a human value judgement on temporary

and inherently illusory opportunities to realize transcendence.

9) We are the creators of our experiences. We create both through transcendent choices made outside of the material realm and through actions and decisions made within it.

10) We are co-creators together with other souls and with the divine reality

These basic beliefs mean a few things in practical terms:

1) Life is to be enjoyed, not a test to pass or get through. There is as much good/god here as anywhere and we are here to realize that.

2) We have a calling to encourage others on their journeys towards realization, because we are all one at this level of realization.

3) Though all suffering is illusory, we are nonetheless at our best when we are finding ways to transform it into states of higher transcendence (e.g. freedom, love, pleasure, abundance, health, well-being)

4) Because we are primarily energy, transformation comes not through effort or material work, but rather through recognizing illusion and realizing our transcendent Selves. This is done primarily through choosing our emotions and beliefs.

5) We all have equal access to realization, regardless of our circumstances. Circumstances create conditions which can be used either as obstacles or assistants in realization. Either way, they are moving us towards realization of transcendence. Honoring our circumstances, no matter what they look like, while being eager for new ones is beneficial.

6) Wholeness is greater than superficial qualities like convenience or expediency, so practices (such as meditation, yoga, prayer, etc.) that help us to sustain attention to the greater whole, and to our own transcendence, are valuable.

7) True self-good—i.e. experiencing our own transcendence both within and beyond this reality—is inherently of service to our fellow beings. My highest good and well-being always serves the highest well-being and good of others. Self-care is the greatest act of service.

8) There is no competition, no lack. The universe is infinitely abundant, though how that looks may, in practical terms, be different than our own limited mental expectations would suggest. Celebrating others' successes serves us all.

9) Each of us is inherently worthwhile and valuable as souls. We all have equal access to realization. Our circumstances are not a measure of our progress, but rather an indicator of the choices we have made to move us towards realization. Therefore, it is beneficial to honor others' journeys, regardless of whether or not they match our own journeys, or our expectations.

10) Worth and self-realization extends to all natural beings on the earth and in the multiverse, including plants, animals, rocks, terrain, weather, elements, stars and celestial bodies, star beings, and all that we have yet to meet. It's valuable to honor every single expression of life as sacred, transcendent and infinitely valuable.

These basic premises are the foundation of all the teachings I have learned on my own journey, and that I continue to share with others. They are expressed, in an enormous variety of languages and forms, by the world's many mystical traditions. Yet your own understanding of mystical truths—which by their very nature are beyond language—will probably look or sound a bit different, perhaps wholly different. That's a good thing, since no one of us can grasp or focus on all there is to understand in this vast multiverse.

My understanding of these truths which are beyond words comes from my own, unique experiences. On my own journey, I was forced to find explanations for mystical experiences in my life that began when I was a very young child. Family stories say that, when I first began to speak, I once asked my grandmother, "Grandma, do you remember when I was the mommy and you were the little girl?" So knowing that we are bigger than this one life has always come naturally to me. I come from a maternal line of psychics; my grandmother, my maternal aunt, my youngest brother, and my daughter, all have strong intuitive abilities. We have innumerable family experiences of shared dreaming, precognition of upcoming events, shared memories from other lives and times, and the ability to communicate with spirits, ghosts, angels, etc. In other words, in my family, there is a vast amount of mystical experience and wisdom. And yet this wasn't really accepted by the family as a whole when I was a child. It had frightened my mother when she was a child, and many in the family didn't experience it like I did. That meant that I didn't have much guidance for dealing with these gifts. So I had a number of experiences—visits from friendly and not-so-friendly spirits, foreknowledge of deaths and tragedies, intuitions about situations and people—that were frightening and hard to manage. This was hard for me, but was ultimately a great gift, because it forced me to go searching in a wide range of mystical traditions for answers and explanations.

My beliefs come from finding others—in stories of other religions, in the teachings of great sages and mystics, and through ordinary people I have been blessed to meet—who share the intense, undeniable mystical experiences I have had throughout my life. And because I have been 'talking with ghosts' since I was a child, I simply am unable to see us as anything but immortal. My ability to communicate with beloved friends and family who have passed shows me that death is a change of state, but not a change of essence. Because I have been able to travel across time—to the future and to the past—all my life, I am unable to see time as a solid force. Because I have been telepathic, and had more confirmations than I can count of my knowledge of things in distant places, I am very clear that space does not matter in our connection with one another. And because I developed and then healed a number of energy imbalances, and health challenges, related to my untrained energy abilities, I have learned that it is possible to manage energy in a way that allows us to heal ourselves.

We are all on the journey to awakening together, yet we each take a unique and magical path that no one else shares exactly. My path has involved learning the basic principles outlined here through direct experience, which has then been confirmed by the wisdom of many other traditions and teachers. I believe these truths to be fairly universal, but since each path is unique, how we know, and how we define what we know, varies from person to person. Knowing our own journeys, recognizing the patterns of the places we have visited, the experiences we have created, and the people we have encountered, is a way to chart our own course and choose our own destinations. Looking at where we have been, and understanding where we are *right now*—whether we are thrilled, confused, calm, angry, terrified, excited, or likely a mix of these things—can help us choose the next step. Looking back and within, we see more fully the outline of the magical, divine Self that we are embodying. And we are more able to embrace the divine, joyful purpose we came here to fulfil.

You are a divine emanation of the most powerful, sacred, magical energy this universe has to offer; we all are. And we are now, more than ever, able to recognize that spark of divinity within each of us, to nourish it and encourage it, and live it fully into the world. As beings who have come to this magical earth, we have chosen a path that is filled with wondrous challenges, beautiful mysteries, and amazing adventures. Let us each embrace the power that abides within and among us, and allow the journey to take us farther than we ever imagined possible. The mystical, spiritual journey is a never-ending one. There is no ultimate 'goal' but only the greater and greater awareness of, and expression of, infinite possibility, grace, magic and beauty.

May your experience show you that this is so.

CHAPTER 1

The Key

As long as there have been humans on earth, we have been seeking 'enlightenment' and transcendence. The world's many religions were created as a response to a longing to be freed from the limitations and challenges of human life. Each religious path has its own unique strengths and ways of focusing our attention, and each gives us different tools for the journey. The state that these paths seek is often described as timeless, egoless, beyond the fears and concerns of our normal lives.

Traditional Hinduism describes four basic types of spiritual path, also sometimes described as the four types of yoga:

1) Karma yoga: the search for enlightenment through action, particularly acts of selfless service
2) Bhakti yoga: the search for enlightenment through devotion, religious ritual and contemplation
3) Jhana yoga: the search for enlightenment through intellectual study and knowledge
4) Raja yoga: the search for enlightenment through physical exercises (asanas) and meditation

Many other traditions can be seen as related to these, and include similar practices and techniques. And it is generally understood that most of us will practice elements of all of these in our life, though we may prioritize one variety over another. Some of us may really enjoy practicing yoga or tai chi or another physical discipline, or meditating, while others connect with the divine reality through volunteer work, or reading sacred texts. For most of us, we will be doing these things in the context of our daily lives. Perhaps we are lucky enough to take retreats that allow us to focus entirely on spiritual pursuits for a time. And some of us may ultimately choose to devote our entire lives and careers to spiritual work, either on a monastic path or on a path of service.

Throughout history, spiritual seeking and mystical experiences have often been left for those few who are uniquely focused on spiritual pursuits, while average people focus on the challenges of mundane, daily life. This isn't true anymore, thanks to the conveniences of our modern world, which have given us all a lot more time and access to spiritual information. Given this shift in our global, spiritual focus, it's worthwhile to put the contemporary, personal spiritual journey into a larger context. That we are collectively experiencing a huge wave of spiritual talk, spiritual writing, spiritual television and movies, and spiritually transformative experiences in our own lives is no coincidence. For the last many years we have been hearing about the "new age," predicted for centuries, which is now upon us. It is a powerful and transitional time for the whole of planet earth. Though this planetary transition is complex and multifaceted, there are some simple things we can all understand about what's happening now on earth.

This time, according to many traditions and teachings,

is a time of shifting spiritual alignment for the living earth. As part of the life-family of this planet, we are called to be good stewards of this process, which gives the whole planet an opportunity to move to a higher level of consciousness. It was onto this stage that we were born. We entered as conscious actors in a drama that we are helping to write as we play it out. This drama involves helping all of humankind to recognize its own divine nature, and its potential for much greater expressions of love, beauty, creativity, peace, and well-being.

But even this story of where we are in the evolution of consciousness on the earth requires a little background explanation. Much of this narrative is outside conventional thinking about 'reality.' That the earth is alive, that it evolves in consciousness, that we are one planetary family—all of these are ideas that not everyone takes for granted. So let's start with a few basic spiritual concepts about the nature of reality.

First, I and most mystical teachers, rest the entirety of our beliefs and teachings on the concept that the world, and everything in it, is made of energy. We are not *really* real, in a material way. We, and everything we see, touch, taste, smell, hear and experience are simply collections of energy interacting with one another. We are made of motion, more than we are made of matter. This is the truth that undergirds all spiritual, intuitive, psychic practices. Because we are energy, the 'rules' of material reality can be played with, engaged with creatively. This means that we have access to information and experiences that are seemingly outside of the range of our material abilities. We can know things beyond the range of our first five senses; we can change material reality (the weather, our health, the outcome of events) through working directly with energy;

we can experience the larger reality of the multiverse well beyond the earth. We can do things that seem impossible. In other words, through working directly with energy, we have the ability to generate miracles.

In this context, our range of awareness and influence expands enormously. We can know things, and *do* things, which might to a non-mystic seem impossible. Though most people don't spend much of their time *noticing* this greater awareness, because it can be hard to manage so much information, it is nonetheless available to all of us at all times. And if we accept this idea of our potential omniscience, then we have to consider a second, more theological, concept. If we are all made of energy, and can communicate with all things in the whole multiverse, how are we related to what has been called God? From the perspective of the mystic, there is a direct union between the created and the creator. In fact, we are *part* of the creative force of the multiverse (no matter what you call it), and are collaborating with it directly. In other words, we are part of godde—and this is my spelling for that which is bigger than any name we can give it—and godde is constantly engaged with us in making this physical reality, using the tools of intention, emotion and energy.

But how in the world does that work? As the teachings of many centuries suggest, we create our reality both individually and as a collective, through our *feelings*. As so many have said: emotion is energy-in-motion. Our feelings are what mediates between our spiritual intentions, our mental beliefs, and our physical experiences. Feelings are like signposts along our way; they show us where we are, where we are headed, and how we might get to the next place on our journey. They are *not* us, per se, but are essential to how we move. Think about it for a moment: how many times has your mood affected the outcome of your day? How often does the decision to 'let something go' make everything else in your day, or week, or life, a little easier? How we frame our emotions sets the tone for most of what we experience; what sort of energy we put in motion determines what gets created out in front of us, in what we perceive as our future.

So, if I start my day angry, frustrated, or upset, the chances are good that I will increase my negative experiences throughout the day. At the simplest, psychological level, this happens by determining how I choose to act. I'm angry, so I might move my body more abruptly as I'm getting ready for work. I might choose a breakfast that gives me a rush of 'better feeling' energy (e.g. sugar, high calorie carbs, etc.) rather than taking the time to cook a healthy breakfast with the appropriate balance of proteins and other nutrients. I will focus my attention on what's not working: on what others are doing wrong, on how I'm failing, on all the possible worst-case scenarios. By the time I get in the car, I'm so distracted I don't drive as well as I might, putting myself at risk for road rage at best, and an accident at worst. If the process continues, and I don't interrupt it, I may have all manner of terrible experiences throughout my day. All because of the vibration of energy-in-motion that I started the day with.

From a psychological, behavioral perspective, it makes sense to try to find a way to get in a better mood before I start that day. It makes sense to do a little yoga and a little meditating, or listen to some music, or talk with a good friend who will reassure me, or take the time to pray quietly. It makes common sense to work with our moods to help us simply enjoy ourselves more, and to be kinder people. But the effects of emotion, of our energy in motion, go well beyond this immediate, direct psychological sphere. The general emotional stances we hold, and perpetuate, determine at the deepest level, our whole experience of reality.

As the brilliant and humorous Abraham channel, Esther Hicks, has repeated over and over, getting to a better feeling thought, getting to our highest emotional state, brings us to the doorway of our optimal experience. Abraham calls it 'the vortex,' the place where our wishes, dreams and highest intentions are all held for us, waiting to be experienced. Being in this *vibrational state*, rather than taking any particular material action, determines what we experience in our lives. This means that our emotions have a very long-term, less direct way of determining how things go for us.

The way this works is that what we might call *chronic feelings,* patterns of emotion that persist over time so that they become nearly or entirely unconscious, determine what we believe is possible. And this, in turn, determines what *is* possible for us. So, if I have had experiences that left me with a deep sense of disappointment in the world, and a feeling that my needs are never met, I may turn this into a belief like "I can never get my needs met in this world." Holding this vibration will ensure that, in fact, I never get my needs fully met. Because the multiverse takes our intentions directly, it hears this belief as "I trust that I can't get my needs met, and will now create proof of this belief."

The nature of energetic reality is that it returns whatever we vibrate out, using our emotions and intentions and thoughts as raw material. Like tuning forks that emit a sound which is quickly matched by others around it, we are senders of vibrations (emotions and thoughts) that are quickly matched by our surroundings.

But here's an absolutely essential thing to know: *this doesn't mean we should censor our emotions!*

Too often, mystical seekers translate the idea that

emotions shape our reality to mean that we should never think a 'bad' thought. They quickly try to suppress 'negative' thinking with positive affirmations, and get frustrated when challenging situations in their lives don't go away. This approach misses the point of how energy really works. Forcing ourselves to claim to be something we're not— happy instead of sad, excited rather than disappointed— simply won't work. If we are *feeling* sad, even if we try to convince ourselves and others it's not so, we are *emoting* sad. So simply mentally claiming a new emotion doesn't get us where we want to go. Instead, what helps is to be conscious of whatever feelings we are having, and making the choice to *transform* them to a higher vibration. This takes some time, and some compassion, and some persistence. And much of the alternative healing work available to us right now is about doing just that: finding ways to transform old energy patterns into newer, more beneficial ones.

So for the greatest joy on this spiritual journey, it helps to accept that the multiverse is made entirely of energy, that this energy connects us directly with the divine presence, and that through consciously using our emotions and intentions in a positive way, we can direct how our lives play out. We need to recognize the origins of our limiting emotions and beliefs, honor them, and invite something new to replace them through real, lasting transformation. This is not a mental exercise, though the mind plays a part in it. Instead, it is an *energetic* exercise which uses all the tools available—mind, body, heart, and spirit—to truly shift energy patterns that have become set in our systems. In this way, our 'negative' emotions become teachers and guides, helping us find where we are limiting ourselves and offering us a gateway to something more. Much of the spiritual journey is just this process: liberating ourselves from the limiting patterns of thought and feeling that hold back our powerful spiritual energies.

But if we look at the spiritual path as a process of letting go of limitations, we are faced with another question: why come here in the first place? So many people embark on the spiritual path only to become disillusioned with earthly life entirely. They become renunciates, wanting to leave behind this world of illusion for the more 'real' spiritual realms. If we're infinite, eternal divine beings, they ask, why bother with all the trouble and hassle of earthly life? Is there any reason to be here, at all? Of course, people have been asking that question for millennia, and none of us can really answer it completely. But it seems to me that, if we are indeed energy beings that are an expression of Source, playing in the world, we have come by choice. Not by another's choice, but by our own choice. We have selected this experience, this expression, for some good reason.

Some religions suggest that the purpose for the earth is to decide who 'deserves' to go to heaven. From this perspective, the earth is a place of punishment and/or testing, and we are here to fulfill some task or test set by another, bigger force. By contrast, the integrated mystical mindset tends to see this earth as a place of either developing or remembering our divine essence. And though both perspectives suggest that there is more than this earth for us to experience—that we are, in fact, citizens of a much larger reality—an integrated mystical mindset doesn't accept that the earth is therefore *less desirable* than any other place. It's my understanding that we came here to experience the creative process, the infinite variety of life: godde expressing herself in a material realm. We are godde playing on the earth for the sheer experience of it. And perhaps even to participate in the expansion of the divine presence.

But what, we must then ask, about suffering? Most religions were created (and are still being created) to deal with the question of suffering. Mystical approaches are no different. They, too, attempt to address the question of suffering, but choose to see it, in the words of the channeled Abraham, as "contrast." Pain and pleasure are relative states, often shifted and affected powerfully by emotion, and belief, and intention. Take for example the pain of childbirth: though I can attest from personal experience that this is very intense pain, it was in no way *unpleasant* for me. Because I had an attitude of great joy and excitement about the *meaning* of the pain, I was able to experience it from a different vantage point. The human mind likes to interpret things in a dualistic manner, but this is not necessarily the perspective of the energetic mulitiverse, in which all things are just energy moving around and interacting. The same has been true for me in moments of great loss. When dear friends have passed on—some of them in very tragic circumstances—I have experienced the same grief and pain that all humans have in these circumstances. And yet, because I see the world from an energetic perspective, this pain is easily transmuted into a deep feeling of love and abiding connection. The challenges we face, and the transitions we make as we leave this life, offer us opportunities to experience our transcendent reality. Seen through this lens, even great suffering is transitory and offers gifts or blessings.

We know from medical studies and personal experience that our attitude makes a huge difference in how we manage pain and fear. Going to the dentist, taking a test, washing the dishes: all can be made better, or worse, by how we handle our emotions—the energy we put in motion. The same is true of the larger suffering we can experience in this life. Happiness can come to those who have suffered great losses and challenges, while at the same time those blessed with lives of ease and comfort can struggle with despair and depression.

This is not to make light, in any way, of the horrible injustices of our current world situation. These are part of the 'negative' experiences we all came here to transform. Moving these imbalances out of our experience—our collective, global experience—is an important part of raising the consciousness and vibration of the whole planet. *These global instances of limiting energy patterns (like personal feelings and beliefs) are meant to be transmuted and transformed, as well.* By stepping back and *focusing on what is possible*, by turning our attention to what is working, we can bring greater hope, joy and light to the world. If we are energy beings, and if we have the power of godde within our reach, then we have the ability to shift the traumas and tragedies of our own personal lives, and of our world, and turn them into springboards for transformation. *But we don't do this by focusing on the negative.* Putting our attention on all the sorrows, the wrongs, the suffering, will only reinforce their existence. Instead, we can use our energy, our intention, and our attention, to bring more power to the good, the healthy, and the hopeful.

So, here we are, expressions of divine energy, acting in a material world that is mostly illusion, trying to figure out what we came here to do. And at a time when the whole of creation, the earth herself, is ready to move to a much higher level of peace, well-being, and creativity. It is in this context that we find ourselves on a spiritual journey, wanting to be part of this exciting, awesome transformation, but wondering "what next?" Where do you, and we, go from here? Whether you have an attitude of open, patient curiosity or of frustrated impatience; whether you already feel certain of your life purpose or are searching in the dark for some sense of meaning; taking time to reflect on the journey is worthwhile—taking a moment to pull out the map and get our bearings can make the next part of the trip more fun and powerful.

So let's begin at the beginning.

CHAPTER

2

From Spirit to Form

Birth: Setting the Stage for your Journey

The first, and most inevitable, stage of our mystical journeys here on earth is birth. It is the one thing we all absolutely share, though of course our experiences from that moment forward vary greatly, and even our births are highly individual. But we all, coming to the earth plane, must experience those first months of gestation, the hours or days of the birth process, and the initial shock of being separated from the divine unity from whence we come. What do you know or remember of your own birth process?

In general, the messages we receive during our gestation and first moments of life tell us important things about what it means to *have a physical body.* In other words, some of the most basic vibrations we carry about even being here on earth in the first place come from that time period. So, at the very beginning of our spiritual path, our first task is to create a physical body which will take us through every other step on our journey. We don't do this part alone; we do it in collaboration with a host of other beings who influence us: mothers, fathers, siblings, doctors, etc. It's important to start charting our spiritual journeys on earth at the very beginning, by looking at the circumstances and the energy patterns that greeted us when we arrived.

I have been told that I came early, and was quite small when I was born. Before I really took hold, as an adult, of my own spiritual journey, this story perplexed me. I was a chubby child, and have always been a curvy woman, so how did that fit with being an underweight baby? At some point, though, I realized that this energetic connection made perfect sense. I used to joke that I was born craving a burger, since my mother (like most women in her generation) was discouraged from gaining any weight during pregnancy. She focused on staying slim, and minimizing calories, rather than focusing on what we now think of as necessary, healthy weight-gain during pregnancy. That might explain certain metabolic patterns, but how, you might wonder, could that be part of my *spiritual* make-up?

If we consider ourselves energetic beings, and accept the idea that our very physical bodies are comprised of energetic blueprints set in motion by intentions, beliefs, and expectations, then our physical gestation and birth circumstances are like the basic, foundational framing for how we will express ourselves physically here on earth. In my case, the experience of a vibrational framework that focused on "don't gain weight' and "stay slim" and "count calories" was a *vibration* that was powerfully present during my soul's transition into physical form. All diets and exercise plans aside, only directly addressing and shifting that basic vibration, as it persists in my physical body and energy field, will change those basic messages. I will always focus on "don't gain weight" and those other silent, vibrational settings unless I change them at the vibrational level. I can look at all the struggles I have had with food sensitivities—essentially vibrational imbalances—as arising directly from those earliest messages about food.

So the basic context, the mood, the tone of our birth sets the foundation for much of how we experience physical life. Let's take a moment to consider our own experiences of arriving on the earth-plane.

Exercise #1: Remembering Your Arrival Here

Have you heard stories about your birth, or about the months of your biological mother's pregnancy? Was it an easy pregnancy, or a hard one? Did your mother work during her pregnancy? Take a moment to make a list (either mentally or on a piece of paper) of all the things you know about your actual gestation and birth. Were you born by C-section or vaginally? Did you mother have any drugs to assist the birth? Or did she have any other chemicals in her system (illegal drugs, alcohol, medications for other conditions)? Were you born at home or at the hospital? And if you don't know the answers to these specific questions about your actual birth, don't assume you 'don't know anything.' Consider what you know of the year you were born. What was happening in the world? What country were you born in? How old were you parents? What do you know of the circumstances of your family, or your mother's health? What religion was your family? What were the social or cultural contexts into which you arrived? And if you know nothing about your physical birth, and were adopted and know nothing about your birth family at all, consider what your *body* has told you about this experience. What sorts of impressions or conditions do you carry now, that you know are tied to that time?

As you think about the way your physical body was formed, what stands out as important to you? Sometimes, the physical condition our mother was in at the time of her pregnancy and our birth is extremely important, both energetically and physically. But the emotional condition of our family members can also be very significant. There may have been strong messages floating around at the time you arrived about the nature of this life, or about what it means to be human. Messages like the following can set us up for challenges as physical beings:

- The earth plane is dangerous, and full of troubles and trials
- Life is a test, and the punishment for failure is really, really awful
- People are inherently bad, or sinful; to be in a body is to be less 'spiritual' or holy than to be *not* in a body
- Bodies are corrupt, and will always tend towards failing us
- People can't be trusted
- I don't want to be here, I don't like it here
- It's a bad time to have a baby; I wish I wasn't pregnant
- We cannot afford this baby (this one sets us up for steady issues with self-worth and financial challenges)
- We wanted a girl/boy instead

Or, on the more uplifting side, messages of affirmation and vibrations of excitement and hope can give our energy a boost as we arrive:

- Isn't life wonderful! This is such a miraculous place to be.
- Pregnancy feels wonderful; I feel better than ever pregnant

- Life is a wonderful gift, a chance to experience so many great opportunities
- My body feels great, and I love all the ways it can taste and smell and hear and see and feel
- We are so excited this baby is coming
- We can't wait to see what a cool person this baby is going to be

Of course, most of us arrived to a mix of these different messages. Most expectant parents feel both joy and terror, excitement and constriction as they greet a new baby. There is no 'right' or 'wrong' type of birth experience, from an energetic perspective. If you are an eternal being who has come to experience the wonderful variety of human life, then your birth experience is not so much a "good" or "bad" start as it is the original classroom you entered when you arrived. It sets the tone for your basic concerns, interests, and focus as you shift from spiritual to material in form.

Just as our astrological chart describes the alignment of vast, grand cosmic energies we chose as the stage for our entry, our birth experiences set the scene for our personal human experience. Imagine yourself, a pure spiritual being before this life, chatting with guides, angels, the divine presence, and whomever else you see helping you arrange the story of this life. You had to choose the right stage, the right characters, the sets, the props, the costumes, and the lighting, to match the "play" you wanted to experience in this world. Once here, you have the opportunity to stay on the basic script you've written in advance, or do a fair amount of improvisation along the way (especially since all your co-characters are doing the same sort of creating, and may go off-script at any time). Your birth is not so much a 'blessing' or a 'curse' as it is a good guide to the sorts of questions you wanted to consider while you were here. Seeing it this way gives you power back over circumstances for which you may feel you had no control.

We might want to say about our births, "Well I had no choice in any of that!" But the energetic, mystical framework says that we do, in fact, have incredible power over our life circumstances. Because we are eternal, infinite beings, we get to choose the story we act out in each life. Taking this level of responsibility for our own life experiences is an incredibly liberating act. If you can begin your assessment of where you are with the basic assumption that *you intended to be here*, right here, right where you are, it's much easier to decide what you want to do next. In short, this attitude takes you from being a victim, to being the creator, of your experience.

From this perspective, all suffering can be re-examined, and re-understood, as a tool for focusing our attention. Once we stop insisting on valuing every experience as either 'good' or 'bad' and allow ourselves to see them all as just experiences, giving us the opportunity to get clearer and clearer about who we are and what we want, we are freed to make new choices in all areas of our lives.

So let's go back to that primal, earliest experience of coming into a human body. In my story, I chose a mom who focused on her body weight and on the need to be slim, as a primary vibration. Of course, this affected me psychologically, but it also affected me vibrationally. It set a vibration in motion in my body that made me not only cautious about taking in nutrients, but also made me sensitive at the most basic level to the quality of my food. Having chosen this entry point, I accepted, at least for a while, a psychological and physical framework that involved experiencing food as dangerous, and experiencing eating as something about which I need to be hypervigilant. This meant I had food sensitivities, eating disorders, and problems with my digestion and physical health.

But note that I said I accepted this framework "for a while." Once we can see all experiences as conditions we have set for ourselves on our spiritual journey, we have the opportunity to transform them into the blessings we came here to receive. I came here not to experience food as a *bad* thing, but as the amazing, luscious, wondrous treasure it is in human life. Having put myself through the experience of vibrationally rejecting food, I became much clearer about what I *really* wanted: to experience food as uplifting, and as a wonderful part of being in a human body. Purely energetic souls without bodies do not get to eat! What an incredible part of being human, and most of us take it for granted a dozen times a day. I came here wanting to not just eat, but to luxuriate in the sensual wonder of eating; not to be miserable, but to truly relish each and every bite of food that this earth-walk makes available. I might never have appreciated food at this level without the contrast of struggling with it first. On an even more global level, I came here with the intention of helping to transform the imbalances that have arisen in our food supply as a result of disconnecting from the land, which is our basic physical source and balancing point. Because of my own journey to reclaim the miracle of eating, I have had the opportunity to share this information with many people, and to help them to find more sustainable, healthy ways of enjoying food.

Looked at from this perspective, I am able to see my birth experience as a gift, rather than a burden, and my vibrational uniqueness as a powerful tool for transforming the world. Because the vibration of 'eating' was a big issue at the time of my arrival in human form, I have become vibrationally able to assess the quality of food through its vibration. I can stand in front of a pile of vegetables in the grocery store and select the ones with the highest, purest vibration of health and vitality. I can tell from outside a restaurant if the vibration of the food served there will enhance, or diminish, my overall well-being. And I can be a teacher about the ways we are all connected to one another and to the earth through our food.

So ask yourself this: what amazing teaching, or blessing, that you wanted to bring to the world, might be revealed in the uniqueness of your birth experience? I guarantee you that, like the clichéd diamond in the mud, there is a treasure in whatever challenges your birth situation brought you. Within whatever limitations or 'problems' were present in your body, your family, or you circumstances when you arrived here, you will find buried treasures therein.

Breath: The Meeting of Spirit and Form

The first thing we do when we emerge from the womb, no matter what our birth experience is like, is to breathe. And this one act, this one tool, is the most important of the whole spiritual journey. Simply to breathe is the greatest gift we are ever given as earth-beings, and it also the greatest portal we have to our spiritual selves. At the center of every sort of meditation and mindfulness practice is the breath. At the center of the yogi's asanas, and at the center of the hospital patient's potential for healing, the breath is the channel through which spirit enlivens form. Without the breath, spirit remains pure spirit, and form is lifeless. It is our source of *inspiration*. So, take a breath. Deeply, right now. Just breathe.

What do you notice about your breath? Really pay attention, without trying to control it, to how your breath feels in your body. Is it full and flowing, or constricted and fraught with effort? How deeply does it move into your body? Can you feel it in your limbs, and fingers and toes? Or does it stay just in your chest? Every breath we take is an opportunity to see how we're doing, spiritually, and to transform limits into possibilities.

Throughout many cultures over millennia, the baby's first breath has been treated as a mystical moment. In the modern world, this has become more of a medical experience than a magical one, but we are nonetheless awed by that first moment when the fetus becomes the newborn baby, when the child becomes present with us *out here*. That first sound, the cry that comes with the breath, is seen as a clear message that we have arrived, ready to express ourselves physically. And every breath of our lives offers another opportunity to take that first step over again; we can literally be reborn into human experience with each and every breath. This is the central truth behind many body-spirit practices, such as yoga, tai chi, singing, and bio-feedback. Think about the times in your life when you focus on your breath. As an athlete, a meditator, a musician, a hiker, a public speaker… in what ways does breathing affect how you express yourself, your spiritual self, in the world?

As a clinician and pastor, I find that watching how people breathe is one of the most effective tools I have to diagnose their spiritual and energetic well-being. If the breath is constricted, usually this means the jaw is clenched and the throat muscles are contracted, preventing full voice and expression; the chest is tight so that the heart is protected; the belly is not free to move, so the digestion is limited and ineffective; and energy is not flowing fully through the physical, emotional and spiritual system. Noticing where the breath is being held is the first step in figuring out where the greatest energy roadblocks have been set up.

The body presents us with wonderful metaphors for how we are managing our energy and spirits. Is the jaw clenched in anger, the mouth clamped shut to prevent saying things we 'shouldn't'? Is the throat tight with unshed tears? Are the shoulders hunched to protect a hurt, vulnerable heart? Is the belly hurting from experiences we just can't 'stomach'? All of these physical patterns are ways we constrict the breath. Open up these bodily positions, and suddenly we breathe more deeply. And once the breath is flowing more fully, our energy surely follows. When we breathe deeply, we have the urge to express our held emotions—our energy that has been prevented from being in motion. Fear of expressing ourselves, of calling out like we did with that first loud cry at birth, can prevent us from repeating the act of taking a full breath.

And so the breath is the key to getting ourselves back to full flowing, the key to reconnecting with our divine selves.

Take a minute to play with your breath, and notice what messages it is offering you about the flow of spiritual energy.

Exercise #2: Breathing

Sit or lie in a comfortable position. Place your hands on your belly, and allow yourself to simply breathe normally. Don't try to control your breath; just notice what it's doing. Can you feel it all the way down into your belly? Do your hands rise when you breathe in, and sink when you breathe out? Or does the breath stay mainly in the chest? Can you feel it equally in the back of your body as in the front? Do your shoulders feel tight? Notice what position your mouth is in. Are your teeth clenched? Are your lips parted, or sealed? What are your eyes doing? Are they shut, or open? Are they tight, or relaxed? Where is your body straining, and where is it at ease?

Now deepen the breath consciously. Allow yourself to drop your shoulders and sink into the chair or bed or floor or whatever surface you are resting upon. Let the in-breath be a little longer. What do you notice? How does that feel, to your body and your heart? Do any emotions, even very subtle ones, come up? Or do you have the sense that you should stop and 'hurry up' with some other task, something 'more important' than this? Do you feel a sense of comfort or discomfort as the breath deepens?

And what happens if you sigh, audibly? What happens if you make a sound? It doesn't have to be as loud as that first cry the baby makes, but it might be. Do you feel the urge to make a particular kind of sound, or do any physical or emotional sensations get stronger? Notice again if you are tightening any part of your body. Are your hands open and relaxed, or clenched? What about your toes and feet?

By noticing how our bodies are allowing or preventing full breaths, we can see much more clearly where our spirits are free to move and grow, and where we are holding ourselves back.

Many conditions or chronic patterns of limited breath are also effected by the quality of air, food and water we have available to us, so take a moment to consider what sort of environment you find yourself in. Are there ways in which your current circumstances mimic the space you came into with that first breath of life? Sometimes, we recreate circumstances that feel familiar, even if they are not the best for us. Also consider what habits you are participating in that limit your breath, perhaps as a way to limit your emotions. Smoking, for example, is a powerful way to cut off the breath which, if felt fully, would bring emotions we don't know how to manage. Similarly, asthma and other conditions can be exacerbated by eating foods (processed grains, sugar, chemical-laden products) that cause inflammation in our airways. Again, these all help us avoid our feelings by substituting false energy rushes in our system, but they ultimately hinder our ability to fully breathe and experience ourselves. I personally experienced asthma symptoms for a few years when I was living in an area that had unhealthy air. But dealing with the *feelings* about my circumstances, about why I found myself living there in the first place, was as important to my healing as physically moving to a new place.

The shortness in my breath forced me to consider a number of things. First, I had to ask, was where I lived a good place for me? Did it match my best vibration? Clearly not—it was a dry, dusty, polluted place and I couldn't thrive there. But, perhaps more importantly, I asked myself why my breath was short in the first place. I could easily have blamed second-hand smoke experienced in my childhood for 'damaging' me in ways that couldn't be repaired (in fact, I did just that for a good long while). But what I realized was that, while my lungs had been away from the toxin of the actual smoke for years, they were still pickling daily in my anger and negative emotions about the experience! My breath was short more because I was holding anger, grief and disappointment that I *associated with cigarette smoke*, than because of the actual smoke. My body had been trying to make new, healthy cells for years, but I was holding the vibration of all that pain and upset, and so it kept right on duplicating the shortness of breath. I was used to living in a toxic-air environment, and had recreated it for myself because it was familiar. I *expected* air to be toxic, and my lungs to be unhealthy, and so that's what I got. I found a place to live that had toxic air because my spirit and energy were calibrated to "bad air." My asthma was the doorway to accessing those long-held emotions, beliefs and energy patterns so that they could truly be changed, once and for all.

In a way, living in a more toxic environment as an adult gave me the opportunity to unpack the held emotions that were really limiting me. No amount of controlling my environment, my diet, or others' behavior could help me feel better until I cried, yelled, laughed, and expressed all that pent up emotion in my chest and lungs. Since then, though I will occasionally feel a tiny bit of tightness when exposed to cigarette smoke, I have not used an inhaler in over 16 years. It was compassion, for myself and others, and a good dose of forgiveness, which ultimately cured me of my asthma symptoms and allowed me to create a healthier diet and living environment for myself.

Food: Building a Body

Shortly after we take our first breath, we begin the second most important act of a baby's life: taking in nourishment. Our first months are all about building a body through taking in food, air, and human touch. And imprints to our energy field from early experiences of eating can have long-lasting impacts on how we allow ourselves to be nourished, both physically and symbolically. As my own birth story shows, early experiences with food often shape our relationship with eating for many years to come. This is true not just on a personal, individual level, but also for our cultures globally, as well. How and how well our mothers and families are fed, and how they feed us in turn, determines what we believe about food, and what we expect from food. These expectations then determine how we grow food, process it, purchase it, cook it, and share it with others. Take a moment to consider your relationship with food and eating.

Exercise #3: Eating

What is your relationship with food like? Do you consider it a pleasure, or simply a necessity? Do you eat home-cooked meals, or a lot of fast food? Do you know where your food comes from, what the sources of the animals and plants were? Do you like to cook? Think for a moment about whether or not you eat "deeply." Just as we can breathe superficially, quickly and in shallow breaths, we can also eat in ways that are quick, abrupt and shallow. If we eat foods with care, intention and attention—taking the time to savor them—they will have a different impact on our bodies and our energy than if we eat them mindlessly. Consider the following aspects of your relationship with food: (1) When you eat: do you eat regular meals, or sporadically? Do you eat first thing in the morning, or wait until your body is starving for nourishment? (2) Where you eat: at the kitchen sink? Your desk? Or at a nicely set table, in a home you love? (3) With whom you eat: Do you enjoy the company of others when you eat, or do you eat alone? Do meals with others bring you stress, or pleasure? Which people make it easy to eat fun, healthy food, and which people encourage eating foods that don't really nourish you? Do these people mirror people from your family or childhood? (4) How you prepare your food: Do you cook your own food, or only eat food prepared by others? Do you grow your own food? (5) Why you eat (or don't eat): To relieve stress? To fit in? To control your weight? To control illnesses?

All of these factors are important in understanding our relationship with nourishment not only on a physical level, but on the emotional and spiritual levels as well. Can you remember especially wonderful or awful food moments in your life? How might they be impacting your experiencing of taking care of yourself now?

One of the great benefits for me of being sensitive to my environment was learning which foods cause inflammation and which foods are truly beneficial to my body. Just as I had to un-learn some patterns around my breathing, and what energy I would allow to flow in through my breath, I also had to rediscover what healthy nourishment meant for me. I grew up associating food with love, as so many of us do. In fact, to a certain extent this is a healthy thing. Food can be a wonderful way to show care, affection and attention to others. Too often, though, it replaces more important expression of love and being honored for who we really are. At the same time, our culture sends all sorts of upsetting messages about food. Food is bad for us—it makes us fat, which makes us unlovable. Food is also a source of guilty pleasure, a way to prove our freedom and immortality. Food is medicine, and only careful control of our eating can save us from the terrors of a human body. Food is dangerous, and evidence of a corrupted earth. The list goes on and on. The recent epidemic of eating disorders in girls and boys, and men and women, is evidence that we as a community have gotten out of balance in our spiritual and physical connection to food.

I learned just how out of touch we are with our food when I was teaching community college many years ago. During one conversation with my class of young adults, we somehow got on the topic of farming and food sources. During the discussion, I realized that not a single young adult in the room of about 25 people knew that pickles are made from cucumbers. They had no idea that there was any connection between those two foods. And I was horrified. Having grown up in a farming community, it was unthinkable to me that people didn't know that their McDonald's pickles came from an actual plant that someone grew in dirt. But this sort of disconnection is not uncommon. As you travel the spiritual path, though something as basic as eating may seem terribly 'unspiritual,' there is in fact nothing so central to the spiritual journey. How we breathe, and how we eat, are at the very core of how we *embody spirit in human form.* To ignore these most basic actions as central to our spiritual journeys sets us up for significant energy blocks down the road.

Because I developed food sensitivities around the same time I developed asthma symptoms, the process of getting comfortable being in a body took many steps. I had to clear the imprints of second-hand smoke, and also the imprints of being raised in a culture whose diet is largely contaminated with unhealthy toxins and excess processed sugars. For me, eating processed sugars and grains—especially conventionally raised wheat—and conventionally raised dairy products, is just not healthy. And yet products raised in more old-fashioned, earth-friendly ways, work just fine for me and many other folks with sensitivities to mass-produced products. Knowing how our food was raised, how healthy the fields and farms that sourced our food are, is essential to our spiritual journeys.

Remember: we are all one, and that includes all those plants and animals who give their bodies to provide energy for our bodies. The law of Conservation of Energy applies here: the quality of life that those plants and animals experienced determines the energy that goes into their bodies. And this determines the quality of energy that food made from them puts into our bodies. Some of our most prevalent physical, emotional and mental illnesses in western culture come from ignoring the *feelings and vibrational well-being* of the creatures (both plant and animal) who provide our food for us.

What we take into our bodies—food, water, air—carries the vibration of whatever went into it. So if we pollute our water, not only do the actual toxins come into our bodies, but so does the vibration of all those chemicals we use in the filtration process to purify poisons out that should never have been there in the first place. Rather than drinking in the cool, flowing, wild, invigorating energy of a mountain stream, rushing down a hillside covered in vibrant plant and animal life, we take in water that carries the energy of concrete walls and metal bars, water that holds the vibration of numerous synthetic chemicals that have been removed materially (to some degree) but not vibrationally. When we eat meat raised in deplorable, incredibly cruel conditions, we take in the sorrow, the suffering, the exquisite agony of all those beautiful animals whose lives we have truly devalued. When our bread is made from grains grown in a field where poisons were poured into the soil, killing all the *life* in which that food was meant to grow, we are eating the devastation of a whole ecosystem that was destroyed for our seeming "benefit." Cheap food generally means cheaply-treated lives: plant lives, animal lives, human lives, and the earth herself.

This impact extends also to how our foods are processed and prepared. If our food is gathered by underpaid workers, who are forced to live in unhealthy conditions and whose lives are not valued fully, we are taking in the imbalance, and the despair, that comes with those conditions. When our food is processed in giant manufacturing-style plants, stored in giant warehouses, and travels thousands of miles to get to us, we are building bodies made of asphalt, diesel fuel, concrete, and plastic.

Once the food is in our home, we have some ability to shift or enhance its vibration by how we prepare it. How our food is cooked, how the cook *feels* while cooking, matters more. If we eat or drink foods prepared with carelessness, anger, resentment, or the intentions of a quick fix, or a quick buck, we are minimizing even more the actual health and value those foods can deliver to us. If we eat these foods in situations filled with family strife and tension, rather than with calm, grateful appreciation for the gifts of the earth and of our loved ones, we are building bodies and lives made of tension and upset. But if we choose to truly honor and thank the plants and animals who give us nourishment, and prepare them carefully with loving intention, we can raise their vibration and our own as well.

Consider taking the time to reevaluate your own food consumption. Are there ways you might make eating a part of your spiritual practice? Are there ways you can contribute to a higher-vibration for your body and your spirit by eating with more presence and joy? And I'm not talking about one type of 'diet' being better than any other. Each body is different, and needs a unique set of foods to fully nourish it. What I'm talking about is the *vibrational quality* of what we choose to eat. As we shift our attention and intention around food, we have the ability to lift ourselves to a new level of energy, which will then fuel our other spiritual projects. Just as breathing more deeply makes way for more energy to flow through us, improving the quality of our eating experiences provides us with higher quality energy to run through our systems.

Vibration moves through, among and within us with every exchange we have with our world. Our bodies, our very physical beings, are comprised not only of the substance, or matter, of what we take in, but also of the energy, or vibration of what we take in. There is nothing more spiritual than breathing, eating, and drinking. As the great Buddhist teacher Thich Nhat Han has so perfectly expressed in all of his works, it is in the simplest acts of life—eating, drinking, walking, growing food, washing dishes—where our spiritual journey is most deeply felt and expressed. So, no matter what else we may do on our spiritual journeys, simply returning to awareness of these most basic aspects of our lives as human beings on a living planet can transform everything within and around us.

If you do nothing else on your spiritual journey, become aware of how the vibration of your most simple, necessary, daily acts of taking in food and water for sustenance, and of taking in breath for life, are profoundly vibrational acts which impact every single living being that you are connected to. To bypass this in favor of more "spiritual" and less "mundane" endeavors misses the point entirely. We are here to *embody spirit*, and to do so requires honoring the wellness of the physical body as fully as we honor the elevation of the spirit. The two, in fact, cannot in any way be truly separated.

CHAPTER 3

Wonder

Childhood Wonder

The experience of our births and our first welcome to the earth plane sets the tone for our entire experience as both physical and energetic beings. At the earliest stage of life, we are pre-verbal, expressing ourselves mainly through pure emotion. Like very sensitive tuning forks coming into a cacophony of sounds and sensations, we are—to some extent—at the mercy of the vibrations around us. The good news is that, no matter what circumstances we arrive into, we have come as pure beings of light and energy, with an intention to experience the earth for our own upliftment and the upliftment of others. Though in some ways we might appear (and feel) like utterly vulnerable, helpless creatures, we are nonetheless powerful beings even as infants. No matter what experiences we have set for ourselves in this life, we have the ability and intention to make wonderful use of our time on earth.

In fact, most infants and young children have an advantage over those of us who have been here longer: they remember more clearly that they are part of godde. They have not yet been conditioned to think of themselves as 'separate' from the divine Source. They understand that so much more is possible, and that they are magical beings. Think of a small child you know, who still has his or her sense of infinite possibilities intact. Aren't they wonderful to be around? And what about that almost inexplicable, amazing feeling of being around an infant? They are completely miraculous! They pull us right into the feeling that miracles are possible, that life can be pure and innocent and perfect. This is one of the most amazing gifts of the earliest stages of life: direct connection with our true natures. Perfection, innocence, pure love, openness, possibility.

As we grow from infant to young child, we begin to project this sense of infinite power and possibility outward onto the world around us. We believe in the power of the larger people who teach, feed, hold and care for us, and we see the world with eyes wide open in expectation of the miraculous. We believe in things that older children and adults consider 'impossible.' In early childhood, most of us (if we are fortunate) are not yet jaded or cynical about the world we live in. At this stage of life, we naturally operate from the state known to Zen Buddhism as "shoshin" or beginner's mind. In this place, we look at the world as something new, something yet to be discovered. Rather than thinking we already have it figured out, and that we know what to expect from things, we are open to surprises. We are more comfortable experiencing and learning from that which is *unfamiliar.*

Coming so recently from the world of pure oneness and perfection, babies are predisposed to give full expression to their feelings, to let their energy flow fully, and to find things around them to be more perfect. And so a sense of wonder at the smallest things fills our infant days with openness and curiosity. It is this quality of beginner's mind, and the state of perpetual wonder it evokes, that we must retain or re-claim from our early childhood. From the infant who spends hours discovering her toes, to the toddler who loves digging in the mud, creating feasts out of dirt and water, to the young child whose favorite playmate is invisible—we are called to return to our innate sense of possibility, magic and hope.

Think back for a moment to your own early childhood— what do you remember of your own sense of wonder? What kinds of magic did you have access to in those days? Were you a child who loved nature, or the stories in books, or imaginary friends, or the seemingly infinite possibilities that growing up would offer you? In even the most difficult of childhoods there are moments of light, when the brilliance of life shines through. Take a moment to touch in with that part of yourself.

Exercise #4: A Childhood Memory

Take a moment to remember your childhood. Allow yourself to really feel what it felt like to be a child. If it helps, you can write down the details you remember, or draw them, or perhaps even make a collage. I find that just picking up crayons, markers, or scissors and glue can return me to a more childlike state. You might consider playing music that takes you back in time, as well. Call to mind a favorite place that you liked to play or rest, a place where you felt safe, comfortable, and at ease, or perhaps where you felt filled with excitement and enthusiasm. Notice if you liked to be in that place alone, or with others, and see if you can remember who you most liked to be with (either physical or imaginary friends). If you can, actually call to mind the sensations of this place: the

---

smell and the temperature of the air; the feeling of your body moving, sitting, or lying; the color of the light; the texture of materials—grass, rock, sofa, bed—around you; any tastes or other sensate impressions you have of this place. See if you can put yourself fully into the feeling, the *vibration*, of that place. Now imagine yourself doing whatever made you most happy there—reading, playing, drawing, swimming, climbing, running, dancing, talking, sleeping, whatever it was. Notice how your body feels as you remember this. Notice how your heart feels, and what emotions come up for you as you remember. Can you find the sense of wonder and possibility you felt then? Even if you can only remember a slight glimmer of this wonder, relish it for a few moments before shifting your attention back to the present. See if you can retain some of that feeling as you look around at your current world.

If you are fortunate, you have made it to adulthood with this sense of wonder intact. Whatever sense of wonder we carry in our daily lives is an incredible gift, to ourselves and to everyone around us. As children, we begin by *seeing* the world as magical. As we grow, in an ideal situation we begin to apply this perception to our own actions: we begin *doing* magic. So, in order to become the divine expressions we are meant to be on the earth-plane, we must be able to both recognize magic, and behave magically.

Recovering Wonder, Rediscovering Magic

This state of perceiving things without the residual soot of traumatic life experiences has been called "innocent perception" by intuitive artist Glenda Greene, who channeled the spiritual master Jesus. It is the ability to look at things and see them *as they are,* with a sense of simple wonder and recognition. This innocent perception in turn gives way to a belief that we have a place in this world of beauty and wonder, that we belong here. This wonder-ful world exists, and I am part of it, therefore I am also part of its magic. Unfortunately, too many of us leave behind our sense of wonder as we leave behind childhood. As the trials of puberty, imperfect families, and surviving in a less than ideal world wash over us, we find our vision clouded and our hearts losing some or even all of that openness. Depending on our circumstances, we may even have had to give up this open mind and heart quite early on, in order to survive.

Most of us were also conditioned by our society to believe that life it decidedly *not* magical. Our modern, westernized culture teaches us that life is difficult, and magic impractical. It teaches us that we must be reasonable and logical, rather than intuitive and emotional. It says that 'clear seeing' means taking all the magic and wonder out of our perceptions. And yet our intuitive, emotional selves are important guides for keeping our sense of wonder and hope intact. If we are to retrieve all the infinite potential that is our destiny as divine beings in physical form, we need to cultivate an ability to see both quantitatively and qualitatively, to see both the form and spirit of whatever we encounter. As adults guiding children towards their own destinies, we have to cultivate in them the ability to *retain* this magical capacity, just as we must retrieve it for ourselves in adulthood.

What aspects of wonder are still present in your life? Do you have hobbies, or people, or even a career that evoke that same childhood wonder in you today? And what about the children in your life? How do you interact with them? Do children make you uncomfortable, because they are so impractical and unpredictable? Do you encourage their wonder, and participate in it? Or do you avoid and discourage it?

That children believe in magic can either energize us or frighten us, and this fear can express itself as impatience, disdain, or just a simple discomfort. Usually, discomfort with children gives us a hint at the parts of ourselves that we have set aside in order to cope in our adult world. But an inability to integrate that childhood wonder into adult behaviors can cause us problems. The trick is to find ways to bring magic into mature, creative play in our daily adult lives. And, to do this, we must integrate all the aspects of ourselves that we left behind in our childhood.

The most important thing that childhood wonder brings to our spiritual journey is *direct experience of magic.* Most of us were taught early on that 'magic is not possible.' We were taught that 'magic' is really all hocus-pocus and trickery, and that there's no such thing as "real" magic. We also may have been conditioned to disregard our own magical experiences as 'simply imagination,' by which it is implied that imagination is somehow inferior to 'reality.'

But nothing could be further from the truth! Deep down, we know that somehow magic is real. It's clear from our cultural obsession with Harry Potter, fantasy genre television, books and movies, our insistence on Santa Claus and the Easter Bunny, and so many other 'hobbies' of the western mind that we *love* magic! And yet, for most of us, knowing how to make magic real in our daily lives seems impossible. It is something left for make-believe and special holidays, and treated as a diversion rather than the very practical work of creating our reality.

So we live in a world of contradictions: on the one hand, we seem to want very much to believe in and engage in magic, and at the same time, we dismiss this as at best a waste of time, or at worst a dangerous distraction. But from a mystical perspective, there is *nothing* more important than using our natural magic to create lives we love. The tools we have to use this are, first, imagination and fantasy and, second, our mystical and intuitive abilities.

Fostering Imagination and Fantasy

The first way we have deep access to the world of wonder is through our imagination. Our early childhood dreams and fantasies offer wonderful clues to the magic inherent inside of us. When you were a child, what did you dream of becoming? What did you love to imagine or daydream about? Did you have imaginary friends and playmates? Or magical worlds you travelled to? Think for a moment about the dreams and fantasies that engaged you and made you happy as a child. Have these things remained with you as an adult? Were you fully encouraged in these dreams and fantasies, or did adults attempt to make you be 'more realistic' in your hopes and aspirations? Did you ever give up a treasured dream because you got the clear message that it was 'impossible'?

One of the first questions we ask small children is, "What do you want to be when you grow up?" And yet, often, we don't really take their answers seriously. We have an expectation that the fantastical dreams of childhood must give way to more 'realistic' adult expectations and goals. In my own life, I had many dreams about following creative pursuits. I wanted to be a singer and a writer; I wanted to make music and creative writing the center of my life. I loved to sing to the television and the radio, and to write for hours in my journals. I created stories and songs in my spare time, happily, for years. But there was a catch: these childhood pursuits were considered more "play" than for "real life" and I was soon encouraged to set them aside for the more practical concerns of schoolwork and growing up. Well-meaning adults in my life honored my musical and creative writing pursuits, but I always had the sense that they were not meant to become *a job*. It's hard to say just exactly where this feeling came from—home, teachers, society as a whole—but I knew that art (i.e. intuitive and creative pursuits) were not good fodder for finding work, paying the bills, and becoming a respectable adult.

Of course, the adults had some basis for their concerns.

First, the simple truth was that, despite my intense conviction that I was meant to be a singer, as a young child I was very nearly tone-deaf. It took years of persisting in my passion for singing before my vocal chords caught up with my *inner knowing* about who I am. I *knew*, unequivocally, that I am a singer! But my voice wasn't ready to begin sharing that with the world until about 8th grade. Fortunately, my mother and father, and school choir leaders, humored me until my voice caught up with my intentions. No one, though, ever considered encouraging me to take singing seriously enough to pursue it professionally, or with any intention of making a career of it. That sort of 'work' is left only for the very rare, very talented few.

Fortunately, I never really gave up on this 'hobby,' and continued to sing in choirs and in ritual settings. Eventually, my voice not only grew up to match my original sense of knowing, it became one of the most powerful tools I use as a pastor, teacher and healer. My voice was there all along, waiting to be gently released by intention, patience and loving support. Had my own inner sense of magical possibility, my dreaming, been what my society used as a guide to help me fulfill my destiny, the journey might have had much less shame, discouragement, and pain in it. But those adults were only doing what they had been taught to do, by other well-meaning adults who had themselves discouraged 'impossible' dreams.

The same is true of my early desires to be a drummer. I was a girl, and I was summarily informed by a well-meaning band director that I would be "better off" playing a more feminine instrument, like the flute. So I played the flute, very well and very seriously for many years, all the while longing to be a drummer. I lost many, many years of joy and pleasure—not to mention the sheer *magic* created by the drum—through deferring my drumming until adulthood. In fact, because drumming is central to shamanic and magical practice, I might have accelerated my own divine purpose and calling quite a bit had I been encouraged to drum from an early age. Now, I play many different styles of drums, and use them often for rituals and healing ceremonies. But I made the best of playing the flute, as well. Because I was willing to embrace *all* the gifts I was encouraged to pursue, I also play North American flutes and use them for healing and ritual purposes. In this way, we can all make lemonade out of the disappointments and discouragements of our childhood and teen years.

Though I managed to keep alive my love of music, and eventually turn back to the instruments—my voice and the drum—that first called me, my primary creative love has always been writing. As a young child, I memorized poems and read constantly. In elementary school, I wrote stories that won local competitions. By high school, I was writing poetry seriously, and devoting a great deal of time to my creative writing projects. But writing fiction and poetry is, like so many creative endeavors, seen by our culture as highly impractical. We believe that only a very few 'successful' writers can make an actual living doing this sort of work, and most of those folks are considered a little bit suspicious anyway. Writers and artists are often seen as a bit crazy, or socially rebellious. "Regular" people can't be writers, or painters, musicians, or actors, or any of the other fully artistic professions. And, if a regular person *is* going to be an artist, he or she will either need a practical day job, or have a wealthy patron or a large inheritance to make it work. Writing fiction or poetry, or painting murals, or heading to New York to become a professional musician, aren't real professions in many people's eyes, and are certainly risky choices to make for one's future career.

This was made clear to me, in many ways, with the message that I could enjoy my writing and artistic endeavors as long as I was a child or teen, but when I became an adult I was going to have to put aside all that fun and start working for a living. Writing might be pursued in a 'serious' way if I chose to go into journalism or some other form of 'practical' writing, but writing about magic and fantasy was reserved for the fortunately wealthy, the mildly crazy, and a few brilliant exceptions. None of these categories seemed to apply to me, so I took the next-best path: I became a professor of reading and writing. Getting a PhD in literature and writing, I was satisfied for a while with this almost-but-not-quite my dream.

In what ways have you done the same? In what ways have you compromised your actual dream for a close approximation? If you are really honest with yourself, have you given in to pressures to surrender you true dream for something that is only partially satisfying, that comes close but isn't quite what you want? This is precisely what 'adulthood' means to many of us. As we move out of childhood into our teen years and into our adult lives, we often gradually reshape or entirely give up those 'youthful dreams' which gave us so much pleasure and hope when we were children. It often takes many years, and numerous twists of fate and intention, to find our way back to that childlike sense of wonder and possibility. But it is always there. Like beautiful places on an actual map of the world, the places we have dreamed of, or even visited briefly, they do not go away simply because we've been spending time on other terrain. It's possible to go back to them, or visit them for the first time, no matter how long we've been gone or how far afield we've travelled. And every experience we have picked up along the way can be used to help us find our way home to our true Selves.

Exercise #5: Where is Your Wonder Now?

Is that sense of wonder something you still have access to in your present life? Where in your life do you still act or feel like the child who knew what he or she wanted, who knew what felt great to you? Consider the following questions:

- What would you do if you were given all the money you needed for the rest of your life today? What activities would you do regardless of how much or how little you were paid for them?
- What things in your life feel truly "yummy"? How do you cultivate that good feeling now in your life?
- Do you have any secret or so-called 'guilty' pleasures that you engage in just for the joy of them? Perhaps favorite foods, special activities, or beautiful places you like to visit just because they make you feel good?
- When you let yourself fantasize, what do you find yourself imagining? Is it being in another place or time? Or perhaps another lifestyle? With another partner? In another career?
- Is there someplace you've always wanted to visit, or a class you've always wanted to take? Something you've always wanted to learn or try?
- What is the *feeling* that these dreams bring up?

Most of us find safer avenues for our imagination, and set aside the 'childish' fantasies we once cherished. What about you? When did you start getting the message that your imagination was not for all-the-time use? What sorts of limits or constraints were put on magic and wonder in your life? And who were the people bringing that message to you? Often, well-meaning parents, family members, and teachers discourage the very sorts of magical thinking that would best support our divine, energetic well-being. They mistakenly tell us that we should "work hard" and put in "good effort" if we want the rewards of a happy life. In fact, from an energy perspective, all this gets us is more 'hard work' and 'effort.' If we want to have happiness, or success, or well-being, what we actually need to do is vibrate at the *feeling* of happiness, success, and well-being. In other words, we need to spend our time doing what makes us feel wonder, joy, abundance and well-being—whatever that is!—if we want more of those things in our lives.

So how can we cultivate this sort of imagination, fantasy and wonder in ourselves and in our children? Doing this often requires changing our ideas about parenting, about relating to the children in our lives and also those hidden within our hearts.

Children naturally lean towards what makes them feel good, and pull back from what makes them feel uncomfortable. As children, we resist things that feel yucky, because we know intuitively that "yuck" will not get us more "yum" in our lives. When we force our children, or ourselves, to do things that we truly feel are not in harmony with our most joyful selves, we only limit their, and our own, progress towards our divine destinies. Though our contemporary world asks us to function mechanically in a structured, rigid system, our natural well-being flows through much more intuitive, fluid channels. Of course, children need help from older people to figure out how to live in this human context. When we arrive on this earth-plane, we are not necessarily well-equipped for the limitations of physical form. So guidance from elders who know a little bit more about things like food, sleep, gentle touches, and good hygiene are very helpful to vast souls trying to figure out how to exist in very small bodies. But we can offer this kind of guidance and support within a context of affirming the child's basic sense of what works for her

We can, for example, offer children choices about their lives that allow them to feel empowered in being happy. Rather than telling them they have to eat/read/watch/ play/do things we specifically have chosen for them, we can instead suggest that, while they need to do things that are healthy, they can choose from a range of options which would all be workable and acceptable. When a child 'misbehaves,' we can ask "What do you need?" and suggest better ways to get those needs met, rather than simply telling them "no!" or insisting that they have done something "bad." Remember, we are all divine being trying to find ways to express ourselves in a limited world. All actions have 'good' motivation; they are all efforts to express something important. It's more important to get to the deepest intention of the expression, no matter how ineffective it was, than to dictate specific behaviors. In this way, we must not only *parent intuitively*, but also encourage intuitive insight on the part of our children.

As small children, we are most concerned with pleasing our parents and care-givers, and understanding the 'rules' of the material realm. As we grow from childhood into the teen years, our desire to be accepted, to be 'normal' and to fit in, often means that we replace our inner knowing of what feels right to us with the voice of external peer pressures. At this age, the voices of friends, friends' parents, and the media become as loud as, if not louder than, the voices of our family. And if we have not developed a strong sense at home that our intuition and inner-guidance matter, then the voice of social constraints will drown out our natural desires and inclinations. Many of the interpersonal struggles teens experience with friends and peers are the result of trying to resolve differences between what they want for themselves, and what others expect of them. Many of the struggles that young people experience in their families and schools come directly from the conflict between what they know is inherently right for them, and what we adults think will 'help' them.

Too often, at this point in a child or teen's life, adults try to ease the pain of growing up by offering specific ideas about how the young person should manage his or her life. But helping a young person negotiate the challenges of this world does not include determining for them *who they are or where they are meant to be.* Too often, well-meaning adults try to 'coach' a child or teen into the adult's idea of what might be the best profession, or life-partner, or religion, based on the adult's own experiences and ideas. We would serve our children (and ourselves) better if we thought of ourselves not as teachers, but as facilitators. Our job, from this perspective, is not to know in advance what they need, but rather to be resources for tasks they have set for themselves. If we begin by assuming that they are in fact infinite, eternal, wise souls who came here for a good reason *that they know*, at some deep level, we will handle supporting them differently. We can ask, "What do you love? What brings you joy? What are you curious about?" and then offer whatever tools, resources, insights, and inspirations we might have to help them achieve their own greatest desires. We can follow their intuition, and our own, on a journey of joyful exploration, rather than on a prescribed path to supposed 'success.'

As adults trying to reclaim our own sense of magic and wonder, this same approach works best for ourselves, too.

Unfortunately, most of us got more 'coaching' than facilitation in our early years. But, no matter what age we are, we can retrieve that magical inner knowing about who we really are and what we really want. As adults, we too often stop our imagination and fantasies with arguments about money, responsibility, respectability, etc. We begin to dream and within seconds, WHAM!, we've shut ourselves down with the thousand reasons we can't/shouldn't/mustn't pursue that dream. We have internalized all the voices of 'no' that we heard as children, and become very good at speaking their words inside our own heads. But what would we have liked to hear, as children, that we can now say to ourselves instead?

Here are some suggestions for things you might say to your inner child and dreamer when he or she starts imaging new possibilities:

- That's a fabulous dream! We don't have to figure it out now, but it sure feels great!
- I love the way it feels to remember this kind of hope and possibility
- Wow! I'd forgotten how much I love to do that
- What else would you love to have be part of that dream? Is there more we can imagine?
- Imagining for imagining's sake is really healthy and nourishing.
- When I imagine, I get so much energy to do other things.
- I would still love to do that, somehow! Let's see if we can find a way.

And when the negative voice starts saying things like, "You don't have enough money" or "You have too many responsibilities" or "It's too late for that" try these:

- It's never too late to do things that I love and that make me happy
- I don't have to do the biggest version of this right away; I can start small
- I can write one poem/paint one picture/take a day-trip—I don't have to publish/have a gallery/move to France right away
- It will be fun to do *any part* of my dream, even a little bit
- I bet there are other people who have the same dream, and would enjoy talking about it and supporting me
- When I'm doing what I love, I give more love to other people
- Being happy is the best way to give my true gifts to the world
- My dreams are a clue to my best, highest self

In an energetic world, we are *creating* so-called 'reality' by the very *act of imagination*. Imagination is the most basic tool of magic, and their root—"*mage*"—reveals that connection. The "mage"—think of Merlin in the stories of King Arthur—creates through wish, will and intention. His greatest tools are desire and faith. There is nothing more critical to our own well-being than being able to imagine what we want, need, and wish for, and to believe in their possibility. I have heard adults dismiss or condemn what they call "magical thinking," suggesting that such an approach is dangerous and unrealistic, even delusional. They would argue that our fantasies, while useful perhaps as guides to our desires, have no impact beyond that. In fact, they caution, fantasies are a distraction, and can get in the way of creating a healthy 'real' life. The energetic or mystical mindset says something quite different: mystics believe that what we imagine—for good or ill—is precisely what we call into our lives. That is to say, imagination directly creates experience, and we are all doing it all of the time, whether we are conscious of it or not.

Think about something you managed to create in your life that felt good to you: a new house, a partner you dreamed of, a great job, healthy children. None of these things could have been possible without first at least imagining some action that gave rise to them occurring in your life. You had to think about them first, then go on that date, or send out that resume, or take action (intentional or not) to get pregnant or adopt. Our thoughts and feelings lead directly to conscious and unconscious actions which lead directly to our reality. And this happens on a much more subtle, pervasive level than we often realize.

On the purely psychological level, we have to believe something is possible to take steps that would allow it to happen. And on an *energetic* level, we must be able to *vibrate in harmony with an outcome,* if it is going to flow into our experience. If we want to heal chronic illness, for example, we have to be able to first at least imagine some sort of healing possibility. And, beyond that, we must be able to raise our own vibration to one that matches the quality of 'health' in order to allow it to flow into our experience. Likewise, if we want a relationship to become more rewarding and loving, we have to be able to replace our sense of disappointment and anger with the belief that something better is possible, and then to truly *feel* what it would be like to have that partner in our life.

And here's what's really important: we can't just *say* we

want something to be possible; we can't just think our way into it. We have to *feel* the possibility. The wonder, the sense of possibility in our hearts and minds and bodies, has to be strong enough to overcome our old hurts, disappointments, and conditioning if we are to truly create new things for ourselves. We have to tune ourselves to a tone, a pitch, a vibration of well-being that is louder and stronger than old vibrations that don't feel good. Imagination, day-dreaming, and fantasy, are all tools for doing this. They turn up the volume on hope so that it can override our sense of hurt or hopelessness. So wonder, then, is not a concept; it is an experience, a whole-body, whole-being experience. It is like beginner's mind that is carried through your whole system of being. This sense of wonder, so easily accessible in childhood, is the gateway back to real magic for us as adults.

When I was a child, I found magic in nature and in books. I spent my summers sitting on the screened porch reading and wandering the woods behind my parents' home. By travelling into these worlds, I was able to access things that were not otherwise present in my day-to-day 'reality.' I went to lands far distant in the past and future. I spoke with trees and birds, and with the spirits of the ancestors who roamed the forests. Because I was often alone, there was no one there to say "you did *not* see that!" or "that's not possible!" My imagination was free to go where it liked, uninterrupted. We all need time and space like this in our lives, no matter what age we are. We all need to give ourselves permission to dream and have fantasies about what new, wonderful things we might explore and experience. We all have not only the *right*, but also the *responsibility* to pursue our greatest fantasies, for they are the guides along the way to our very best lives of service and joy.

Intuitive Inventory

That our society is mesmerized by, and yet deeply fears, magic and fantasy is nowhere more obvious than in the realm of psychic or intuitive abilities. All it takes is a look at the movie listings in your local paper to see that we are drawn to the paranormal. And yet we treat this as somehow 'unreal' or freakish, and often see it as bad and dangerous. Many religious traditions tell us that 'magic' of this sort is not only impractical, it is downright heretical and evil. And yet, as most mystics will tell you, intuitive abilities are as natural to humans as breathing and using our other senses.

Though we have a modern fascination with the ghoulish and gory, many of us hit a wall of powerful resistance when our mystical abilities show up as psychic or intuitive skills. It's fine for the adults around us, usually, when we are simply describing what they can ascribe to childhood imaginings. But it's another matter entirely when we start getting messages from deceased loved ones, or predicting the future, or receiving messages from people in other places and times. It's fairly threatening, to those who haven't been trained in the magical, when small children start talking about things the child couldn't know through the first five senses, or demonstrating abilities that seem beyond 'normal.' When a child moves naturally along the spectrum of intuition from imagining to expressing magical abilities, often the adult world systematically dismisses them, often shaming or ridiculing the child in the process.

These gifts are some of the most important tools we have for retrieving our divine Selves, and for blessing the world with them. So let's take a moment to wonder about what intuitive, magical gifts you may naturally have, whether or not you have developed them.

Rev. Carol Bodeau, PhD

Exercise #6: A Survey of Psychic Gifts

As a child, you most likely had some basic intuitive abilities that started to show through. These can come in many forms, and express themselves in a wide range of circumstances. Look through the following list, as see what qualities or experiences matched who you were as a young child:

~ *empathy:* feeling strongly the emotions of, and around, other people; picking up their feelings even before they become aware of them; having feelings you can't explain or understand where they are coming from

~ *telepathy:* being able to communicate with others using only your thoughts and feelings; knowing when someone is thinking about you, and having this confirmed later (e.g. knowing moments before the phone rings that someone is calling you)

~ *mediumship:* being able to communicate with those who have passed; seeing, hearing, or feeling the presence of deceased people and animals, and being able to communicate with them; may include *crossing work*, or being able to help those spirits who need to transition to another plane make that next step

~ *precognition:* being able to predict the future; having awareness that something is about to happen before it does (the range of precognitions can be anywhere from a few minutes or hours, to weeks, months or even years)

~ *retrocognition:* being able to directly experience or know things from the past without any physical, material source of information; this often happens when visiting a specific location, in which you hear, see, feel, or know information about the place from a different time

~ *other-life recall:* having clear memories from other places or times (in either the past or the future) and/or knowing and identifying people from your current life as family, friends, acquaintances, from other times; remembering places you have never been before as if you had lived there

~ *healing abilities and medical intuition:* feeling energy in your hands or other parts of your body, being able to use this energy to effect change in yourself or those around you; being able to notice when someone is sick, perhaps before they even know (sometimes involves feeling the illness in your own body, as if you were yourself ill)

~ *animal, plant or elemental communication:* being able to communicate directly with animals, plants, rocks, or the elements of the natural world; finding yourself easily able to intuit what other living creatures need; healing abilities with these other members of the earth family

~ *clairvoyance, clairsentience, clairaudience:* being able to, respectively, see, feel, or hear information about a person or situation without any physical, external source of information; can include seeing auras and energy fields, or hearing the voices of ancestors, elders, teachers, etc. giving information to you

~ *channeling:* being able to serve as a conduit for spiritual information coming through you from a spiritual source, such as ascended masters, guides, angels, teachers, or ancestors

All of us are born with some basic intuitive gifts, though many of us do not consciously develop these until later in life, if ever. Often, the choice—conscious or unconscious—to not develop our psychic abilities comes from feeling as if they are 'bad' or unacceptable to our families, our friends, our religion, or our society in general.

And yet it is our intuitive or psychic abilities—no matter how subtle—that give us direct access to the realm of spirit beyond form. We are typically encouraged to hone our first five senses, and often discouraged from paying any attention to the senses beyond these. And yet these abilities, like muscles that need exercise after long years of not being used, do come back and grow stronger with practice and intentional care. As so many internet and coaching courses now teach, it's possible to cultivate and hone our psychic abilities so that they become tools we can use to serve ourselves and others.

We will delve more deeply into this topic in later chapters, but let's begin by asking the question: what intuitive or mystical abilities would you like to have or enhance, in order to enhance your own life and the lives of those around you? Are you an allopathic healer who would like to be more intuitive with your patients? Or perhaps a stay-at-home dad who wants to be more telepathic with his children? A business woman who would like to cultivate her clairvoyance or clairsentience? Perhaps you have a basic connection with animals that you sense could become even more powerful and profound. Or an ability to predict the future in ways that might help others shape more fulfilling, healthy lives. Perhaps you are a medium who could ease the suffering of those grieving. No matter who you are, you can develop your intuitive abilities just as you can develop your physical muscle tone and flexibility.

By developing our intuitive abilities, and by cultivating our imaginations (two practices that go hand-in-hand), we begin to rediscover our innate magic and recover our sense of wonder in the world. As you practice using these tools to create the life you dream of, you will find more and more wonder-filled signs of support and encouragement from the magical multiverse. Coincidences and synchronicities will increase in your daily life, and seemingly impossible magical events will rise up to help you get more and more of what you envision. Rather than creating from unconscious and deeply ingrained messages that magic is not possible, you can take action now to begin creating from the deepest desires and wishes of your own heart and soul.

Suffering

A belief that the world is filled with possibility, and that we have access to wonderful and magic opportunities, is essential to living the lives we dream of. Unfortunately, many of us have experienced circumstances that made us feel that the world was dangerous, hurtful and terribly unkind. Too many children experience either acute or chronic traumas in their early years. Too many children's lives are shaped by loss of one or both parents; by poverty and hunger; by physical, emotional, or sexual abuse; by substance abuse; by neglect; or by illness or other traumatic circumstances. For children whose lives are far from safe, comfortable, or easy, wonder can be a rare commodity. For children who suffer extreme or frequent trauma, imagination often becomes a way to escape the harsh realities of daily life. If you or someone you love has been effected in this way, the journey back to the divine, whole self may be more complicated. And the first step may be making some sense, to the best of your ability, of why such things happen in the first place.

How do we account for such horrible circumstances in the lives of children who are, by all accounts, completely innocent? This is one of the most difficult and tricky questions for the mystical mindset. Before we spend more time on the subject of creating the lives we dream of, let's take a moment to consider the suffering that we may have already encountered.

The challenge of dealing with suffering in mystical terms is that we find ourselves caught between identifying with our three-dimensional, this life, this earth selves, and with our bigger, eternal Selves. We are both kinds of beings at the same time, and the two do not always (or even often) experience life the same way. As Prince Siddartha learned on his journey to becoming the Buddha, suffering is not something that can simply be dismissed on the spiritual journey as irrelevant. Too often, spiritual seekers find it convenient to focus solely on the spiritual and metaphysical realms, while pushing aside the concerns of the material world as if these were inferior, or at least secondary, to the concerns of the 'high Self.' Often, this is a survival strategy that lets us connect with a part of ourselves that is less harmed by the traumas we have endured. But in the journey to becoming our most divine Selves, embodied in human form, it's essential that we integrate Spirit and Form, the infinite/eternal and the earthly/temporal as fully as possible.

The greatest of spiritual teachers—the Gautama Buddha, Jesus of Nazareth, the Prophet Mohammed (PBUH), and many others—have repeatedly taught that enlightenment serves best when it alleviates the suffering of our fellow earth beings. So connecting our spiritual selves to the traumas of our lives, and those experienced by other beings, is essential.

Nowhere is this more apparent than in the suffering of innocent beings such as children, animals, and the planet herself. These are creatures we see as having done nothing 'wrong' to create the suffering that plagues them. Often, we separate 'justified' suffering—suffering created by clear cause-and-effect actions committed by the sufferer—as understandable, while all other suffering is seen as senseless. We are willing to attribute some suffering to a person 'getting what they deserved' while other situations seem the cruel acts of either an unfair divine presence, or of a universe that is at best neutral, at worst downright unjust. But this doesn't give us much sense of the actual, co-creative power we truly have, to alleviate *all* suffering.

Human experience is indeed fraught with contrasts: pain and pleasure, joy and sorrow, loss and gain. Spiritual traditions have used innumerable methods to try to help us come to terms with this contrast. Some traditions attribute suffering to original sin, or the inherent 'brokenness' of the human being. To some traditions, our very presence on earth as humans, as 'sons and daughters of Adam and Eve,' means that we must endure suffering as a sort of punishment for our inherent, unavoidable 'wrongness.' By this formulation, the only way out is through atonement and release from the earth plane. But, if we believe that we are pure energy beings, and that we are co-creators with godde, this makes no sense at all. We are one with godde, and therefore punishment as the overall purpose of the earth-plane just doesn't ring true.

Other traditions suggest that suffering is always a direct result of actions, in this or other lives. So all suffering is 'justified' suffering, though the circumstances by which we 'earned' our challenges and hurts may come from outside this current lifetime. For the mystical mindset, this comes a little closer: patterns set outside the limited framework of this one time and place may indeed create energy imbalances that lead to greater contrast in our lives. But to see this as a sort of karmic punishment also is out of sync with knowing ourselves as divine, holy souls who are part of the greater good/godde.

For many of us who embrace the idea that we are

all divine souls, here to experience a re-awakening or realization of our own infinite, eternal Selves, suffering can be seen as a motivator, not a punishment. It brings us opportunities to shift our perspective; to change our patterns of thought, behavior, and emotion; to explore more deeply what we are capable of in the face of challenges and difficult circumstances.

But, we ask, if we are infinite, eternal, powerful creators, why would we choose to suffer an abusive childhood, or a traumatic assault, or a difficult life-threatening illness? This question stops many of us in our tracks, and it can make us turn tail and head back the way we came on the path to awakening. And this is true no matter how severe our suffering has been. I have seen people with life stories of incredible suffering claim their own inner divine power more easily than those with far easier, more pleasant lives. It's not so much the condition of our life experiences that determines how much personal responsibility we claim for our own journey. Rather, it is our readiness to hold that sort of power going forward.

In other words, if you have come to the place on your journey where you are truly ready to be responsible for *every single thing* that comes your way, knowing you called it to you by conscious or unconscious intention, then you're ready to look at your own suffering in a new light. If you are not yet ready to do that, *it is perfectly okay*! It is okay to need more time, maybe *lots* more time, to feel the pain and suffering of our wounds. It is good, and healthy, to take as much time as we need feeling the hurts, processing the grief and rage, and doing whatever it takes to be compassionate with ourselves as we recover from any number of physical, emotional, psychological, and spiritual traumas. If this is the case for you, then give yourself time to go back to the original traumas and do whatever it takes to transmute and transform those energies, understanding that *your own compassion for yourself, giving yourself as much time as you need, immediately raises the vibration of your mind, heart, body and spirit.* Give yourself whatever you need to heal.

And then...return to a place on the path where you claim divine agency in your own life.

Eventually, we come to the place where we no longer wish to see ourselves as victims. We come to a place where we see ourselves as having the power to move forward, regardless of what did or did not happen in the past. No matter what we lost; no matter who hurt us; no matter how long it takes us to heal; we can come to this moment, right here, right now, as if we are new. We have that power within us, and I believe that we will all claim it in the right time and place for us. Each breath is a new opportunity to be reborn.

So, on the spiritual journey, contrast is—again, as all the mystical and practical teachings tell us—inevitable. And while it is necessary to take the time to make sense of our own suffering, we must ultimately remember this:

We are not our suffering.

At some point, we must cease to be defined by it. It is a story we can stop telling, and replace with another story, when we are ready.

Often, critics of the mystical approach argue that the idea of co-creating our own reality suggests we are 'blaming the victim.' But this is a misunderstanding of the basic principle. The mystical truth that we are powerful beings who have come to the earth-plane to experience our joy and creative ability means that we have also come here *to overcome suffering.* Not just for ourselves, but for the whole of all living beings. As the boddhisatva vows of the Buddhist tradition suggest, enlightenment for one requires conscious desire for enlightenment of all. Liberation from suffering is something we desire as spiritual beings, as well as human, three-dimensional beings. But liberation, seen from a spiritual perspective, is somewhat different than liberation seen from a material perspective.

Where a human perspective would have us believe that the solution to suffering lies in liberation from the *acts and events and circumstances of suffering*, the mystical mindset suggests that it is liberation from the *perspective of suffering* that is necessary. In other words, we will all feel pain—partly as a way to help us see that human difficulty can either be interpreted as suffering, or not. Pain is inevitable, and for someone very sensitive, a small hurt can be as devastating as a large trauma is to one who is less sensitive. But how we mature in response to pain is part of our spiritual progress towards liberation from a *mindset* of suffering.

When a child experiences great difficulty, he or she is not necessarily programmed to experience this suffering in a specific way. We are all given some resources to handle the challenges we face. We have loving peers or teachers; inner resources of humor or compassion; a willingness to be optimistic or cheerful despite difficulty; miraculous gifts of help and kindness from outside ourselves. These and many other forms of assistance come to each and all of us in the face of whatever difficulty life brings our way. And we can take credit for accessing, and accepting these, as magical creators of our reality! To be sure, there are some very serious and significant impacts of childhood trauma on the psyche and the development of a person, emotionally, physically, and spiritually. It is ultimately not our primary task to search for blame for these, *either in ourselves or in others*. Rather, it is our primary task to focus on the resources we have to overcome, and transform these challenges into liberation, hope and possibility. This is the spiritual task of any being on the earth plane: to use what Abraham calls 'contrast' to call us towards something better.

Once we have this perspective, we are more able to ask the question "why is this happening?" with an open mind. When we are still in the place of processing our pain very directly, the question "why?" can often be translated most accurately as "Why me?" It is a cry for help, saying, "This is unfair! This does not work for me! This is awful!" It is also a statement of theological uncertainty, which means something like, "I have no framework for making sense of this experience." But when our consciousness shifts to a mystical understanding of ourselves as divine co-creators, the question "Why?" takes on a new meaning.

From a mystical perspective, "Why?" means something more like "What was I wanting to learn? What was my purpose? What greater good was or is being served here?" Or, at the very least, "What greater good might I choose to use this towards now?" There are as many answers to these questions as there are individual stories, and only you can decide for yourself what lessons, opportunities and gifts have come, or can come, from your challenges.

One more thing: often, we think of these challenges as 'lessons' we are learning to become 'better' selves. But such a way of thinking assumes we were somehow inadequate before, and takes us right back to seeing earth as a place of testing and judgement. This may not be a compassionate (or fair) way to look at the situation. Here's another possibility that occurred to me years ago, and stopped me in my tracks the first time I considered it: what if you signed up for some of those awful circumstances as a gift to others? What if they were an act of service, in some way? If we are all one, then many of our choices are likely tied up in service to the greater good.

The story that brought this teaching to me seemed fairly simple initially, but has since proven to be immensely important. One morning, when my daughter was only about 14 months old, I felt the urge to go to the mall on some trivial errand. But I also felt a little uncertain about the trip, as if I was being told to both 'go' and 'not go.' I chose to go, thinking it would only be a little jaunt across town. No big deal. I strapped the toddler into her carseat, and her dad and I headed out. On a whim, I decided to drive the back way—a route I had never taken before. Coming through a nice little residential neighborhood, I suddenly realized, looking out the corner of my eye, that we were about to be hit full-impact on the driver's side (my side, and the baby's side) of the car by another car going about 40 miles per hour towards a stop sign. He was clearly not going to stop, and I had only seconds to recognize this, put on the brakes, and wish for the best.

Then something odd happened: I literally felt a force, a presence, surround our car and 'bump' that on-coming car around the front of my vehicle. He hit our front bumper, going 40 miles per hour or so right through the stop sign. And yet while we were shaken up, and the car sustained some damage, we were completely unhurt. When we got out of the car, we learned that the other driver was 16 years old plus one day, and that he was driving his grandmother's car. He begged us not to report the accident, but since I am the daughter of an insurance agent, I said 'no way.'

After getting the appropriate information, and heading home, I called my trusty spiritual guide, my favorite aunt. When I asked her the question, "Why would I have chosen that?!" She had an interesting answer. She acknowledged that I had clearly had foresight that something less than pleasant might happen; I wavered and waffled about going, and almost didn't get into the car for that trip across town. And yet I went anyway. My aunt suggested that perhaps I had intended to somehow be of service to the other person involved, that young 16 year old driver. I was, frankly, a bit mystified. But only for a couple of weeks.

A few days after the accident, we received a call from the boy's grandmother. She pleaded that we not report the accident, that we all protect her grandson from having it on his record. I was not home at the time of the call, and my husband essentially agreed to go along with a plan to have the grandmother pay for repairs without involving insurance agents. But when I learned of this plan, I refused to go along. I had a very deep, gut feeling that this was a bad idea. So I called the grandmother, asking for her by name when the phone was answered. The woman on the other end replied, "That's me" but seemed very confused. As it turned out, the boy's mother and grandmother (who lived in the same household) had the same name. The grandmother and the boy had not told his mother about the accident, and when I said to the woman on the other end, "I'm calling about the accident the other day" I was quite unintentionally spilling the beans to his mother about what had happened.

So, first, I intercepted what could have been a troubling secret in the family. It was clear that there were forces at work in this young man's life engaged in a spiritual struggle. On the one hand, his grandmother was encouraging shielding him from taking personal responsibility. I, on the other hand, was acting in a way that insisted he be held accountable for his actions. After I explained the situation to his mother, and let her know that I had reported the incident to the police, and that my insurance agent would be handling it, I thought that would be the last I would hear of it. I felt relieved that there was some 'sense' in my involvement—perhaps my insistence on making a report would help this young man take his driving more seriously, and help him to learn some accountability for his actions. But the story wasn't over yet.

About two weeks later, as I was watching the local evening news, a story came on about a young man who had tried to race a commuter train with his car. My attention was caught by the name of that careless, flagrantly dangerous young driver: it was the name of the young man who had hit my car, two weeks earlier. I suddenly had a very clear sense of the bigger story going on in this young man's life: here was a young person trying desperately to get attention by being reckless, and endangering others in the process. When he hit me, on the day after receiving his license, the accident was small. People in his life tried to protect him from taking responsibility for this action, but my instincts told me it was *essential* this accident be reported. When he was hit by the train, he had swerved out of a line of waiting cars, gone around those cars and then around the railroad crossing gate, and had been hit by an express train that couldn't stop in time. Though the young man lived, he left the scene on a stretcher (reports said that he was grinning and waving at the crowd of on-lookers as if he were a TV star).

So, why would I have gotten involved in all that drama? To try to give him a chance to avert disaster before it happened. To put one more accident on his very short driving record, and perhaps make the pattern clearer sooner—to police, to family, to even the young man himself—in hopes of helping him to avoid an even worse, more deadly event for him or some other unsuspecting person. In other words, perhaps I subconsciously chose to get into that little accident as an act of service to that young man, hoping to help him learn a lesson the easier way, rather than the harder way.

In the years since that event, I cannot count the number of times I've caught myself choosing situations for this very reason—to be of service to someone else who was looking for a spiritual contrast for the sake of learning something. Fortunately, I've gotten better at recognizing this is advance, and making more conscious choices about how and when I choose to be 'helpful.' In fact, one of the great spiritual lessons for *me* in accepting responsibility for *choosing* this experience, is that I've learned about my own pattern of sacrificing myself for the spiritual growth of others. And I've begun to reverse and transform that pattern. So, that young man did me a pretty big favor after all, too.

Exercise #7: Transforming Suffering

Take a moment to consider the traumatic or challenging events in your own life, either in childhood or later. Can you see ways in which you have used these experiences to serve your own greater good, or to serve others? Are there ways you could yet choose to transform some of your own suffering into upliftment for your own life, or for those around you?

There are no easy answers to the questions of why suffering happens, or how we can alleviate it, but there are some good teachings out there about how to respond to it. When we consider our own lives, and the lives of those we love, we must face the fact that difficulty—contrast—is inevitable. And yet we have choices about how we interpret and make meaning out of our challenges. From the perspective of an infinite, eternal, divine being, these are experiences designed to maximize our potential for spiritual awakening, and expressions of generosity and love. As we co-create our lives with those around us, and with the Source of our being, we have the ability to see ourselves not as victims, but as brave souls choosing to attend 'earth-school' with an eagerness to learn as much as possible each time around. And also with an intention to ease and support the journeys of our companions here.

If we've signed up for really hard classes, we need to be patient and compassionate with ourselves. And we need to consider the possibility that it's time to choose easier, more pleasurable learning opportunities. We can do this *no matter what our life circumstances are, or have been.* Believing that we can reclaim all that was lost, that we can become all that we are meant to be, is an essential part of the spiritual journey.

4

A Sense of Adventure

Cultivating Curiosity, Fostering Fearlessness

One of the most important tools we will need to return back to our own sense of wonder and magic is a sense of adventure. Also an important part of many of our childhoods, a sense of adventure gives us the courage and daring to take steps which might otherwise seem too risky. A sense of adventure helps us step into the unknown, and travel through relationships and experiences that are new and unfamiliar. Though these situations may be frightening and challenging, a sense of adventure allows us to face the fear and difficulty with a certain curiosity and courage.

In childhood, we are more likely to have fearlessness about our environment and our actions. This fearlessness comes partly from the security of being cared for by others, and partly from a state of innocence about our world. The less harm we have experienced, the less likely fear will overrule our curiosity about the world. For some, this sense of curiosity and adventure gives way far too quickly to fear and an expectation of danger, as the traumas of life on the earth-plane come too hard, too young. If this has been true for you, you may have responded by giving up your sense of adventure entirely, in favor of caution and anxiety. On the other hand, you may have gone to the other extreme, embracing danger and rebellion as a way of insisting 'you can't stop me.' Either approach makes it hard to feel truly safe and enthusiastic about the world we share, since even defiant risk-taking is based on an inherent fear that our freedom will be stolen from us. Usually, we adopt a mix of both of these stances in response to the losses and traumas of our lives. We may take great risks in one area of our lives while being much more cautious in other areas. For example, for many years I was very willing to take great emotional and spiritual risks, while remaining very hesitant to take material (e.g. financial and physical) risks. I lacked confidence in my physical body and my own ability to physically support myself, but was very confident and adventurous in intellectual, emotional and spiritual realms.

From the time I was a young child, I was fearless about intellectual and spiritual pursuits. I made the decision quite young to separate myself from the dogma of my family's religion, and began my own spiritual explorations. I was even more audacious in my exploration of what some call the "paranormal" realms—the world of psychic phenomena and mystical encounters. When others thought ghosts and the supernatural were best left for campfire stories, exaggerated Halloween costumes, and scary movies, I immersed myself in the paranormal and ESP section of our little school library. I walked in the graveyard whenever I could, finding it to be the most pleasant, comforting place in town. While there, I felt at peace, in good company, and very much connected to the timeless stream of my community. I knew the people named on the tombstones weren't 'dead' at all, just in a different form or place. Though others often considered me weird, I persisted in exploring things that my culture told me were impossible. This interest and exploration grew more intense as I grew older, and my own experiences intensified.

While I was somewhat shy and socially backward with my human peers in school, I was a brave adventurer with spirits who were not in human form. By the time I was a teenager, ghosts were visiting me at night, and I was experiencing a growing wave of precognitions and intuitions. I began dreaming about deaths in our small town, always 2-3 days prior to those events. For me, the separation between life in physical form and what comes after was a very thin one. When a beloved elderly neighbor woman died in the early summer after my freshman year of high school, she woke me very clearly from a deep sleep to let me know she was passing. Though in my half-awake state, and given my inexperience with these things at that time, I didn't quite understand cognitively what was happening, I still knew that the world had shifted completely. I looked at the clock, noted the time and, realizing that something significant had happened, went back to sleep. In the morning, when her body was discovered, I knew it was her passing that had awoken me. When the coroner's report came back, it noted the time of death at exactly the moment I had looked at the clock. I knew that she had said goodbye, and my grieving was lessened considerably. We learned that she had also wakened her cousin, her closest living relative, upon her passing.

Even more interesting were the nighttime visits (usually at about 3am) by spirits who were hoping to communicate with me, but whom I couldn't identify. I got in the habit of trying to acknowledge them without being bothered by them, but one particularly persistent spirit forced me to take what I can see now were very brave steps for a teen without any formal training in this sort of work. For many weeks, I had awoken in the middle of the night to the presence of a young man, about 24 or 25, who had apparently died during the American Revolution. He always came in a soldier's uniform with a somewhat battered tricorn hat. He was in breeches and shirtsleeves, and seemed very patient but determined to talk to me. Of course, the problem was that I had too little experience and training to communicate effectively with him. So one night, after losing sleep for too many days in a row, I finally just sat up in bed and had a very direct conversation with him.

I simply told him that I was 'too young to handle this exchange right now.' I asked him to please leave me alone, and come back later, when I was older. He politely left, and I went to sleep. The next morning, I found small white flower blossoms spread around atop my dresser and on the cedar chest at the foot of my bed. It was pretty impressive, actually. He didn't come back for many years, until I was in my twenties and had gotten enough training and support to be able to help him. I knew he was back when those little flower blossoms began appearing around my apartment. When I began to see these tokens of his kindness, I simply invited him back into a conversation—he politely waited for the invitation, sending the blossoms as a sort of 'calling card' while he waited to be asked back into my conscious space— and then we talked through what he needed. I assisted him in his journey, he assisted me in mine, and we went our separate ways as soul friends.

So, for me as a child and teenager, having a sense of adventure and daring involved exploring deeply into the realms of the mystical and the intuitive. My curiosity and excitement for the spiritual realms was simply greater than my fear and hesitation. This curiosity also led me to taking risks in relationships in order to learn more about the world of the 'paranormal.' By the time I was a high school senior, I had read all the books I could get my hands on. I had met ghosts, had precognitions of deaths, and had greatly developed my telepathy and intuition. I had also been corresponding some with an aunt who openly shared her intuitive abilities, and was experienced and knowledgeable in this area. I knew that she was the person I needed to have teach me! So, upon receiving money for high school graduation, I decided to get on an airplane and head out to visit her. I initiated the visit, which surprised her and the rest of the family.

I flew off to spend a week with her, and my eyes—especially my third eye—were opened in incredible ways. In that one week, I learned a number of excellent tricks for balancing and developing my intuitive abilities; I spent time communicating with her truly telepathic cat; I visited places where she and I had spent lifetimes together, and was affirmed in what I could 'see.' That week started what was to become the most formative spiritual relationship of this lifetime for me. It started as a mentorship and has over three decades turned into a deep, engaging and wonderful friendship. Flying off to get to know her was a risk, a step of daring, that has paid off many-fold.

As a teen, I was willing to take risks and go on great adventures to explore the mystical realms. I did this in spite of resistance from people I loved, in spite of being seen as weird by some of my family and friends, and in spite of cultural norms that warned me against it. I also moved forward despite lacking adequate training and mentorship for many years.

Think for a moment about your own sense of adventure. In what areas were you daring and brave as a child? And now, how are you adventurous and willing to take risks? And in what areas are you cautious, expecting harm and therefore less open to trying new things? Typically, we can trace our willingness to take risks and be adventurous to experiences that have given us confidence, and our fears or hesitations to situations which have undermined our sense of personal power. And yet all of these were merely experiences, not truths. Even the slightest shift in our curiosity and sense of adventure can make a huge difference in what we are able to do, experience, and know. Even the willingness to entertain a new idea has enormous power in our lives. Perhaps, in fact, this is the single most powerful act of adventure we can undertake.

Exercise #8: Where do You Take Risks?

Take a minute to explore the areas of your life where you find it easy to take risks, and the areas where you avoid risk. Are you a person who is adventurous in a physical way, perhaps travelling a lot or playing sports? Have you had lots of broken bones, or injuries from reckless or daring behavior? How about mind-altering substances? Sometimes we use what anthropologists call 'entheogens'—plant helpers—to access other realms in a way that is (more) culturally sanctioned, and which give us a sense of danger within the confines of somewhat proscribed outcomes. Or are you a person who takes emotional risks—getting involved in problematic or challenging relationships? Perhaps you use your mind, rather than your heart, to take big adventures through inventing things, or trying alternative approaches to healing, learning, or growing.

> And now consider areas where you avoid risk and danger. Are there areas where you are especially hesitant or set in your ways? What areas of your life are limited by a lack of adventure or curiosity? Do you have a sense of apathy, or lack of motivation, in parts of your life that might benefit from a little bit more inspiration and daring?

Looking at our patterns of adventure and risk-taking helps us assess where energy flows fully in our lives, where it is blocked, and sometimes where it overflows. We often develop these patterns in response to a mixture of family and social conditioning, and powerful experiences that we've had. As young people who very much needed to belong, to fit in and to be included in society, we were all faced with tough choices about ways to step out and take risks, and ways we needed to conform. Sometimes, we had to conform by taking a certain type of risk that we in fact didn't want. And sometimes we had to put aside things that really stirred our curiosity and excitement, because they weren't accepted by our peers or our religion. What were the ways you altered your natural sense of adventure to match your social context? How did your family, your economic situation, your religion and your education, shape the way you chose to channel your own exploring energies?

To claim eternal, infinite co-creative power with the divine is, by its very nature, a daring act. At the very least, to do so means we will be considered 'crazy' or 'heretical' by a significant number of people. It may cost us our job, or relationships with people we care about, or a sense of being 'normal.' It may mean that we have to rewrite a tidy plan for our lives that we had grown comfortable with, or that we have to make changes that are difficult. But we can balance our curiosity and our caution through a healthy sense of adventure. Looking at the balance of risk and adventure in our lives also helps us assess how we are managing our own energy flow. By taking the time to make this assessment, we give ourselves the chance to send some powerful new energy into areas that might let us become more fully who we are and who we were meant to be. And becoming conscious of patterns we have for sending 'go-get-em' energy to places that bring trouble, helps us rein in unnecessary risk. We can begin to take more measured risk in areas that need more energy, and ease back in areas where we are taking unnecessary and sometimes destructive risks.

An Aside on Public Education

As we talk about how children explore and experience their place in the family, the community, and the larger social context, it's important to take a moment to talk about the role of public education in our lives. For most of us who attended public schools, there were pros and cons to that experience. School is a place to meet people, to participate in activities, and to gain access to information that may not be available at home. At the same time, the format of public school can present a serious challenge to developing our innate abilities, particularly our intuitive ones.

Our modern schooling system arose during the industrial revolution, and is formatted to be much like an assembly line. Large groups of children go into a system whose intention is to have them come out looking very much like one another: they are all meant to know a proscribed set of information, to be able to perform a certain set of 'standards,' and to execute the same basic skill set upon graduation. Unlike previous generations, who learned by the apprenticeship method, children for the last century and a half have been churned out a bit like cogs from an assembly line. Though we have tried to insert some basic encouragement for creativity and individuality in this system, that frankly isn't working so well. Too often, the 'creative' kids are considered failures by the system, or 'creative arts' programs are eliminated in favor of more 'practical' and 'realistic' ones.

Though of course the older, apprentice-based mode of education was flawed in that it meant a child could be forced into a trade that didn't match his or her interests, there was still an advantage in giving a child a chance to specialize early on in a subject he or she was passionate about. Though much of my public school education was valuable, to an extent, there was just no point in forcing me to learn trigonometry and calculus. What I mean to say by this is that, while a broad liberal arts education foundation is valuable for all children—it gives each child the chance to gain a broad base of knowledge from which they can *select their own specialization*—we have taken this a bit too far. We are forcing children to take in an *enormous* amount of information in a range of areas that simply do not serve each child equally. Some mix of broad education and apprenticeship, it seems to me, would benefit our children immensely.

In more traditional societies, this balance would be especially true for children who demonstrated intuitive or mystical abilities. Recognized early on as having gifts that needed special training, such children (and if you are reading this book, chances are you were such a child) would have been given special attention by the appropriate elders to assist them in handling and developing their abilities. While they might, depending on the specific circumstances and culture, have had some level of contact with their peers, they would also have received training specifically in the mystical arts. Some, like His Holiness the Dalai Lama, would have been separated entirely due to the importance of their callings. Others might simply have had extras 'lessons' as deemed necessary by elders.

In my own life, I can say without a doubt that, had I had such training, I could have been spared an awful lot of fear, confusion, shame and imbalance. As an educator myself—I am the daughter of a mom who taught middle school math for 40 years, and I taught college English and Native American studies for a decade, before homeschooling my own child and then teaching numerous courses in a wide range of settings as a minister—I see two core problems with our contemporary education that are particularly hard on intuitive, creative, artistic children. One is a problem of what we *do*, and the other a problem with what we *don't do*. First, we actively discourage intuition, artistry, and magic making. We tell children that they should not be spending too much time imagining, and we steer them towards a particular type of career. In fact, we have a system of learning that intends to develop the left brain (the analytical) over the right brain (the intuitive and relational); we take children *off the land*, which has devastating effects (more on this later); and we value conformity, rather than the cultivating strong individuality.

Secondly, we fail to give our intuitive and mystical children—and the truth is that *all* children are intuitive to some extent—anywhere near adequate training in these abilities. While the true evolution of a society absolutely requires actively intuitive and innovative people (people like Albert Einstein, Steve Jobs, etc.), we don't actually take the time, collectively, to provide training in these areas to our children. And the remaining communal places where our mystical or spiritual sides might be developed—our houses of worship and our religious communities—in fact often condemn mystical abilities. It's can be a tough society in which to grow into an intuitive, divine co-creator. I believe that this situation is the primary fuel for the popularity of 'new age' culture.

When our natural drives towards intuitive, creative exploration, and individuality are suppressed or squelched entirely, the result is depression, acting out, rebellion and 'failure' at social norms. On the other hand, when individual, innate creativity and exploration are nurtured, the result is children growing into healthy, confident, energized adults who know their purpose and calling. It is possible to nurture young people in a way that helps them set good boundaries without requiring them to conform; it is possible to nurture a good 'work ethic' by harnessing passion rather than using force; and it is possible to have a healthy society in which people have very different skills, interests and abilities. Chances are that, if you were a particularly intuitive, empathic, or otherwise 'sensitive' child, public education had some limiting effects on you. So how do you undo those effects for yourself? You begin, of course, by thinking back on your own experiences, and recognizing both the blessings and drawbacks of the education your received.

Exercise #9: School Days

Think back on your education, and make a list of the most beneficial, positive experiences you had there. Were you homeschooled, or did you attend public or private school? Did you have a favorite teacher or mentor? How did the people who really supported you do so? Were there favorite classes or subjects that you had the chance to explore and learn about during your education? What opportunities did your particular school setting offer you? Consider all of the following aspects of education: academic content, artistic expression, social setting and peers, teachers and mentors, the physical environment, the values or ethics encouraged by the school, and the overall mood or feeling of the environment. Now, make a list of all the ways you felt restricted or shut down by your educational setting. Were there areas you would have liked to explore more fully, which were unavailable or off limits? Were there hurtful people or practices in your school system? Were there any values encouraged or enforced that didn't match your own internal sense of what was good for you? Did the physical environment feel healthy and supportive, or were there qualities to the physical space that were upsetting, limiting or unhealthy? Was your learning self-directed, or controlled by other people? Think about any ways you might have done things differently, if you had been in charge of the education you received.

In order to consider how our education might have suppressed or limited our creative, intuitive impulses, it can be helpful to look back at the assumptions and core values of the system in which we were trained. More powerful even than the actual academic content of the schooling we received is the unspoken, unconscious lessons we learned about 'what life is all about' and what has value to our society and peers. These messages—embedded in the very concrete blocks and fluorescent lights of our learning environments, in the ways eating and bathroom breaks were treated there, and in the tone of voice and type of language used by teachers and leaders—have at least as much, and probably more impact on us than what was in our textbooks. Did you feel treasured and special in your learning environment? Was open discussion and play encouraged? Were you allowed time to follow your own desires and interests? If not, then you can do some recovery and repair work now to reclaim the magic within you. Be sure to complete exercise #12, below, for rescripting your own childhood, including your educational experiences. And consider reframing your life now in ways that offer you the chance to learn some new things, in new ways, in an environment that is supportive and exciting, and that feels good to you.

For many of us, we arrive at full adulthood without realizing all that we've given up in order to fit into our society's ideas of 'success.' We may have spent years and tens of thousands of dollars on a college education, or a professional training, that we're not sure really matches our inner calling. Or perhaps we've made commitments that seem to limit our freedom to start over. We have home mortgages, children to support, aging parents who need our care, business debts to pay off, and a long list of other responsibilities and obligations. No longer the seeming free-agents we were when we were twenty, we might find it difficult, if not impossible, to imagine reframing our own life paths. What if you've already spent half a lifetime in a profession that you now realize you just don't have the heart for anymore? What if it seems too late for your dream of painting, or singing, or studying environmentalism, or of doing non-profit work, or of becoming an alternative healer? When we talk about finances and professions later, we'll go more in-depth on your innate 'calling,' but for now consider the possibility that it's never too late. There are a thousand ways you can embrace and re-claim your creative and intuitive self now, if you are willing to step out of your comfort zone into unfamiliar territory (either financially, professionally, or personally). And you don't have to overturn your whole life to do it.

Going back to a forgotten dream requires a sense of adventure, but as a spiritually maturing adult, you now have the skills and resources to find ways to do that with steadiness, calm, and balance. Whereas a twenty-something might be more inclined to go for it in a way that takes high-level risks, folks who are older and who have a longer list of responsibilities and dependents can still follow their hearts in gentler, subtler ways. Building slowly upon a solid foundation of commitment, with a willingness to take small and medium-sized risks, you can pursue whatever dreams were set aside earlier in your life.

And how can we support young children and teens is holding onto their dreams, empowering them to pursue their true callings right away? Though homeschooling, unschooling, and various alternative school options are becoming more and more common and widely available, there are still many families who—for a wide variety of reasons—opt for more conventional educational settings. In each of these settings, there are benefits and drawbacks. The single most important thing to do to support children in their educations is to acknowledge the benefits and detriments of whatever system they are in. Recognize, and be honest with children about, the ways their particular educational setting prioritizes certain things—whether that be creativity or social conformity, science and technology or the arts, self-direction or teamwork—and support the child in making conscious decisions to balance this setting with his or her needs. Regardless of the child's educational context, it is possible to adapt in-school tasks and projects, and out-of-school activities and circumstances, to foster the unique interests, abilities and passions of each child.

Maybe the best way you can help a child to cope with their learning environment is to *let go of expectations*. It's especially important to let go of the idea that, since your child is 'smart,' he or she should perform equally well in all areas. Stop expecting all A's! If that's something that comes easily to your child, wonderful. But none of us is meant to be an expert at all areas of study, or equally adept at performing in math, science, history, writing, music and athletics. We are individuals. Pressuring children to excel in all areas puts them under undue stress and requires of them that they prioritize *performance* over their own innate well-being. My own very intelligent daughter put herself through sheer agony earning very high grades in high school. I kept encouraging her to go to bed, to sleep, to rest, to *play* some for heaven's sake! But she lived in a culture that insisted her 6 hours of homework per day were worth it, to earn a 'good' job doing something that would be measured not by how much it matched her dreams but by how high the paycheck would be.

I was beyond relieved when she allowed herself to take a year off after school, before college, to paint and recuperate. She went into college knowing who she is and what she loves, and committed to being both financially responsible and working in a field that serves others *and* brings her joy. After ten years working as a college professor, I can say with certainty that the vast majority of young adults who come to college directly from the high-pressure environment of our current secondary school system have rarely been asked "who are you?" They have been told who they *should* be, and what career options they should choose from, but rarely given the freedom to just explore their own crazy, creative interests. The most important subject young people need to study in order to grow into productive, happy, successful adults is *themselves*. They need to be exploring what they truly love, what gives them joy, and where their passions lie. For those who happen to have dreams and passions that fall within our society's accepted range of professions, things may go a little easier. But this isn't most young people. The young people—perhaps you were one of them—whose interests and passions don't fit into prescribed boxes too often turn away from things they would really like to explore, and go into professions that their parents and teachers have chosen for them.

No matter what your dreams are, whether your internal goals fit easily into a social norm or not, and no matter your age, you have the right to pursue your passions fully. In fact, you have a *responsibility* to do so. Each of us is completely unique, and has gifts to offer that only we can bring. No one else on this planet has exactly the same mix of vision, knowledge, wisdom, interest, and resources that you have. And your passions and wishes are the best guide you have to uncovering how you can best serve the whole of society and our planet. If you don't listen to this inner calling, we all lose.

So it's absolutely essential that you follow your dreams, and let your inner guidance show the way to your very best, most powerful and divinely creative self. We need that version of you in the world!

Daring To Dream

Whether we are working with the children in our lives, or with our inner children, one of the important stages of the spiritual journey is daring to dream our best dreams for ourselves. These may be small or large dreams—your dream may be to own a successful business and become a millionaire entrepreneur, or your dream may simply be to have your art work shown in a local gallery. You may want to support a child in competing in a local essay contest, or help a teen get into the college of their dreams. Our dreams can take on many different shapes, sizes and textures. Take a moment to list every single dream—no matter how small or large—that you harbor in your heart. This exercise is meant to unpack the longest list of dreams you can find within yourself, since you have a divine right to receive not just one or a few of these, but all of them.

Exercise #10: Your Dream List

List every single dream or wish or desire you have in each of the following areas. Don't censor yourself at all—there's nothing that should be excluded from this list. Make your lists as long as you possibly can, and when you think you've run out of dreams to write down, come up with a few more. Go into great detail, and really enjoy imagining all the wonderful things that you would like to have in your life. Consider all these areas, and any others you can think of for creating the life of your absolute highest dreams:

~ Home and Living Environment
~ Spouse, Partner or Lover
~ Family (children, parents, siblings, extended family)
~ Friends and Social Life

~ Work, Career
~ Finances and Material Resources
~ Health and Fitness (including diet, exercise, medical care)
~ Leisure (travel, hobbies, play)
~ Spirituality, Religious Community, Philosophies, Beliefs
~ Service Activities
~ Creative Projects and Endeavors, Self-Expression
~ Education and Exploration of New Ideas and Experiences
~ Sexuality and Sensuality
~ Leadership and Success
~ Mentors and Guidance (physical or non-physical)
~ Releasing Fears and Blockages, Healing, Recovery

You can complete this list as many times as you like, and for as many people as you like. It's okay to dream for those you love, as well as for yourself. In fact, dreaming in general terms (e.g. saying "I wish for her happiness and freedom from all financial struggle) rather than worrying about specific outcomes ("I sure hope she gets that job I recommended her for") sends positive creative energy towards the people we love. And dreaming for ourselves—really allowing ourselves to imagine every possible great thing we can—sets in motion all kinds of good energy and help from the multiverse.

One of the biggest obstacles to dreaming is disappointment; we feel that, once we've had a dream delayed or derailed entirely, it's just too dangerous to dream again. Perhaps you thought you had found your one true love, only to have the relationship end in heartbreak and loss. Perhaps you began a business venture that truly excited you, and made you feel as if you had found your calling, only to find it unworkable in a practical way. Perhaps your disappointments have come with your physical body, through illness or injury, or with your hopes for home and family. Whatever form our disappointments have taken, they often diminish or eliminate our hope entirely.

It can be easy, in the face of pain, loss and regret, to shut down our dreaming. We can inhibit our own desires, limiting our wishing and imagination to 'safer' levels of expectation, or to less risky areas of our lives. If we have been hurt in intimate relationship, we may shift our visionary energies to our work; or if we're been disappointed by our health, we may focus entirely on relationship or home.

Sometimes, on the other hand, disappointment can lead us to become overly zealous trying to "get it right" in that part of our lives. We can try to prove to ourselves and others that we have overcome that loss, or somehow been unaffected by it. We may jump too quickly into new relationships or new endeavors, and simply repeat the hurts of the first time around. If we take this approach, like Don Quixote charging at windmills, we will likely end up getting hurt again. Not taking the time to heal from and integrate our losses often results in repeating our own painful history.

As any experienced psychotherapist can attest, human beings tend to repeat patterns, simply changing the set and the cast of characters while keeping the same basic plot and repeating it over and over again. So as we dare to dream again, reclaiming some of that adventure and risk-taking we had as young children, how do we make sure we're doing so in a way that will turn out well for us? Just as recovery from the traumas of childhood requires patience, intention and time, so does recovering from adult disappointments. We have to balance our willingness to try again with wisdom gained from past experiences. The secret of such balancing comes from trusting our inner guidance system, and listening to our hearts as much as (and perhaps more than) our heads. Only our deepest guidance can tell us if we are being curious and courageous, or careless and dangerous. In this way, disappointments are an opening, an invitation, into a deeper relationship with our highest Selves, with our divine guidance, and with our inner knowing.

If we use disappointments as an opportunity to cultivate Self-awareness, they can be invaluable guides to the life of our dreams. But in order to do this, we must transmute the energies of those losses into wisdom and knowledge. And that means spending quality time with the losses themselves.

Think back to a time you took a risk, and were disappointed in the outcome. What did you lose through that experience? Was it a sense of innocence or idealism? Was it a home, or financial resources? Was the loss material (e.g. of a physical ability, or material objects) or was it more ephemeral and subjective (e.g. the loss of a quality in your personality, or of an idea or belief)? The process of transmuting losses into wisdom begins by taking a sincere look at the nature of the actual loss.

Exercise #11: Assessing Your Losses

Choose one big disappointment from your life to spend a few moments with. First, identify what hope or dream was involved in this experience. Next, consider exactly how much of the dream *came true*. We have to recognize both what we gained and what we lost in order to measure our disappointments fully. Once you have a sense of what you gained from this dream, consider what exactly you lost when things turned out differently than you had hoped. Did you lose money and materials? People or relationships? A sense of belonging or an identity? An emotional quality like faith, or hope? Give yourself time to actually *feel* each aspect of the loss before moving on. And don't draw any conclusions about the meaning of the loss—the goal is simply to feel it fully.

If we never *really* assess our actual losses, and honor the significance they have had in our lives, we cannot move beyond them to make newer, wiser dreams. But, by the same token, if we remain stuck in our losses, constantly replaying them in our minds and holding tight to them in our bodies and hearts, we are likely to recreate them. As beings of energy, we must handle our disappointments as energy that is both real and manageable. Once you have a good sense of the nature of your loss, you can take the necessary steps to transform it into usable energy.

Let's take the example of a painful divorce, something that is very common in our world. Many marriages begin with great hopes and optimism; we create dreams together with another person for a life that may include children, a home, careers that fit together, a whole lifestyle that depends on our shared experience. These dreams give us fuel for the challenges we face together, and offer us a way of approaching the future that gives us something to move towards. But, quite often, as we grow individually, our relationships begin to change shape. Couples that at twenty had many shared dreams may find at forty that they no longer are headed in the same direction. When this happens, we are faced with choosing between staying together despite the loss of shared dreams, or ending the relationship in hopes of finding companions who better match our new dreams. Of course, ending such a shared dream involves loss on many levels: material, financial, emotional, psychological, and social. We may lose treasured objects, including our home. We may lose friends who chose the other partner after the divorce, or connections with extended family that we valued. We may lose our sense of self-respect, feeling that we failed, or our sense of identity, no longer knowing quite how to 'fit' in the world as we start over.

Such a loss, much like the loss of a career or of our physical health, causes us to completely redefine who we are and how we belong in our own lives. These losses, and the disappointments and pain that come with them, require some significant attention and compassion before they can turn into workable new dreams. If we hurry to remarry, we will likely find ourselves in the classic 'rebound' relationship, which traditional wisdom says probably won't last long. If we start a new business immediately out of bankruptcy, without taking the time to rethink, reassess and rebuild, we'll likely find ourselves with another financial headache to manage. Instead, the first step to take is to work with the *energy* of the loss—which presents itself most often as *feelings*—and experience it fully.

We often hesitate to set free the full energy of our losses because they frighten us. We somehow believe that, if we let them out of the tight container we have built for them in our bodies, psyches, or emotions, they will bring us even more loss. But this is an illusion. What happens when we feel these emotions, these energies-in-motion, is that they dissipate. So we begin the healing process by naming and experiencing our losses as pure energy, which can move through us. As we sit with the feelings, we may have insights into larger, older patterns in our lives. We may remember things that happened even before this loss, that feel similar. Or we may see things in a completely new way, recognizing great teachings or benefits we have gained from the experience. As the energy *moves*, it will often unveil all sorts of insight and information that was previously unavailable, hidden behind the wall of resistance we put up to avoid feeling those losses.

In the case of a completed relationship, we may begin to feel a new sense of peace and possibility, grateful for everything that the relationship taught us but ready to move forward. When our bodies change and lose some of their previous abilities, we may discover new abilities and gifts that had been unnoticed or unused. When we let go of the energy around old careers or callings, new and exciting ideas and interests may have space and fuel to grow. This process of transmuting the energy of loss into new awareness might happen quickly, or it may take many years. But our task is to *allow the energies to flow freely again.* As children, our free-flowing energy gives us courage, confidence, and curiosity. As adults, restoring this free-flowing energy is essential to building and manifesting new dreams.

Once the energy of loss begins to loosen up and move, we can use it to imagine new possibilities. One of the best tricks for freeing up stuck energy from the past and creating a new, more vibrant future is a trick sometimes called 'scripting,' taught by Abraham Hicks and Abraham students, Lynn Grabhorn and Christy Whitman. You can use it to imagine something in the future or, as I suggest here, to re-create events from the past in a way that makes you feel more alive, and more whole.

Exercise #12: Rescripting an Event

You can write an imagined 'script' or scenario to help you visualize the way you wish things had been. You aren't doing this with a sense of self-pity, though, but with the feeling of re-creating your inner landscape as if you'd gotten everything you truly wanted. When you rescript a scenario or situation, you get a chance to see what it would *feel like* if the disappointment hadn't effected you. This, in turn, changes the energy in your field and allows you to actually feel the feelings, and hold the energies, of your preferred, alternate experience.

Consider the event you reflected upon in the last exercise. If you could rewrite that situation or event exactly the way you would like, what would have happened? If you had been given all the resources, support, ease and grace you could possibly have wanted, what would you have experienced in those moments? And what would you feel like now? You can include the people, the experiences, and the adventures you would like to have had. You can eliminate illnesses or traumatic experiences, and replace them with joyful, pleasant experiences. Or, if you feel the difficult experiences were essential to who you are now, you can shape your and other people's responses to them.

The purpose of this exercise is not to feel sorry yourself, or say "it's such a shame I didn't get what I wanted." Instead, the goal is to imagine who you really are, separate from those experiences. You are re-imagining the whole scenario in a way you like better. Once we have named the losses that have imprinted on our energy, moved that energy out of our bodies, and begun to shift the vibration from loss to freedom, we can use this moving energy to imagine what it would feel like *if the loss had never been there at all.* This exercise relies on the basic premise that all of our experiences are, first and foremost, energetic ones. As such, the energy we hold surrounding them can be played with, altered, and redirected however we like.

You can do this with any experience that you feel has limited you, or with whole segments of your life. I have taken time to rescript my entire childhood, imagining all sorts of wonderful energies coming in that would support and nourish my current dreams right now. As I do this, I am conscious that I am directly working with the energies of my life, and I am intentionally using these visualizations to direct new energy into my energy field. The same practice works great with imaging things that have not yet happened. Abraham teaches that if you can maintain a high vibration, through exercises such as this, for at least 17 seconds, you can materially change the quality of the experiences you create in your life. This, in turn, makes your dreams more available, and gets them moving towards you.

CHAPTER

5

Seeking Safety

Most of us are able to retain some portion of our deepest dreams and mystical abilities, despite the traumas of human life. Though disappointment may have dimmed our childhood enthusiasm and faith, we often find ways to weave our deepest desires into the fabric of our lives. Still, we often limit the size of our dreams, keeping them as hobbies or only giving them a portion of the time they crave. We usually do this because our dreams are tied up with feelings of pain, loss, and fear. The full flow of energy that would give us our greatest joy, and fulfill our greatest wishes, would also break down the barriers we have constructed to hold back unresolved feelings. Like water from a garden hose running through clogged rain gutters, a greater flow of spiritual energy through our systems would release the built up debris of pain, anger, fear and unresolved hurts that is clogging up our emotional and spiritual systems. We compromise with ourselves by allowing ourselves a slow flow of energy: we settle for a modified, reduced version of our deepest dreams, while maintaining a relatively tight lid on the old hurts, disappointments, and losses that are still stuck in our energy fields.

There are three primary ways we lose touch with our innate, open, magical Selves. First, we may have traumas unrelated to our mystical abilities which cause us to shut down and become cautious. These sorts of experiences require us to divert spiritual energies to survival skills. We need to focus our attention on recovering from shock, managing the overwhelming emotions of loss and tragedy, and getting by in a less-than-ideal world. This sort of trauma comes, to some degree, to all of us. But for many, such traumas can tie up so much energy that our spiritual journeys become secondary, if not totally irrelevant to our conscious minds. (Of course, this is all part of the spiritual journey, but we may not recognize that until a later stage.) Paradoxically, sometimes the intense survival needs of a traumatized child can in fact *enhance* some of his or her intuitive abilities. Many children who perceive danger in their environment will develop a heightened sense of empathy, telepathy or intuition in order to predict danger and avoid it. These sorts of traumas usually result in coping strategies to help keep us safe from harm. The most common of these strategies are hypervigilance, perfectionism, rebellion, and numbing.

Two other ways we lose touch with our magical Selves come directly from dangers associated with being intuitive or sensitive. In this area, the danger can come either from intuitive, psychic experiences themselves, or from other peoples' reactions to them. Mystical experiences may be dangerous because they are emotionally, spiritually, or physically threatening. Or they may be dangerous because they make others uncomfortable, and then we feel rejected or judged. Let's take a closer look at each of these three circumstances that can lead us to consciously or unconsciously shutting down our intuitive, magical abilities.

✦ ✦ ✦

As we've already discussed, physical and psychological traumas in our childhood and teen years can cause us to shut down some or all of our intuitive abilities, and our sense that the world is a magical place. Injuries, illnesses, abusive circumstances, poverty, and other traumatic events can force us into survival mode, and we may not even realize that's where we have been until many years later. Most of us have had at least a few traumatic experiences that have left their marks—sports injuries, break-ups with boyfriends or girlfriends, hurtful words from parents or teachers. Some of us have experienced more extreme traumas, such as homelessness; physical, sexual, or emotional abuse; life-threatening illness or injury; or other life-altering traumas. In either case, these experiences can have wide-ranging effects on our bodies, our emotions, our beliefs and our spiritual expansion.

In any of these circumstances, we adopt strategies to help keep us safer. Some of the most common strategies children and teens use to protect themselves include: hypervigilance, perfectionism, rebellion, and numbing. There are many other strategies, as well, but let's start with these very common ones.

Hypervigilance

Hypervigilance is a way to ensure safety by accurately predicting how others will act. If a child or teen (or adult, for that matter) is exposed to repeated dangers and hurts, they become very alert to cues in the environment warning them when it might happen again. In a hypervigilant state, you will notice things much more acutely, and take signals of danger much more seriously, than someone who is not hypervigilant. For example, if you had an alcoholic father who always drank on the way home from work, then was abusive upon arriving at home, you may be especially agitated at the end of the work day. You may jump at the sounds of garage doors, or cars pulling in the driveway. You may have learned how to tell very quickly, by the look on his face or the way your father carried himself as he came through the door, whether it would be a 'good' day or a 'bad' one. This heightened attention to detail carries over into other aspects of our lives, channeling our energy from creativity into self-protection. Once out of the dangerous situation, we may continue to spend lots of energy noticing sudden noises, or reading between the lines of what others say. We may remain on 'high alert' even when others perceive things to be safe, and we may develop symptoms of depleted adrenal glands as our adrenaline levels—kept high for long periods of time—begin to dwindle.

Hypervigilance is a classic symptom of Post Traumatic Stress Disorder, and is one of the most important ways young people attempt to protect themselves from dangerous people or situations. From the energetic perspective, hypervigilance means that you are diverting large amounts of energy from *creating* and *enjoying* to *watching* and *expecting*. Your energy is being used to carefully scan the environment for potential dangers, so you don't have very much left over for meandering thoughts, or imagination of the positive sort (i.e. seeing yourself having fun and experiencing pleasure). At the same time, you are devoting a large amount of time and attention to expecting unpleasant experiences. So, in a way, you are devoting your creative energy to imagining unpleasant, upsetting outcomes. All of this keys your system to watching for, and finding, things around you that you don't like and that feel threatening.

Hypervigilance is a useful tool for someone who is truly in danger, but once the material danger has passed, this mind-set can leave us feeling depleted, upset, and like we are surrounded by danger and threat at all times. Hypervigilance also can leave us feeling like we have to work, work, work and never have any fun, since we develop the habit of never relaxing or letting down our guard. Linked up with some of the other strategies we develop as children and teens for coping with trauma, hypervigilance can make our lives an endless cycle of looking for danger, trying to get around it, and getting caught up in unpleasant situations which affirm our belief that the world can't be trusted.

At its most basic, hypervigilance is based on the assumption that life isn't safe. And, for some people in some circumstances, this may be materially true. And yet, once the energy pattern has been set in place, it's hard to shift out of it and can become a self-fulfilling prophecy. In other words, we can experience danger, become hypervigilant, decide that the world isn't safe and then, no matter what new circumstances arise, we continue to believe and act as if things are unsafe. This exhausts and depresses us, resulting in further circumstances that are depleting and out of balance.

Exercise #13: Hypervigilance Checklist

Do you have the symptoms of hypervigilance? They include: (1) a heightened awareness of what other people are doing, saying, or (possibly) thinking, accompanied by a feeling of needing to 'watch out for' what someone might do next; (2) finding it hard to have fun, let down your guard, and just relax; always feeling like you need to be 'on top of things' and in control of the situation; (3) a heightened intuition about other peoples' future actions or behaviors; (4) symptoms of adrenal fatigue or depletion. You may also notice that you are very sensitive to loud noises, or to abrupt or dramatic body language.

If you have any of these symptoms, ask yourself when they began to develop. Did they start when you were very young, perhaps before you can even remember? Or was there a moment when you made the decision to 'not be caught off guard again'? Noticing when and how hypervigilance developed is the first step to freeing yourself from its limitations. If you have symptoms of hypervigilance, in addition to doing the energy work needed to heal these patterns in your energy field, it is a good idea to work with a trained psychotherapist who can help you release the psychological layers of trauma that generated them.

Hypervigilance is a very common response to traumatic experiences encountered in childhood and the teen years. Whether the trauma was caused by another person, such as in an abusive home, or by an accident or illness, we can develop an instinctive response to protect ourselves by 'watching out' for similar circumstances in the future. Once we develop this pattern, though, it can get wired into our energy systems in a way that later can be more limiting than helpful. Unfortunately, our culture actually *rewards* hypervigilance in its less dramatic forms, by paying higher salaries, offering more praise, and giving more promotions to those of us who have sacrificed some basic health and balance for an over-developed sense of alertness and being ready-to-act.

Perfectionism

The same reward system is in place for an over-developed sense of performing for others' approval. Perfectionism is one of the most insidious, and destructive, of the ways children and teens respond to traumatic circumstances. Too often, we learn that if we can behave perfectly—never making a mistake, never causing any upset or conflict, always acting in ways that make others happy—we can avert or avoid situations that cause pain. Children and teens who adopt perfectionism as a safety strategy can seem to be doing very well, on the surface. They make good grades, they are leaders in sports or clubs at school, they excel academically or in social contexts. But sometimes all this high performance masks a deep feeling of fear, that the child is just barely doing enough to stave off judgments, rejection, condemnation, or other forms of emotional or physical abuse.

Perfectionism is rewarded highly in contemporary society, and it does provide some level of protection against the dangers of the world. But there is a difference between doing our best, and expecting ourselves to be perfect. When we do our best, we take into account being *at our best* in all areas of our lives. When we are *at our best*, we take care of our physical health by sleeping well, resting often, and relaxing and having fun. When we are at our best, we know that our time and energy are limited resources, which must be stewarded wisely and cared for with self-respect and self-awareness. At our best, we know when to say "no," when to stop *doing* and just *be*.

By contrast, perfectionism is that driving force that won't let you rest until all the dishes are done, the house tidied, the lunches packed, and the reports for work completed. It's the force that insists it isn't 'good enough' to take a B or a C in a class that's difficult, but instead that you must push yourself as hard as possible to achieve the A. Perfectionism won't let you rest until you've excelled above others, outperforming both your peers and your own limitations. Perfectionism feels like pressure, like urgency, like necessity. It's a drive to go beyond your limits, to push yourself, to prove yourself, to perform.

Though it can sometimes be healthy to challenge our own limits, and excel where we thought we might not be able, perfectionism requires us to do this in all, or at least many, areas of our lives. And this includes areas that are very challenging and difficult, or for which we have no interest or ability. And when we are unable to meet our own or others' expectations, we criticize ourselves and push ourselves even harder. We tell ourselves that "if only I had..." worked longer hours, or studied a little harder, or tried a little more, I could have/should have/would have accomplished more. It is a strategy that prioritizes succeeding at goals we think will please others, and make us more acceptable, or worthy, in their eyes. But this all comes at the price of sacrificing our own basic sense of self-esteem, self-respect, and self-love.

Perfectionism forces us to put a very high value on others, while placing a very low value on ourselves. Because it is essentially designed for self-protection, perfectionism makes us heighten our attention to external markers of 'wellness'— grades, titles, awards, leadership roles, money. It necessarily forces us, at the same time, to turn away from *internal markers of wellness*—feeling well rested, feeling calm and at peace, having a strong sense of self-worth and self-respect, having time for play and leisure, and having good balance in all areas of our lives. Too often, we mistake satisfaction at a job well done, or pride in our accomplishments, for a deeper sense of having followed our own hearts. Though we gain the approval of others, we lose our own internal gauge of what *feels good* to us. We are often told that focusing on our own well-being is 'selfish' but, in fact, if we don't pay attention to our own well-being, our own self-interest, we end up exhausted, depleted, and lacking a clear sense of who we are, and what's really true for us.

During my days as a college professor, I counselled innumerable young students who sat in my office, crying tears of despair and confusion, who simply had no idea who they were or what they wanted. They were excellent students; they had gotten good grades, led in sports teams and school clubs, volunteered in all the right extra-curricular activities, and yet they were miserable. They had performed perfectly in all the ways their teachers, parents and peers had demanded, thereby protecting themselves from judgments of failure, laziness, lack of discipline, and the like. They had done everything right, and while it made them look good to the outside world, their inside worlds were crumbling.

When I asked these students, "Well, what do *you* want? What do *you* like to do? Who do *you* want to become?" they simply couldn't answer. For many them, they had never even been asked that question. They had been scolded and molded, through both unintentional pressures and intentional bullying, to become people that were 'perfect' on the surface, and yet utterly disconnected with their own true Selves. If we remember that perfectionism is a strategy, not for 'success' but for *survival*, we can understand this all a lot better.

At its most basic, perfectionism is a strategy that children, teens and adults adopt to protect them from rejection, criticism and punishment by others (from the most subtle verbal jabs, to being deprived of things we love, to outright physical pain). It is not a strategy which arises in a context of curiosity about, or compassion for, a child's inherent needs, passions and uniqueness. It is highly rewarded in our society, precisely because so many of us feel a deep need to protect ourselves from these experiences. As adults, we want to protect our children from the same sort of social rejection and pain, so we continue the cycle of forcing perfectionism on our children as a way to 'help' them to be safe in a dangerous world. In other words, too often parents and caregivers *teach perfectionism* as the best strategy for dealing with the dangers of modern life.

And yet perfectionism has an incredibly high cost. It deprives us of our deepest connection to our inner, magical, knowing Selves by telling us to focus on others' goals, rather than our own. This means we may lose touch with our passion for things we love, unless they fit neatly into society's box of 'acceptable' interests. Even worse, perfectionism teaches us that *it is okay, even good, to sacrifice our physical, emotional and spiritual well-being for the cause of performing well.* We let go of our own internal monitors for balance and overall health, prioritizing instead performing in a few limited arenas of life. And we divert energy away from our own spiritual paths, in the service of comforting others who have themselves often lost track of their own inner truths.

Take a few moments with the following exercise to consider how your life would feel different without any pressures—external or internal—for perfectionism.

Exercise #14: Life Without Perfectionism

One of the things I often found myself asking young college students, most of whom had mastered perfectionism by the time they reached their late teens, was this: "What do you really want to do? Or be?" If you could go back to the age of ten or twelve, and ask yourself that question, what would you answer? Imagine yourself as a young person just on the verge of puberty sitting with some caring family member or friend, someone you trust who you know would want for you exactly what your deepest self wants for you. If you can't think of anyone, imagine yourself sitting in my office, having this conversation directly with you. Imagine this person asking—with deep sincerity and curiosity—"What would you really like to do when you grow up? What really interests you? What do you love?" This person doesn't care one bit about whether or not your interests match society's ideas of 'success' or performing well. What would you say?

Secondly (and this is the really important part for dealing with perfectionism), imagine what they would tell you to *stop* doing, *stop* paying attention to, in order to focus on what you love. What would they counsel you to ignore, or let go? What areas of your health and life would they encourage you to care for more, as you make your way towards becoming your best self, rather than a version of you created by other people. In what ways can you imagine them counselling you in your life now, as they support you to *be at your best*, in the most whole, balanced way?

Rebellion

Where some children and youth adopt a strategy of following the rules perfectly in order to secure the love, approval and acceptance of others, there are certainly many young people who adopt the opposite response: outright rebellion. And many of us choose to conform in one area while rebelling in others. Though perfectionism and rebellion appear to be very different, their vibrations have some similarities. For starters, both arise primarily from fear, and both attempt to convert fear into control. Conforming closely to the rules and expectations of others allows us to convert fear into control by saying, "I can handle myself so well that I can out-distance any danger you put in front of me." Rebellion, on the other hand says, "I can control *you* by refusing to agree to your terms, no matter what. Your rules don't apply to me, so I am in control of this situation." In both cases, we attempt to gain control over a dangerous and fearful situation by manipulating the energy exchange between ourselves and the source of the danger.

Rebellion always rests on a fear that one's personal choices will not be welcomed or accepted by others, but will instead be rejected and condemned. Therefore, the rebel chooses to act as s/he wants *anyway*, usually with defiance and a heightened sense of assertion or aggression. Often, rebellion goes even further by selecting actions which may not come from our deepest desires, but instead from the knowledge that they are explicitly *not desired* by people we perceive as dangerous. When teens rebel, they are saying "No!" very emphatically to being shaped and molded by external forces. They are asserting their personal power for self-direction. Unfortunately, rebels often turn to other rebels for the social welcoming, community and acceptance that we all need, and end up conforming to a secondary peer group while rebelling against primary influences like family. We all need to belong; if a child or youth feels like true belonging is unavailable within his or her family, they will seek it elsewhere. They will choose to say "no" to family or teachers or other influences by saying "yes" to whatever those influence most want them to avoid.

This can certainly be a good thing if our family or teachers are, in fact, dangerous to our innate well-being. Too often, we label rebellion as a 'bad' behavior when it may be a young person's absolute best defense against others who are trying to seriously damage their sense of autonomy, inner-knowing, and self-direction. Often, a young person knows clearly that they must protect their authentic identity against any attempts to destroy it. Unfortunately, though, too often their only options for support are other young people who are themselves in rebellion and *also* lacking in good adult support structures. In a healthier environment or context, these young people would have healthy adult advocates who could teach them how to maintain autonomy, and protect their authentic selves, without endangering themselves in other ways.

It makes sense, when our sense of personal freedom and the right to choose is threatened, that we do whatever it takes to protect our basic human needs. We all have a right to follow our deepest inner knowing and wisdom. We all have a need to make our own choices, including our own mistakes, and to explore the world from our own spiritual centers. Many children and youth are deprived of these basic freedoms when they are told they must act in certain way, prefer certain interests or certain people, and follow a path laid out for them by adults who don't fully respect the young person's inner direction. If we are to truly support ourselves and the young people in our lives, we have to accept that our inner direction can be trusted, and that we are all on unique spiritual and physical journeys. Allowing ourselves, and our children, to explore the world in our own unique, sometimes unpredictable and often counter-cultural ways, is where all hope for the future lies. If we keep insisting on doing things the old way, the way they have been done, or 'should' be done, then we will keep getting the same results—including all the problems and limitations and difficulties that have plagued our world for millennia.

Rebellion, then, can be a very healthy strategy. If guided by spiritually mature and responsible mentors, a young person rebelling against cultural norms and overly-directive parents, teachers, and care-givers can in fact blossom and flourish. However, remember that the primary motive here is *fear and self-protection*. When we are afraid, we tend to be reactive, rather than responsive and therefore we tend to make hasty decisions and choices we may later regret. So often, young people with a legitimate reason to rebel have no good guidance for a new path. They tend to choose paths that are as far from their parents' or teachers' choices as possible, to put distance between themselves and the source of the danger. This often leads them into even more troubled situations, and it can be hard to find the way back to balance from there.

Exercise #15: Healthy and Unhealthy Rebellion

In what ways are you a rebel? Are you someone who strongly rebels against cultural or family norms? Or someone who rebels in quieter ways? We all have some areas in which we 'go against the grain' of society or family, choosing to do things our own way, rather than conforming to how 'everyone else' acts. For me, I am a bit of a food rebel: I insist on eating organic even if it means I bring my own food to big family dinners, or insisting on buying naturally raised meat for the

---

whole family. Though this isn't a dangerous rebellion, it does go against the grain of my family conditioning. Sometimes we rebel by choosing a different religion than our families, or leaving religion entirely. Political beliefs, holiday traditions, religious affiliation, clothing and food…all are areas in which we might challenge the 'shoulds' given to us by others.

Once you identify a few of the ways you rebel, consider if these rebellions are healthy for you in all ways, or have some unhealthy aspects. Does your rebellion preserve your autonomy, but cut you off from your family or community in a way that hurts you? Does your rebellion in any way hurt your physical body? Or expose you to other dangers (including dangerous people or substances)? As you consider your own personal rebellions, ask yourself two questions: (1) what am I trying to protect or preserve through this rebellion? And (2) what, if anything, is it costing me to rebel in this way?

Numbing

Another strategy that often accompanies rebellion is 'numbing': shutting down or numbing the pain and fear in our lives by using substances or behaviors that cut off sensation or feeling. The most common and obvious way we numb ourselves is through substances that chemically alter our state of consciousness. Illegal mood-altering drugs, over-prescribed painkillers, and alcohol get the most attention in western culture for this, but many other things serve to numb us, as well. There are any number of completely legal, socially accepted ways that we numb our pain and thus limit our flow of energy. Cigarette smoking, overeating, excessive consumption of artificial sweeteners (especially in diet sodas and other diet products), excessive exercise, over-spending, and work addiction are just as destructive and dangerous as drugs and alcohol. But because these legal means are considered 'okay' by our society, we often ignore their destructive effects until significant damage has been done.

Western culture has a serious addiction to prescription and over-the-counter medicines for treating, and suppressing the symptoms of energy imbalances. A few years ago, there was a television commercial for a popular stomach medicine (one used to treat indigestion and heartburn) that showed very busy people, running around frenetically to overwork and manage incredibly high levels of stress in their lives, who were having symptoms of stomach problems. The commercial went on to say something to the effect of, "You could change your lifestyle, or you could take our product." I was horrified by this commercial. It openly acknowledged that the *healthy* thing to do would be to address the underlying causes of dis-ease—to change the lifestyle that was clearly out of balance. But, instead, the commercial freely tapped into our resistance to changing our addictions; we'd rather take a chemical that promises a quick fix (no matter how temporary) than do the deeper work of changing core patterns and beliefs and getting a more real, sustainable healing.

We take cold remedies rather than resting. We drink energy drinks rather than eating a healthy, slow-food diet. We use caffeine to fuel our hyper-speed lifestyles. And we think it's perfectly okay. So many times, we don't even make the connection between the things that aren't working in our lives, and the very basic ways we choose to neglect our bodies and minds. We think it's too time consuming to purchase and prepare unprocessed food, and too expensive to select products that have been filled with nutrients by nature, rather than by a chemistry lab. At the most basic levels, we often prioritize 'convenience' and speed over sustainability and health. And we often consider our own legal addictions acceptable, while judging others' addictions as failures.

As a society, we are quick to condemn people who are using substances that have been deemed illegal. We see these people as weak or immoral. But the very same parent who condemns a teen for smoking pot may be addicted to tobacco and diet sodas. Or to shopping. From an energetic standpoint, there is no difference between the 'legal' and the 'illegal' substances. From the perspective of our energy bodies, they serve the same purpose: to shut down feeling, to suppress anger and grief, to create sensations which help us avoid facing our own, inner truth. In fact, the people struggling the most with addiction are often the ones who are most sensitive to the flow of energies around them.

Children learn very young that numbing the pain is the norm in our culture. Take the quick fix from a pill, or a food, or a new pair of shoes or car—that's easier than asking ourselves what hole we are trying to fill, what pain we are trying to avoid, what grief we are wanting to not feel. As a culture, we teach our children that it is better to take short-term rewards and immediate relief, rather than spend the time, energy, and attention we need to deeply heal ourselves. We show them that surface performance matters more than deep, slow awakening. So when young people are faced with situations that are threatening—whether the threat comes from teachers pressuring a child to become someone they are not, or from abuse by family members, or from incredible loss faced too young—it's a natural thing for them to choose the quick way out of the pain.

Not all shopping is bad, nor all sodas, nor all fast food.

But addiction is epidemic in our culture, and the purpose it serves is to numb us to our pain, to help us deny and avoid our chronic confusion over where we truly belong and who we truly are. A mix of numbing and rebellion can be heady— we take the drugs, have the adventures, take the daring risks we shouldn't take. A mix of numbing and perfectionism can make us feel powerful, as we excel in school, work and finances while deadening the symptoms of overwork, exhaustion and fatigue with medications or food. Numbing mixed with hypervigilance often means we use anxiety medications, and sleep aids, allowing us to function while ignoring our bodies' messages that something is seriously wrong. All of these mixes can be profoundly destructive, to both soul and body. Eventually, this misdirection of our internal energies will *increase*, rather than decrease our symptoms. The credit card debt will become unmanageable; the weight gain will become impossible to shake and the dieting will damage our systems and self-esteem; the pills will stop working and we have to take more and more.

Exercise #16: Identifying Our Addictions

It took me years to admit that I am addicted to overwork, and I still haven't completely gotten over this addiction. I learned young to be a perfectionist, and was rewarded greatly for it by academic honors, praise from teachers and parents, and being seen by my community as a great success. So I became addicted to the high of their acceptance and encouragement, as well as to the actual chemical rush experienced by someone who overworks. Adrenaline is a powerful drug. I would *never* have seen myself as an 'addict' until my symptoms— chronic neck and back pain, exhaustion, irritable bowel

---

and bladder, anxiety and panic attacks, migraines and other odd neurological symptoms—forced me to take a deep, serious look at how I was managing my energy. I developed these patterns in my teen years, as so many of us do, but it wasn't until my mid 30s that I finally began to untangle their destructive effects.

What sorts of numbing patterns have you developed in order to survive? What substances or behaviors do you resort to when you feel upset, frightened, or overwhelmed? Are your preferred numbing tools legal or illegal? Do you consume any substances on a 'gotta-have-it' or 'life wouldn't be worth living without this' basis? Take a moment to consider what it is that helps you *avoid* the tough feelings you are holding inside, or the challenging changes you know you need to make in your life. If you have already overcome the most powerful of your addictions, take a moment to consider if, and in what ways, the residual pain and grief they were covering up still remain.

The only way out of the mess that comes from numbing ourselves is to *feel*. The only way to deal with the destructive effects of hypervigilance, rebellion, and perfectionism is to recognize them. We need to slow down, and give ourselves and others time to really understand what we are feeling, and what we are avoiding feeling. These are really the first steps in creating or restoring a healthy flow of energy. When students or clients come to me hoping to increase their psychic abilities, or get quick-fix psychic answers to life problems, I always tell them this: there is no 'quick fix.' Healing, and flowing in your true life energy, is a process, a journey. There is no great psychic escape from the very real physical and psychological effects of blocking our own energy. Though numerous tools, techniques and traditions exist for assisting us as we unravel the patterns that have protected us, but now limit us, there is no way to completely bypass acknowledging our pain.

We need our defenses while we are in danger. When the danger passes, we need to release those defenses, those safety mechanisms. Yet when we do this, we must be prepared to feel the feelings which were set aside until a safer day. One of my greatest teachers, Megan Wagner, a psychotherapist and teacher of the Kabbalah, as well as head of Tree of Life Teachings with her husband Jim Larkin, used the phrase "spiritual bypass" to describe what many of us mystically inclined folks like to do with our pain. Having established solid and effective defenses in our childhoods, we charge forward into the spiritual realms ready to experience the mystical and the magical. We often feel we have overcome our difficulties by putting them into proper perspective. We know that we are eternal beings, and we have had some therapy, so we believe we have moved beyond those old hurts and traumas. But, more often than not, our defenses are still solidly in place, and we're actually using the mystical path to further avoid the very real pain of the earth plane.

This doesn't work, and can quite frankly be dangerous because as we increase our spiritual flow and power, those blocked areas create an even more powerful potential for explosions. The spiritual path isn't an *alternative* to the very real needs of the body or the mind and emotions; it is a complement to them. They work together, not in opposition. Western culture holds a deep belief in the separation of body and soul, of matter and spirit, and yet they are inextricably interwoven. In order to be on a healthy spiritual path, we must also be on a healthy physical, emotional and mental path. Taking a real look at how we have decided to keep ourselves safe in the face of trauma and danger is an important part of this journey into health and reuniting with our divine Selves.

Social Conditions

Another important source of danger to our young, intuitive, mystical Selves is how other people respond to our psychic abilities. Though some young people have family members or friends who understand and encourage intuitive, mystical abilities, many others do not. For many, the people around us as we were growing up were either confused, politely amused, or downright scared when we told them what we knew or experienced. As I've said before, it's one thing for a child to have imaginary playmates—adults who don't understand the magical world can brush this off as harmless imaginative play. It's another thing entirely, though, for that child to predict future events or pass along accurate information from deceased relatives. Though we may begin our childhood with a curiosity and courage about mystical experiences, the responses of adults and other children can quickly teach us to be more cautious.

I was blessed to have chosen a family in which intuitive abilities were at least recognized, though they were also often misunderstood or treated as a little suspect. Even in this context, I was very careful about what I shared about my intuitive experiences. Luckily, in my extended family, there was a culture of recognizing and accepting, to some extent, intuitive abilities. Too often, though, children are told that intuitive knowledge is a 'tool of the devil' or the work of dangerous or malevolent spirits.

I clearly remember one day, when I was in my 30's, and a mom of you children, when another parent expressed this sentiment. Though I was an adult, and was prepared to deflect the harm her words might have done, I was mindful of the children around us at the time of our exchange. We were standing outside our children's school, waiting for the afternoon bell to ring and for our children to come out at the end of the day. There were many other adults around, many of them with much younger children—preschoolers—in tow. This other woman began describing her latest creative project: a novel she was working on. We began talking about the challenges of balancing writing with parenting young children (I was also working on a novel at the time). The conversation seemed to be going well until she began talking about the actual plot of her novel. The main character, she said, was a young woman who had fallen into the clutches of satan, who was manipulating her through giving her psychic abilities. As I heard this, I felt my stomach clench and my face grow blank in self-protection. The woman went on to explain how the novel was about the evils of psychic and intuitive abilities, which are always tools of the devil and dangerous snares to unsuspecting victims. Oh my.

I was, first, extremely grateful that I had not revealed the plot of *my* book first. It was about a woman protagonist who travels through time, using her mystical abilities to connect with members of her soul family across lives and to pursue her soul purpose. Whew! That was a close call! And then I was angry, really, really angry. All of the old feelings I had experienced as a child who was shamed by her culture for having abilities *beyond the 'normal'* came rushing back. All the feelings of rejection, of being told I was at best confused, deluded, or making things up and at worst crazy or malevolent, swelled in my heart, mind and body. But this time I knew them for what they were: projections of people who simply don't understand, or can't accept, our natural intuitive abilities. I understood that, rather than expand her worldiew to include these things that she simply didn't comprehend, it was easier for this woman to condemn them. But, boy, was I mad.

I was furious for every child who has ever been, or will ever be, told these things about him or herself. And I was furious for all the lost wisdom, the lost healing and beauty, that would be created if we as a culture embraced our intuitive gifts. And I mourned all over again for the years I had spent, and that I knew so many others have spent, trying to recover from being told that our unique and special gifts make us broken. As adults, we have the ability to heal and recover from these wounds, made by the words and physical reactions that others have to our intuitive knowing. But children are too often unprepared for such judgments, no matter how subtle. Not only do these experiences cause us to shut down our intuitive abilities, either by stopping expressing them or stopping experiencing them entirely, they also cause damage to our spirits, our psyches, and our identity that may take years to repair.

Often, such damage leaves us feeling as if we just don't know who we are. We have an innate ability that we cannot ever truly eliminate, and yet we are taught—both implicitly and explicitly—that to live up to this ability will result in being ostracized or ridiculed. So we choose to stop being or doing the things that come naturally to us and try, instead, to be something that we are not. Over time, this act of self-denial makes us feel more and more alienated from ourselves, blocking access to our deepest desires, and forcing us to live out a life path that is not true for us. The damage that can result from such seemingly simply criticism--"Oh, silly child! There's no ghost in your room. You're just making that up!" or "Now, stop that! You're scaring your sister by saying you can see these things!" –even such seemingly innocuous comments have long-ranging and devastating effects.

There's another way our society now distorts our understanding of our own mystical abilities, and this is by dramatizing them and exaggerating them in the popular media. The pendulum has swung back from total societal rejection of psychic gifts and magical realms, but it has swung far past a balanced center. Now, we have television shows, books, and movies that present mystical abilities as if they are either very rare or only held by very odd people. So we have vampires and vampire slayers, instead of herbalists and healers in the movies. We have a surplus of semi-demonic, and semi-angelic creatures with magical abilities carrying out wild adventures and battles between good and evil, rather than shows that depict the rather mundane, everyday work of an intuitive counsellor. And even the most realistic of shows, such as "Long Island Medium" portray very powerful, accurate intuitives as eccentric and odd.

We've made the mystical unusual, rather than normal, and that doesn't help the situation much, either.

We are making progress, though, as a society. There are more and more decent portrayals of mediums, psychics, spiritual teachers, and other mystics doing very good work in fairly 'normal' circumstances. Hay House publications, Gaia TV, and many other media are offering excellent material on a wide array of mystical subjects, accessible to people of all ages. But there's still an awful lot of material out there that makes the mystical seem maudlin, or crazy, or dangerous.

What about your experiences as an intuitive child? What were you told about your gifts, both directly and by implication, by the adults and other children in your life?

> ### *Exercise #17: Mirrors in the Faces of Our Family*
>
> Can you remember a time in your childhood when a family member or other important person acted surprised, upset, confused or otherwise troubled by your mystical or intuitive abilities? What did that person say or do? And what did their body language, especially their facial expression, tell you about how they were feeling? How did you respond to their reactions to you? Did you feel frightened, or ashamed? Or did you have family stories about ghosts or mystical events? What messages did you receive about the 'paranormal' world?

The first response most of us have when faced with criticism, judgment, or shaming is to try to retract our words or actions. Next, we will try to make amends with the other person in some way. For example, I often tried to be the most caring, most obedient child I could be, because I believed that my "weirdness" was a burden to my family. Next, we will avoid naming or speaking about our experiences, at least to some people. And, finally, we will internalize the messages we have heard to the point that we ourselves no longer believe in, or experience, mystical moments. We so thoroughly take in the message that, "You couldn't have seen that," that we dismiss our perceptions as quickly as they happen. And over time, we may simply no longer have them.

Most of us have experienced pressures from family, peers, and teachers to shut down our magical selves. Unfortunately, this is one of the most common stages of the spiritual journey. As the wonder and magic of childhood give way to the social pressures and the challenging experiences of puberty, most of us begin to hold back our visions, our dreams for ourselves, and our mystical abilities in order to fit in. Seeking safety from hurts ranging from mild criticism and teasing, to shaming and outright physical abuse, we find ways to conform rather than stand out.

Psychic Dangers

Social conditioning teaches us that seeing spirits in our bedroom, or hearing the voices of ancestors, or seeing fairies in the forest, is 'weird' or unnatural. So we stop hearing and seeing them. We are told that we must be practical, rather than fanciful, so we stop paying attention to our imaginations and start focusing on externally accepted data. And we begin to internalize the voices of our critics, telling *ourselves* it's 'just our imagination' when magical things happen. As we do this, as we stop using these abilities, they can weaken and even seem to disappear. I have heard too many students and clients describe abilities that, once normal to them in childhood, seem to have disappeared over the years.

This same basic process of shutting down happens when we have mystical experiences that are themselves upsetting or frightening. Just as the responses from others can make us want to stop having intuitive and magical experiences, so too can the intensity or nature of the experiences themselves. It is possible to have experiences that scare us away completely from the other realms. Because we live in a culture that is only now developing a professional class of mystical teachers—such as in a traditional society, where 'medicine' people served as the communally recognized agent of such teaching—children are woefully without training on how to manage mystical experiences. Just as I was left to handle the ghosts in my bedroom on my own, many young people explore the edges of their psychic and mystical abilities only to get 'burned' by experiences that are frightening or troubling.

Though I do not operate in a world of polarities, where 'good' and 'evil' are forces that are battling it out for control of the universe, I do believe that it's possible to have unpleasant, even dangerous experiences in the realms of the mystical. I often explain this to clients and students by saying that, just as you meet people in your daily life who express a range of emotions, moods and personalities—angry, friendly, wise, unwise, helpful, draining—the same is true of those who inhabit the non-physical realms. Or, to put a point on it, just because someone is currently not in a body doesn't make them enlightened. Too often, in our early mystical explorations (as both youth and as adults), we can make the mistake of thinking that spiritual presences are innately neutral or helpful. If we have overcome the cultural bias that says spirits are evil, we can swing too far in the opposite direction and embrace *all* beings from other realms without discrimination. We also can make the mistake of thinking that, since we seem to have mastered crossing the bridge between realms, we must be prepared for whatever is over there.

Both of these beliefs are untrue, and can get us into situations that don't go so well. I have heard innumerable stories by family and friends who embraced their mystical abilities and then got themselves into some pretty scary situations. There are certainly people who have passed from the earth plane in what I'll call a *supremely bad mood*. In other words, they are hanging out on the other side, with a bad attitude and a lot of fear and anger that's still not resolved. Handling these spirits is really best left for the experts—people who have had extensive training in working with unresolved spirits, who know techniques and tricks for supporting their journey forward without unnecessary danger to the assistant. I have seen students who tangled with beings that really needed much more mature help and guidance, end up with physical injuries, emotional traumas, and disrupted lives and energy fields.

But, as young people growing up in a culture that says these being are either 'evil' or just don't exist, we have very few resources for identifying which spirits are healthy for us to encounter. We don't know how to screen our calls, so to speak, from the spiritual realms. On the one hand, we are told to invoke god to battle the evil of these spirits; and on the other told that we should just pretend they aren't there in the first place. Each of these techniques has some potential to be helpful but, used without just the right intention, both will actually rev up out-of-balance spirits. I have heard stories of people being kicked by spirits, of storms being called up that wiped out small buildings, of people being pinned in bed by angry ghosts, and of unsettling invasive thoughts and images visited upon people by unhappy beings. *This does not mean these spirits are 'evil' in any traditional sense of the word.* It simply means they have serious, unresolved issues and have either strayed very far from the light, or are extremely confused or desperate. But this makes them no less unhealthy to be around. What's required for them is appropriate therapy from trained professionals. Just as a lay person should not attempt to treat serious physical or mental illness, neither should an untrained intuitive tangle with seriously disturbed spiritual energies.

And, too often, children and teens and young adults, exploring the mystical realms, appear to such beings as very bright, open lights which are very attractive. Actually, the twin techniques of either denying the existence of spirits, or of seeing them as banished only by a fierce god/good figure do offer some protection. If we are able to shut down thoroughly enough, convincing ourselves completely that such things do not exist, then we might be able to effectively block negative energies from entering our fields. Similarly, if we believe forcefully enough that the divine light can protect us from darkness, then the light will in fact provide great protection. But the problem with these strategies is that, first, we probably won't be able to *completely* convince ourselves it was our imagination, or that they're not real. And, second, if we're relying on being on the 'right side' of a dualistic battle between good and evil, we are probably adding fuel to the fire of believing in, and fearing, evil and darkness. At the very least, an intense belief in and fear of evil, revs up energies that *like* to be feared, that are attracted to the vibration of fear.

So, without proper guidance and training in discerning what is safe for us to explore, and what is best left alone, we may have some frightening experiences that make us want to shut down our mystical abilities all together. As a child, I was sometimes terrified by the ghosts I saw walking the hallways of my hundred-year-old home. I was even more disturbed by the precognitions I had of deaths in the community. Though I was a pretty brave and spiritually curious child, I found myself facing things that were just beyond my reach. Fortunately, I had the instinct to tell the spirits, "Wait, I'm not old enough. Come back later." But many people I know simply shut down and run the other direction, physically or metaphorically.

We've already talked quite a bit about transmuting traumas from social conditioning and other kinds of life experiences. Now let's take a moment to consider this third form of experience that can dissuade us from engaging our most intuitive, creative selves.

Exercise #18: Early Experiences—Pleasant or Scary?

Think back to your childhood and teen years, and remember as many 'psychic' or mystical experiences as you can. Were they mostly pleasant or unpleasant? Did you hear family stories of ghosts that colored your expectations or understanding of what the mystical realms were like? Did you ever have a truly frightening mystical experience, with a ghost or an energy or a situation that felt dangerous? How did you respond to this situation?

Now, consider what resources you had for coping with these experiences. Notice if you had any elders—family, friends, teachers, or even books or famous figures—who gave you ideas about how to handle these sorts of experiences.

And, finally, ask yourself this: is there any way in which I am still being affected by those early mystical experiences? The effects of such experiences can go beyond the decision to shut down our intuitive abilities. We might actually still have traces of spirits or energies in our own energy fields, or have 'imprints' or impacts on our energy system that need healing or repair. Do a quick scan of your physical body and energy field, and see if you notice anything that feels like you've been carrying it since the time of an early experience. You may see these as dark spots or cords in your field. If you observe any of these, set the intention to send them into the light of source and visualize beautiful light surrounding you.

As young children learning about our intuitive abilities, it is best if we have guides and teachers to help us navigate the mystical realms. Just as we wouldn't send a child out into the wilderness without an adult to guide and assist them, it's unwise to send children into the alternate realms without mature, adult help. Many of us are blessed to have been assisted in these realms by *spiritual* guides and helpers— those imaginary playmates, and ancestors and animal spirits who stayed with us as we explored and adventured. But most of us needed more material help, to translate these experiences in ways that our bodies, minds and spiritual systems could integrate.

One of the most frightening experiences I had as a teen was not with the ghosts who came to talk to me, or even the foreknowledge I had of impending events, but rather persistent visits from my own possible past. I remember very clearly when the spirit of a young child who had died in a concentration camp began coming to me. I was about 10 years old, and was standing in the upstairs of my family home, in the bathroom in front of the small, old mirror there. Suddenly, I very distinctly heard a child's voice saying my name. I 'saw' instantly in my mind's eye a young girl about my own age, 9 or 10 years old, with should-length blond hair and a dress that came to her knees. She was clearly a child who was not happy, and yet she was also not afraid or fearful. She was not coming to me for help, as best I could tell, but simply wanted my attention. I instinctively did not feel comfortable with her, but couldn't really figure out why.

Over the course of many months, she came fairly regularly, and her visits made me feel more and more frightened. She was not nice, and seemed dangerous to me somehow. I began to piece together information about her. She was French; once I saw her and her best friend, a young boy her own age, riding a bicycle together on a dirt road through the French countryside. She had been taken to a concentration camp, and had become the 'pet' of one of the officers there. She was allowed extra food and supplies, warmth and shelter, for performing sexual favors for this man in power. Eventually, she died there. Once, I dreamed of her trying to drown me in a muddy, swampy area in the camp, with this man standing nearby. As I've said, I have always had clear memories of many other lives, and it became clear to me that this child was somehow connected to me and my own soul journey. Later, when I was an adult, she came in dreams to my husband, threatening to kill him (this before I had ever described her to him). It took many years, and the help of skilled professional spiritual healers to clear her energy from me. For many years, she plagued my sleep and haunted me when I was awake. But rather than asking for help, she instead seemed threatening and dangerous.

This aspect of my soul had developed an attitude of defiance, of false power and supremacy, taken from her captors, to help her cope with her circumstances. Because my current self could at least see and hear her, she came to me—probably without any real consciousness of doing so—seeking help to resolve her death in the camp. But I was utterly unprepared to deal with her. It took the assistance of a professional energy worker to finally resolve my relationship with her.

I cannot say that she was me in a past life, because I don't think it's that simple. I believe we are all tied to one another, and that there are many threads of connection that bind us together as souls. We have aspects of our greater Selves that live in many times and places, and while they may or may not be simplistically defined as 'me in a past life' they are nonetheless deeply connected to us. For whatever reason, she found me to be a source of something she was looking for. And yet her presence caused me a great deal of distress. Had there been a wise, older mystic nearby, I might have been relieved of her presence immediately. Instead, she travelled with me for years, draining my energy and depleting me in ways that I would only understand much later.

The truth is that most of us come through childhood with a number of 'cords' attached to us by our experiences and the energies of other people. To an intuitive who sees energy patterns, these often look like actual cords 'plugged in' to our spiritual bodies. Some of these are more straightforward: the impacts of traumatic events, the attachments we have to unhealthy people or patterns from our own lives, and the expectations and beliefs we have developed in response to life experiences. But for the psychic or intuitive child, these cords and imprints can be much deeper and more difficult to deal with.

Whether from social conditioning, traumatic experiences, or lack of support and training, difficult experiences can make us change our natural energy flow. Sometimes we are actually doing this to cut off energy flowing out of unhealthy cords. But this often means that our sense of wonder and adventure transform, sometimes gradually and imperceptibly, and sometimes dramatically, into fear and the need to shut down. This serves us very well, for a time, because it allows us to survive and be accepted in a world where the mystical is often denied. But, ultimately, this shutting down has a price: our energy flow is restricted, and our lives begin to show signs of dis-ease and imbalance. As we reach adulthood, sooner or later these unhealed traumas, and the pressure of suppressed psychic energy, will force us to confront and face them once again.

6

Crisis

By the time we reach adulthood, many of our intuitive gifts may have been pushed to the side, as we focused on finding our place in society. Because being intuitive, or mystical, is not considered 'normal' by western culture, outright mysticism is rarely the choice of young adults stepping into mainstream society. Instead, we find ways to do what is expected of us, and generally manage fairly well for some amount of time. And yet...there are often quiet little signs that things are not quite as they are meant to be. We have a little bit (or a lot) of a problem with alcohol or drugs (legal or illegal); we are chronically dissatisfied with our job/marriage/lifestyle; we overspend money, trying to connect to something that will make us feel 'valuable;' we develop patterns of physical illness, or eating disorders, or other symptoms; we struggle through repeated relationships that discourage us; we have a tendency towards violence or conflict. All of these are symptoms of the same underlying problem: disconnection from the Source and flow of our own true energy, and from the balanced energy of the earth which sustains us.

Disconnection, which we often choose as a way to survive, ultimately strips us of our well-being in many areas of our lives. In western culture, this is considered 'normal.' Rather than adjust our lifestyles to our own, inner truth, we are taught to pop pills to numb the ache and to quiet the growing messages from our bodies that something is not right. We are encouraged to shop our way to happiness, and purchase our way out of despair. We tell ourselves that it will all get better when we retire/meet the right partner/earn enough money. Often, this process of denying our inner truth results in a dramatic crisis, a crash-point, that forces us to confront our deeper, more wise Selves directly. It may come as a medical crisis, a financial crash, a divorce, or a 'midlife crisis. All are calls to take a closer look at living our truth. Though a crisis stage on the journey is not inevitable, (and can even by averted in cultures where chosen, guided initiations serve the purpose of focusing spiritual energies and intentions), it is extremely common in western society.

You may be reading this book because you have hit a crash-point, and are now searching for a way to make things right. Or, you may have already moved through your initial crash-point, and are ready to move forward with a gentler, more intentional approach to things. Either way, it's important to look at our crash points as clues to how we have blocked the flow of our natural Source energy. Even if you've already moved through your biggest crises, and are well along the spiritual path, there's value in looking back from your new vantage point, to appreciate just how you have managed energy in the past, and how you choose to do so now.

Exercise #19: Your Crash-Points

What crash points have you already hit, or are you now experiencing? What areas of your life have let you know that you disconnected from the full Source of your own true energy? Are you experiencing physical illness, or psychological difficulties? Do you have chronic depression, anxiety or dissatisfaction with your life? What about your relationships, your job, or your finances? What areas of your life might be serving you by *insisting* that you return to your true Self?

In my own life, the suppression of my very strong natural, intuitive energies, combined with a number of traumatic events, left me a real emotional and physical mess. And because I had shut off the natural flow of my own energy, healing the traumas of my experiences was really difficult. The imbalance was made even worse by my choice to take birth control pills, which further interrupted the natural flow of my biological and spiritual energies. By the time I was in my mid-twenties, I had a serious case of Post-Traumatic Stress Disorder, an eating disorder, anxiety and panic attacks, food sensitivities, and a number of odd neurological and physical symptoms, including migraines auras. It was a mess that took literally decades to unravel and set to rights.

Throughout my twenties and early thirties, I existed in what you could call a *chronic state of crisis*. Though I got married, completed a PhD, and had my first child, I was not really functioning well at all. I felt unhappy and dissatisfied with my life much of the time, and like I was "broken" somehow. But throughout these years something else was happening: I was exploring alternative healing, and learning about the way energy works in the body. I visited chiropractors, energy workers, psychotherapists, massage therapists, and acupuncturists. I studied with cross-cultural shamans and traditional indigenous teachers. I experimented with Tibetan bowls, lucid dreaming, and all sorts of psychic protection and development techniques. Over twenty years of studying and healing myself, with the help of a wide range of teachers and traditions, I not only put my Self back together, I also pieced together a much clearer picture of how body, heart, mind and spirit interact. This process laid the foundation for my ministry, and my ability to companion others on their journeys. And it allowed me to reclaim the innate power, lying dormant within me, of creating my own reality.

This extended time of crisis allowed me to move through an intensive study of energy dynamics on the earth plane. And it allowed me to shift my own life from constant stress and struggle to a much greater sense of joy, purpose and well-being. These are things we all yearn for, and yet they can seem pretty difficult to achieve in our modern, fast-paced, driven world. If you are currently experiencing a major crisis, a mini-crisis, or an extended period of challenge or dissatisfaction, perhaps the hidden gift of your true Self is not far away. Any symptoms of imbalance, if we really listen to them with patience, will reveal our true state of well-being and balance. And this is true whether the symptoms go away completely or not. Sometimes, the symptoms remain but our perspective is changed enough so that they no longer trouble us or limit the way we move forward.

My life partner experienced his crisis stage in a slightly different way. Where I had physical symptoms that drove me to alternative healing methods, it was his business and work life that precipitated much of his spiritual growth. As a young man, he was a conventional farmer, raising cattle in a way that he can see now was completely out of alignment with the natural energies of the earth. He found himself working more as a veterinarian than a farmer—medicating his animals because the system used to raise them was so out of natural balance—and losing animals, money, and enthusiasm to a way of life that simply wasn't healthy. He says that his moment of clarity came when, after trying for many days to save a sick cow, and pouring heart, soul, and body into caring for her, he was forced to put her down. "There's got to be a better way," he thought, and he began researching alternative farming methods. So where I learned about energy and the connection between the physical and the spiritual through my own body, he learned about it, initially, through the body of the earth. This led him to spiritual experiences with other people interested in nature, and to expanding his understanding of the life force in a much broader way. In the process, his own intuitive faculties re-opened powerfully, and his own energy flow began to heal as he healed the land and animals he worked with.

Whether your crisis starts in your finances, your physical body, your personal relationships or your profession, the healing it offers will certainly spread—if you let it—to all areas of your life. My physical healing led me to a calling in ministry, which led me to new relationships, a new home, and a completely new lifestyle. My partner's awakening to new ways of doing agriculture led him to a deep study of indigenous North American cultures, to a new understanding of psychic abilities, to new relationships and a completely new way of living. In fact, our separate awakenings brought us across a seemingly impossible divide of lifestyles and landscape to be together. Had we met before our spiritual crises, and the resulting transformations they triggered, we would never have even considered dating one another. Now, we are excellent catalysts and supports for each other's journeys.

One thing is for certain, if you allow whatever struggles or challenges you are facing to guide you towards new possibilities, your life will open up in unexpected ways. It is truly impossible to predict where they will take you, but you will find at each stage of the journey new opportunities to choose greater and greater well-being, greater and greater spiritual health, and greater and greater peace and purpose for your life. As we meet the challenges that come to us with curiosity and faith, the possibilities are truly endless. Our struggles show us where our energy is blocked, and thus are the gateways to restoring its full flow. By reclaiming this flow of Source energy within us, we reclaim our ability to choose fully who we are, and where we will go next. Of course we will all face human limitations, but we need no longer feel those limitations to be insurmountable. We can reclaim the ability to consciously regulate our spiritual energies. When we do this, we eliminate the need for unexpected crises to open us up. Instead, we can become active creators of exciting, fun spiritual adventures.

Conscious Initiations and Choosing our Teachers

In many traditional cultures, spiritual crises are created purposefully through rites of initiation, which accelerate and support the individual's spiritual journey. In our modern western culture, though, we have far too few intentional rites of passage, and far too many other forms of initiation. Hazing rituals in college organizations, starting drinking or using drugs while in high school, having sex casually or very early—these have all become the ways that teens and young adults attempt to initiate themselves into adulthood. These acts involve some of the essential components of an initiation: they involve risk and physically altered states; they induce a sense of euphoria and ecstasy; and they allow the young person to feel accepted into a new, more 'adult' peer group. And yet they lack other essential components of true initiation.

A true spiritual initiation involves a strong community of healthy, spiritually grounded elders who hold a space of safety and healthy intention around the initiate. In healthy initiation, there is training and preparation for the initiate, which ensures that he or she is ready for the experience. Healthy initiations are focused on the overall spiritual well-being of the initiate, rather than merely on 'having fun' or being included in a group. And healthy initiations take into account the whole, life-long spiritual journey we are on. Taken out of this context, acts which *mimic* true rites of passage become dangerous and destructive. They may indeed give us glimpses of another possible, alternate reality; they may in fact expand our sense of ourselves, but they do so in ways that can have devastating effects on our bodies, psyches, and spirits.

The average teen in western society has gone through a process that distorts our natural spiritual development. Rather than having our mystical gifts recognized, nurtured, trained and tested, in a natural progression from childhood to adulthood, we instead have to find an alternate route to actualizing our spiritual potential. This route often involves realizing that our intuitive gifts aren't accepted; shutting off or limiting those gifts; engaging in behaviors designed to imitate those gifts, but without any actual spiritual guidance or intention; and then suffering difficult consequences from both the initial shutting off, as well as from the false initiations. This process can lead to physical illness, mental illness, unhealthy relationships, and other destructive and life-denying patterns. Whether these painful consequences are acute—like an acute physical or financial crisis—or chronic—like long-term dissatisfaction and the gradual erosion of self-esteem and a sense of purpose—they destroy our connection to true joy and fulfillment. Hence, most of us find ourselves somewhere in adulthood getting on to the spiritual path as a way of repairing damage done and wounds suffered. Had we, instead, been given the right guidance, training and support early on we might have been able to avoid many of these unexpected crises.

But since so many of us did not have the guidance and support we needed to cultivate our mystical gifts, we find ourselves obliged to put ourselves through the process as adults. At this point in the journey, it's important to find helpers that will truly serve us. There are so many possible healers, healing paths, and spiritual teachings available now, it can be easy to spend enormous time and energy looking for help. And it can be a terribly confusing process.

One caveat here, though: there are no 'mistakes' on the spiritual journey. Every path we take, every action we try, teaches us something or gives us new material to work with. Though we may take some steps that seem to get us further from, rather than closer to, our desired destination, they are nonetheless valuable for showing us things we didn't know before. Even on side-trips, we can learn about ourselves and our world. But it does help to have some healthy and wise guides for our travels, and to know how to avoid the worst bumps and bruises that can happen while exploring. It's helpful to have some good tips for choosing teachers who are ready for the task, and for knowing how to select the techniques that work best for us.

In order to make sure that your path is as joyful and supportive as possible, it's important to remember that, no matter how tough your situation, you can trust your own deepest instincts about what you need. Sometimes, we are so desperate for help and support that we are willing to give over complete control and power for our lives and well-being to a more experienced guide or teacher. There are certainly times when we don't have the answer, and we need to trust deeply in another person whose intention is to support our highest good. But it's important to keep our sense of boundaries and true clarity that, though teachers can bring us incredible aid, they are all still just humans, too. (Well, mostly. There are some true Speakers and Great Masters in the world, but they are hard to gain access to and even they have their own moments of being physical beings, in bodies, with limitations.) Most teachers are just people who have gone ahead a little on the path, and are willing to share what they know. This does not mean, however, that they are fully actualized or self-realized, or that they are without flaws and blind spots. Though many teachers will assign you tasks that may be designed to help you let go of ego, and to release old patterns of control which are limiting you, a true teacher will never ask you to do anything that feels deeply wrong to you. You must trust your instincts over the words and suggestions of anyone (particularly anyone to whom you are paying money) asking you to behave in ways that feel inherently inappropriate or out of balance.

On my own journey, I spent an enormous amount of time and money trying to find the best methods and teachers to help me return to balance. Some of these were very valuable and helpful; others simply showed me what wouldn't work for me. I learned that my body loves yoga, but does not like tai chi (even though I tried it many times over

15 years). I learned that while one teacher might be worth studying with for many years, others have only a weekend's worth of material for me. On the subject of food, I learned that there are any number of 'healthy' diet options, and that one size definitely doesn't fit all. After trying many different curative diets, I learned that it's best to listen to my body, informed by what others have said but knowing that I am unique and only I can know what really feels right to me. During all this travelling and journeying through the landscape of alternative healing and spirituality, I had many positive experiences. But I also had some really unpleasant experiences.

In one instance, I ended a relationship with a healer/ teacher because I felt it was becoming unhealthy. Just before I left, though, I completed a few private healing sessions with this person. During one session, she told me that the best way to 'heal' me would be for her to bring a 'spirit' up from another realm into my body, to assist me. The healer did in fact ask for my permission to do this, but the truth is, I was in a such a state of need and fear that I said 'yes' despite my feeling of uncertainty and confusion when asked. I agreed to the process, but almost instantly regretted it. Within moments, I felt the energy of another being in my body. This energy was kind, and not at all malevolent, but it didn't really belong with me. The spirit that the healer called into my body was that of a woman from another time, another culture, and another realm. I was told that, in order to facilitate this spirit's presence in my body, I should dance regularly. For months after that day, I struggled with the presence of this being travelling with me. This presence inhabiting my body and I could communicate pretty clearly, and she was frankly as uncomfortable with the situation as I was. But I didn't yet have the skill to release her myself.

And I had become rather frightened and intimidated by the healer, who was herself going through some difficult personal, psychological crises.

After a few months of struggling with this presence in my body, I happened to attend an event with other seekers from the original group I had met through this teacher. They reported that the healer had begun speaking badly about me in groups and activities, saying that I had 'left the path,' because I had turned away from her teachings. I knew—and by this time the others did too—that this teacher was going through a period of crisis which probably made it impossible for her to focus on anyone else's well-being. I had left sooner than others because I felt instinctively that it was in my best interest to go. The others, who had stayed longer, were experiencing varying levels of trauma and difficulty in the situation. But, though I knew my instincts had gotten me out of an unhealthy situation early on, this teacher had been speaking about me as a 'failure' in spiritual work.

At that gathering, one my friends told me that she had been getting messages from 'a spirit' about the situation going on in my body and energy field. Though I had told none of them about the situation with the presence the healer had called into me, this friend spoke explicitly and directly about the spirit's presence in my body. She told me that the spirit had come to her with guidance about how to allow us both to be freed from the relationship, and she gave me exact instructions about what to do. I told the group about what had happened, confirming to my companion that the message was truly needed and important. And I promised to follow the instructions right away. I did so as soon as I got home, and within moments the spirit left my body. Over the following months, she occasionally visited me to check on me, and to let me know that she was still supporting me, but we were both relieved to end that connection that wasn't serving either of us.

This situation is a good example of a side-trip on the spiritual journey that was uncomfortable and not as healthy as other paths might have been. The relationship drained my energy, and caused me a lot of confusion and unhappiness. But this doesn't mean it was a 'mistake' or a failure, either. I learned a valuable lesson through this experience: *I learned that giving and withholding permission in a spiritual setting is extremely important.* I learned that I am not always in a frame of mind to make the best decisions, when I am struggling or in pain or my energy is blocked, and that sometimes I need to default to "no" rather than to "yes." I also learned that this is true of anyone I may be attempting to assist, as a healer and teacher myself. The Hippocratic Oath applies to alternative healers as well as to allopathic ones: First, do no harm. And now, many years later, I can also see how important it is for me as a healer to recognize when I am depleted, or dealing with personal issues that may cloud my work, and to step back at those times.

Of course, I have learned these sorts of lessons over and over again as both patient and healer, as both student and teacher. I have done things that, looking back, I think I could have done better, or more wisely, or more gently. In every instance where I have given or been the recipient of less than ideal advice, counsel or treatment, I have later discovered a hidden teaching of great value.

Still, it's wise to know in advance that these sorts of things can happen, and to do your best to protect yourself from damaging consequences. This is why it is extremely important to set good boundaries for yourself, and trust your inner voice, even as you ask for help along the way. When we are in a state of crisis—acute or chronic—we can be so desperate for help that we are willing to disregard inner warning signs, and let ourselves be led onto paths that slow us down or cause us additional pain. As we progress along the path, from this point forward we must balance our sense of adventure and curiosity with our internal sense of limits and boundaries. In fact, the balancing of these two aspects of ourselves is one of the most important tasks on the spiritual path. Whether you follow Native North American teachings, or Celtic teachings, or the teaching of a more conventional religion such as Catholicism; whether you are a rational humanist learning about energy or a mystical Kabbalist; whether you choose to stick with more scientific materials or wish to inhabit the realms of fantasy—you must start to become your own inner guide, as you seek other travelers who might have tips, clues or landmarks to share.

On my own journey, I had wonderful teachers and guides—both in the physical and the non-physical realms—without whom I simply couldn't have made it. And yet all of them (yes, even the non-human ones) had limitations. In each relationship, there were particular gifts and teachings and experiences that the person or being had to share with me. But whenever I felt the urge to surrender myself to them completely, I hit a wall where their abilities did not reach into the next area of my growth. It's natural to for us humans to want to find a cozy place (or person) to settle down with for the long haul, and sometimes that is indeed possible. But if you are growing at a fairly steady rate on your spiritual path, chances are good that you will go through a wide range of teachers, techniques and traditions as you move through the lessons you need to learn.

In some cases, your teachers will be excellent spiritual guides, and yet rather poor masters of their own finances and material reality. Or perhaps you will find a teacher who is brilliant at manifesting financial wealth, but who hasn't mastered relationships. In my relationship with the teacher who invited the spirit to abide in my body, I did learn many powerful and lasting lessons about shamanic practices, traditions, and teachings that are still very useful to me today. In other relationships, teachers and counsellors saw some aspects of my journey very clearly, while completely missing other things that, looking back, I am astonished they missed. It took me many years and a huge range of learning situations—ranging from weekend workshops to years of study with specific groups and teachers—to come to the place where I truly feel at ease charting my own course. At first, I was terrified that I would never get the help I needed or that I would even make things worse by trying to follow my own instincts. In the crisis phase, I was in enough pain and confusion that it was hard to know if I was making good decisions, and I often felt like I'd made bad choices. This feeling was compounded by the voices of well-meaning family and friends who were quick to judge my slow, usually invisible inner progress. When they couldn't see dramatic healing or positive external changes, they sometimes criticized the seeming failure of the 'new age' quacks who were trying to 'con' me for a quick buck.

On your own search for teachers and healers, often begun during the crisis stage of the journey, it's important to remember two things: First, you are the creator of your reality. You get to say how fast you want or need to go, what sorts of limits or boundaries you want to put on the experience, and what your most immediate and pressing needs are. Second, you are always being helped by very high level spiritual companions who, while they will respect your wishes and requests, are always nearby to give aid as soon as you ask for it. This means that your intention is your most important tool. It matters less what particular teacher or technique you call up to help you, and much more that you set clear intentions about the sort of help you want. In the case of my trouble with the implanted spirit, my highest helpers found a way to enlist the aid of a friend whom I hadn't seen in many months. They got me to that party where she could deliver necessary information which allowed me to clear the spiritual bondage, and they gave me the tools I needed to repair the situation.

Allowing your higher guides to support you is essential in smoothing the way for your journey, but remember that not all spiritual energies are equally elevated. Being disembodied doesn't necessarily make them enlightened. In other words, set high standards for you non-physical companions, as well as for your physical ones. Sometimes we believe that any being coming to us from spirit must be 'higher' or more advanced than us, and this simply isn't so. Rather, the spirits that come to us are the ones that match the vibration and intention we have sent out.

So rather than saying you'll take whatever help you can get, set some high standards for the help you want to receive. Be clear about what you want from material and non-material guides. State clearly the sort of vibrational, emotional, spiritual and psychological qualities you want them to have, and make sure to include balance and integrity in that list. I began to make a practice of saying the following:

> *"I allow only those who serve the light, and who hold my highest and purest well-being as their intention to remain in my space."*

I made a practice of being clear with the multiverse that I wanted my highest guides and helpers to show me what would truly serve my highest good, and to steer me away from things that I might find attractive because of my own unhealed, unresolved wounds or difficulties.

It's okay to ask for companions and guides who make you feel comfortable and safe, who respect your pacing and your other needs and responsibilities. It's a good idea to make clear at the outset that you want a process that is easy and comfortable for you, and that creates minimal chaos in your life (unless chaos is what you truly desire, and sometimes it is). Though we can never totally predict the third-dimensional form our transformation will take, we can certainly ask our highest Selves and our spiritual guidance system to do things in a way that's workable. As great healer and teacher Caroline Myss has said, it's fine to ask spirit to give you all the tools and resources and guidance you need to complete the spiritual tasks they set for you. If your spiritual Self wants to give you a spiritual assignment or journey that is demanding and adventurous, it is certainly capable of giving you everything you need to have that journey be a more pleasant one.

As we move into the New Age, one thing we are learning is that not all transformation has to be painful. Many of us have believed that crisis is *necessary* for spiritual transformation, but we are learning that this is not so. We are finally becoming, collectively, awakened enough to our own spiritual powers that we are learning to transform through joy and ease, through intention and creativity, rather than through crisis and trauma. In other words, we can recognize initiations for what they are, and deal with them more consciously, directly, and playfully. Even if you are at a crisis point right now in your life, you can claim this spiritual power for yourself. Right now, in this moment, you can claim your right to have the rest of your journey be easier and more pleasurable than it has been. You can start believing that, as you open up to your own divine Self, you are able to make this life what you choose.

Spiritual transformation is not a test of skill or progress. Though we sometimes call this place we live "earth school," I believe it is a school without grades. There's no 'better' or 'worse' way to proceed, there are no tests posed by others, waiting to judge us, only those challenges we pose for ourselves in order to explore our own abilities. We are not being punished for some failure or wrong that we must 'transcend' to be 'worthy' of a 'higher' level of spiritual well-being. These are old-fashioned and limiting ideas about what spirituality really means. Instead, we can see ourselves as creators who have chosen to experience all that this realm has to offer so we can remember (literally, to re-member, to bring back into the body, the 'members' of physical form) who we really are. So if we find ourselves with challenges we'd like to leave behind, we can see them simply as consequences of previous choices—choices which served a purpose and are no longer necessary. We are free to make new choices, and experience things differently.

Guides and teachers, then, are people who have something to offer as we explore new choices, and as we look for new strategies to move us forward. If you have already gone through the process of crisis and recovery, perhaps you can look back on your experiences with new awareness. Consider the ways you trusted in, or gave power to, your guides and teachers. Would you do anything differently, if you had it to do over? Take heed, because chances are good you will have another opportunity, somewhere down the road, to find another spiritual guide or companion with whom you will need to establish clear boundaries and balance power. Or, even if that is not so, you will certainly be given the opportunity to serve as a guide to someone else. We all do things that, with perfect hindsight, we might do differently a second time. We must forgive ourselves and others for these missteps, find the blessings in them, and learn from them. And then we must move forward on the journey a little wiser, and a little more patient and reflective, as we companion ourselves and others.

So be willing to try out methods and teachers and techniques, but be equally willing to let them go. This isn't a sign of failure, so try not to let it discourage you. Everything you try that isn't "it" gets you one step closer to who you really are, what truly matches your energy, and what you really need in order to achieve balance. We learn a lot by knowing what doesn't work for us. And one of the most important ways we reclaim our spiritual power is by being willing to say 'no' to what is not working. This requires some faith that we can indeed call forth what we need, and that we have the resources to bide our time while waiting for it to appear. These, too, are essential qualities of the spiritually mature person. And learn how to forgive yourself and others when things don't work out as well as you had planned.

Just because a technique or teaching worked well for someone you admire, who may have come through stages of the journey that you have yet to complete, doesn't necessarily mean their path is the one you should follow. Though there are some basic practices that cross cultural and historical lines, there is no one right way to proceed on the journey. One of the most important things that seeking help during our crises teaches us is to turn away from external voices and pressures, and begin to rely on our own inner voice for guidance. While others can give us tools and opportunities, we must be our own best companions as we move forward. It is usually necessary to experiment some with different healing modalities, teachers, practices, and spiritual traditions as we attempt to find out what feels like 'home' for our spiritual Selves, but ultimately we are our own best judge of what is right for us.

Another thing we need to remember as we explore and experiment with spiritual techniques and teachings is that others have the right to choose their own paths. It isn't helpful when we insist that a path that worked well for us is the 'right' one for everyone else. It's fine to share our experiences, and offer them as possible tools for others to explore. But we must resist the urge to put pressure on others to join us on a specific path, because this urge usually comes from our fear, rather than our love.

Often, as we start to build momentum on our spiritual journey, we find ourselves talking about particular teachers or concepts in a way that others can find overwhelming. On the one hand, our enthusiasm for our experiences is useful because it helps us connect with people who share our passion and who match our energy. On the other hand, it can add stress to the journey by alienating those we love. If you find yourself "preaching" a particular method or belief system, you might want to take a step back and ask yourself what's motivating you. Are you speaking because you see that your listener is ready to hear, integrate and act from the wisdom you have gained? Are your words coming from a deep feeling of peace and knowingness? Or are you speaking out of a sense of fear and anxiety, worried that others will be left behind? Or feeling a forcefulness that you need to 'change' them? We can never force another's spiritual journey, and the words that truly encourage another to move forward often feel as if they are riding a wave of love or pure energy as they come out of us. Words that are motivated by our own deep sense of insecurity or loneliness, however, or even by an intense desire to change the world, often have an edge of anger, desperation, and aggression in them. The need to have others join us on our path usually arises from a hidden fear that, if we follow our own hearts, we will be forced to leave behind those we love. Or we may be worried that if we allow others to take their own time, their own direction, they may suffer in ways we can't bear to watch. And yet it is essential that we honor each person's right to their own experiences, including what we might perceive as 'mistakes.'

Just as seeking teachers and traditions to guide us on our path can cultivate a sense of inner guidance and self-direction, it must also cultivate a deep sense that each of us is right where we need to be.

Exercise #20: How You Choose Teachers

Take a moment to reflect on your experience of finding and working with teachers or guides on your spiritual journey. Consider whether or not you have any patterns or habits for selecting, interacting with, or parting with spiritual teachers or traditions. You may have had religious experiences that set the tone for your way of going about the spiritual journey, or you may have had particularly pleasant or unpleasant experiences that shape your expectations for the future. Are you inclined to look for a famous guru, that you can interact with directly? Or do you prefer learning through the anonymity of books and on-line learning environments? Do you generally choose teachers of a particular gender, or tradition? Have you had any difficult or unpleasant experiences with teachers that might reveal some deeper need, or unhealed pattern, in you? As you consider your habits and preferences for spiritual guidance, ask yourself whether these preferences feel like they come from fear, or true Self-awareness.

Natural Symptoms of Spiritual Expansion

Another important aspect of the spiritual journey that I came to understand during my own extended crisis is that sometimes symptoms—physical, emotional, or mental—are a natural byproduct of spiritual development. There are many physical and emotional symptoms that are direct evidence of spiritual expansion and awakening, and these can be treated more like growing pains than like illness. For example, many intuitives experience migraine symptoms when they are going through an expansion of spiritual energy. To be sure, this is often the physical body's way of saying that there is a blockage or limitation in the channels where energy is trying to flow, but it doesn't necessarily mean something is 'wrong.' In fact, the symptoms of migraine aura have long been associated with mystical trance states. Anthropologist Hank Wesselman describes them in his narrative of initiation into Hawaiian shamanism, and stories of the Christian mystic, St. Teresa of Avila describe aura symptoms surrounding her visions. Of course, conscious management of these energies often diminishes, or eliminates these symptoms entirely.

Often, when we are expanding spiritually, we are sending or allowing higher volumes and frequencies of energy to move through us. And while our spirits may be ready for such an expansion, the body often needs time to catch up. During these expansions, neurological symptoms are not uncommon. Also, the body frequently goes through adjustments to metabolism and blood sugar regulation in response to psychic input and experiences. There are both biochemical and energetic mechanisms for these symptoms, and as such need to be addressed at both levels. So, if I am experiencing a heightened level of intuitive input, for example, on a day when I see many clients, I need to eat significantly more calories, and a higher load of carbohydrates and proteins than on other days. This both regulates my blood sugar, and also serves to ground my energy through the action of digestion. Meat is particularly grounding in such situations.

Other common symptoms include changes in sleep patterns, increased anxiety symptoms (as the system tries to manage increased levels of energy running through it), and sometimes bouts of depression as unconscious material is forced to the surface by an increase in natural energy flow. These can all be symptoms of health, rather than dis-ease. They may be the body's way of regulating a greater flow of energy moving through a system that is trying to adapt and expand. Rather than suppress these symptoms (especially with synthetic chemicals), it is best to find ways to support ourselves as we simultaneously expand our energy pathways and learn to regulate the flow of energy more consciously. This is precisely what many alternative healing techniques and energy management techniques are designed to do. But it's helpful to just remember that the symptoms you experience on the spiritual journey, while they may be uncomfortable and certainly deserve your attention, need not be seen as proof that you are 'broken' or 'weird' or otherwise unhealthy. *Of course, if you are experiencing significant symptoms, it's wise to make a visit to your doctor. Often, an M.D. who is also trained in alternative healing or energy medicine is a wonderful resource.*

In later chapters, we'll talk about a number of ways to ease these symptoms, and to learn how to recognize what is a sign of unhealthy imbalance, and what is simply a message that you're going through a system upgrade. For now, let's review some of the most basic skills you can use to manage the increasing energy flow that comes with opening up your mystical, intuitive Self.

CHAPTER

7

Energy Hygiene

As we enter the crisis stage, we are often looking for practical tools to make our lives better. If you have found your way to this book, chances are good that you are the kind of person who looks for spiritual and esoteric solutions to challenges, and who is willing to explore alternative approaches. Folks who have a mystical bent, and who likely have some basic intuitive and mystical abilities, aren't likely to settle for simple, purely mechanistic (i.e. third dimensional) answers about 'how to' get to a better place. And yet most of us want some very common-sense, easy-to-follow steps—even of the spiritual and metaphysical sort—that we can implement right away. When I was in crisis and going through the steepest part of my mystical learning curve, I relied heavily on basic practices for what was then called 'psychic' health. Reading books about how to protect and ground myself, learning basic tools and vocabulary, was foundational for me.

So let's take a little time to discuss some basic practices that may be helpful as you delve deeper into your own energy-based abilities. These basic spiritual tools provide a foundation upon which to build more advanced, spiritual lives. They give us basic, structural tools which, once we are experienced and skilled with them, can be adapted or even abandoned in favor of more personal techniques. We could also say that they are like a basic vocabulary we can learn and then later use to create a language or system of our own.

If you have already mastered the basics of energy hygiene described here, use these reminders as a way to assess your own energy progress. How often do you consciously remember to ground? Or to intentionally do the clearing and healing practices you used in the beginning of your journey? Often, once we get past the crisis stage, we become careless about these basic practices. But, just as showering and brushing our teeth daily supports our physical health, regular use of these tools is essential to our spiritual well-being.

As spiritual beings having a physical experience, we must maintain a healthy balance between our material and non-material selves. At the most basic level, we are healthiest when our full spiritual energies can flow fully and freely in our physical forms. In the many esoteric and mystical traditions, this balance is described as the union of ka and ba, of spirit and matter, of form and non-form. All describe a yoking, a merger, of the material and non-material. The practice of yoga, which has become so popular in our modern world, arises from this intention; the word yoga means 'to yoke' and in this system it is the breath that provides the mechanism for linking spiritual intention and physical action. Of course, this simple two-part description has been subdivided again and again, into more and more refined descriptions of our energetic and physical beings. For example, many traditions break the components of earth-life into four elements, corresponding to parts of the self: earth (body), air (mind), fire (spirit) and water (emotions).

I often describe the human system as having four levels of energy flow. This is, of course, an oversimplification. (See for example Barbara Brennan's *Hands of Light* for a much more comprehensive description of the human energy field.)[1] Working with clients and students, I often invite them to imagine themselves as having four 'bodies' or layers: first, the physical layer (which is the most dense, or slow-vibrating); second, we have an emotional layer, which is part non-physical and part physical (as the emotions are mediated by chemicals in the body); third, we have a mental body, which is comprised of electromagnetic bio-messages that travel through the body, but are largely non-physical; and fourth, we have the level of our beings that is pure spirit. Each of these levels communicates with and is connected to the other layers. Trouble in any one of the layers will lead, ultimately, to disturbances in the other layers. For those of you familiar with the chakra system, I see the chakras as reaching into all four levels, effecting and effected by all. Because all four levels—physical, emotional, mental and spiritual—are linked, trouble or imbalance in one can easily lead to problems in another. Emotional upset can lead to physical symptoms, or spiritual troubles can lead to emotional and mental imbalances. Poor diet or sleep habits can trigger relationship problems, and relationship problems can cause digestive issues.

To maintain the health and flow of energies within and between these four levels (and any subdivisions we may perceive within them), we must consciously take good care

---

[1] Barbara Brennan, *Hands of Light: A Guide to Healing Through the Human Energy Field*. Bantam, 1987.

of our physical, emotional, mental and spiritual bodies. Most of us have some basic understanding of how diet, exercise, sleep, and appropriate processing of feelings and beliefs affects our overall health. Too often, though, we neglect the spiritual aspects of self-care and find ourselves experiencing symptoms in the three other levels of our being.

But what does "spiritual self-care" look like?

I like to think of spiritual or energetic self-care as having three basic components: First, connecting to Self and Source; second, cleansing and clearing the energy field; and third, healing injuries or traumas. Consistent practice at all of these levels helps us to establish and maintain a healthy energy flow. At the first level, basic connecting practices create a healthy energy flow between us and our Source. These practices are meant to ensure that our systems are functioning well *before* any dis-ease is introduced, and must be maintained even after we feel we have healed all past traumas and wounds. Connecting practices include deepening and centering ourselves (including meditation); connecting to the earth and our bodies by grounding (including basic forms of yoga, tai chi, and other methods of moving energy in the body, and creating grounding cords); connecting directly to Source, as well as to guides and helpers (including prayer and invocations); and setting clear boundaries, and protecting ourselves from energies that we wish to be separate from. *(More later on the more advanced idea of non-protection based oneness.)* Each of these help us to maintain a strong, healthy, self-differentiated energy field, with which we can maintain personal integrity and well-being.

The second level of energy hygiene involves clearing unwanted energies if and when they are introduced into our systems. This is a bit like resting or taking a day off when we've got a cold or the flu. Clearing short-term toxins and imbalances from our energy system is a sort of 'routine maintenance' that allows us to maintain overall well-being despite the challenges of daily life. Clearing spiritual residue from unpleasant experiences or relationships, removing blockages that attach to limiting beliefs, and assisting ourselves in evolving beyond our current state of mind, body, and spirit can be done through techniques such as smudging, visualization, affirmation, chanting and other modalities that engage all of the senses. This level of clearing is meant to be used before real damage has been done by negative or unwanted energies. We all pick up spiritual debris through our daily lives, in much the same way our hands get dirty when we work in the soil, or our shoes get muddy when we walk outside on a rainy day. Just as we bathe and brush our teeth to clean off the residue of normal living, we must clean and clear our energy fields of the grime of frequent energy interactions with our world.

Finally, we sometimes need to use energy practices to heal injury or damage done by experiences that have harmed us. Chronic patterns of negative thought; frequent experiences of mental, physical or emotional abuse; traumatic experiences on any of the four levels; and even inherited ancestral and archetypal wounds—all of these and many other things can do harm to our energy bodies. And while we frequently have help healing the physical, emotional and mental levels injuries, we don't usually get quite as much help repairing damage to our energy bodies. The lingering hurts can cause symptoms that won't go away, no matter how many vitamins we take, or how many doctors we see, or how many body-workers treat our symptoms. And because the physical, emotional and mental bodies are all *sourced by the spiritual body*, failing to heal harm in this most non-material level prevents full healing in all other areas.

Exercise #21: Spiritual Self-Care Assessment

Before reading more about the various areas of spiritual self-care, do a quick assessment of your own energy hygiene practices. Do you have a regular practice or ritual that helps you establish, maintain and repair your energy system? Which of these three areas are you most consistent with: connecting, cleansing or healing? Which do you need more of? Can you see clearly the distinction between the three, in your own practices and health?

Level 1: Deepen, Center, Ground, Connect, Protect

Deepen and Center

The most basic level of energy hygiene is making sure we are connected to ourSelves. Before we can hope to understand and work with energy, we have to be able to perceive it in ourselves, and work with it consciously. This requires slowing down our fast-paced lives, gathering our attention inward, and finding a deep and real connection to our innermost selves. It also requires making some connection—in whatever form and using whatever language or images work for you—with the greater divine presence that is our own *I Am*. Whether you call this God, or Goddess, or the Life Force, or All That Is, or simply your own High Self, it is essential to have a deep and sustainable connection with a transcendent reality as the source of well-being. Earth-life is, by our own creation, full of contrasts and challenges. In order to experience optimal well-being in this world, we need to understand ourselves as *in it,* and partially *of it,* but also able to exist *beyond it.* There are many practices that facilitate building a relationship with our energy bodies, the transcendent aspect of our own nature, and the greater reality. Various forms of meditation, including chanting (kirtan and mantras, saying the rosary, etc), za zen or sitting meditation, walking meditation and other forms of deepening, all assist us in tuning *out* the outside world, and tuning *into* our inner, energetic reality.

The effect of this sort of meditation, according to teachers of many traditions, is that it brings us fully into the present moment. Present moment awareness is essential to energetic well-being. Since time itself, from a mystical perspective, is actually an illusion, present moment awareness is critical to accessing our divine Selves and a key to the highest functioning of our energy bodies. As many teachings repeat, to lose ourselves in the past or the future is to divert our energy away from the power inherent in the present moment. We *are* eternal beings; therefore, our energy need only be fully present *now* to transform both the future and the past. In addition, focusing in this way also brings us fully present in the *here* as well. In other words, not only do we need to be fully present in this moment in time, we also need to be fully present in our bodies, in our actual physical space.

One exercise that works well to do this in a group setting involves standing in a circle, leaving enough space between individuals for each person to take four steps forward without banging into anyone.

> ***Group Exercise to Come into the Present:*** As the group stands in a loose circle, the leader speaks these words. "In invite you to come fully into your physical bodies, feeling any discomfort or comfort, tightness or ease, etc. When you feel fully present in your body, take one step forward." Pause. "Now, come fully present into this place (and naming the precise location, "in a circle of people in the community room at the village library in Wholeville, Ohio, USA")and when you feel fully present here, take one step forward." Pause. "Now come fully present into this moment (and naming the precise moment, "8:02pm on Sunday, June 12, 2015"), leaving behind all thoughts of the past or the future, and when you feel fully present in this moment, take one step forward." Pause. "And finally, come into the Mystery: though we like to think that we know what will happen later today, or this week, and even in our lives, the truth is that life is a great mystery—we don't really know what will happen at all, so when you are ready to step fully into the Mystery, take one step forward."

This exercise, when practiced in a group, really focuses the circle on its transcendent aspect, and allows the individuals to feel themselves fully present as the divine, high Selves that they are. Often, when I use this exercise with groups, we immediately follow it with the important next step of grounding this energy into the earth. As we come into our physical bodies, in the present moment, we also come into contact the physical source of our lives: the earth. And grounding our energy into this material plane helps immensely to stabilize our physical embodiment of our spiritual Selves.

Grounding

One of the most instinctive ways we do this grounding is to simply be in nature. When we go outside—to hike in the woods, or swim in a lake, or work in our garden—our minds, bodies, hearts and spirits naturally synchronize with the rhythms of the earth. These rhythms, which we are evolved to match, entrain us automatically to a much higher level of balance and functioning. This is why nature so often makes us feel better, and is an important symbol for beauty, well-being and flow. We also use nature to help us understand our less-desired states: storms give us metaphorical images for the inner storms of our emotions; blocked waterways suggest inner blockages that we feel but can't quite name. And just as spending time in healthy parts of nature helps us to strengthen our natural, healthy energy flow, encountering *unhealthy* nature, places where human intervention has poisoned or damaged the earth, can cause us greater imbalance and dis-ease, as it points out ways we need to come back into balance.

It is essential—for both humans and the whole of the earth—that we establish healthy connections with beautiful and healthy natural places. Whether this place for you is your garden, a national park, a forest path, or simply the plants on your balcony does not matter; what matters is reestablishing a strong connection with the larger *physical* whole of which we are a small part.

Basic grounding is often best accomplished through connection with the earth herself. You might just keep a few rocks or flowers nearby at all times. I usually carry small rocks in my pocket, allowing them to carry the energy of a particular place or vibration that supports my needs for that day. And my home is filled with stones, plants, bones, wood, pinecones, and feathers. By intentionally and mindfully putting my attention on these things, and by seeing and feeling a connection to them, I become more grounded and whole. But even if you are stuck in a cubicle for hours each day, with no windows, no plants, and no natural objects around you, you can still connect to the earth. Simply using your mind, and your ability to imagine and *feel* the energies around you, you will be able to access the immense and calming presence of Gaia. One of the most well-known, and effective ways of doing this, is to use a 'grounding cord.'

Exercise #22: Grounding Cord

You can do this exercise in any position—sitting, lying or standing. Begin by simply taking a few deep breaths, and allowing tension to ease out of your body. Feel the weight of your body, and the pull of gravity as it hugs you towards the earth. Allow yourself to focus inward, and let the sounds and movements around you fade into the background. Breathing slowly in and out, take a minute or two to become as calm and relaxed as possible. Once you feel centered, visualize your spine stretching through your body, and imagine extending from the base of your spine a cord, ribbon or root. This can be a ribbon of beautiful light or color, a tree root, a tube of liquid gold, or whatever image comes to your mind. You are simply imagining a connection extending from your body down into the earth itself. You can imagine it moving through the furniture you are resting upon, and then through the floor of the building if you are inside. See it moving through the foundation of the building, or the top layer of earth beneath you. Simply imagine this cord or root or ribbon winding its way down deeper and deeper in the earth, moving past topsoil and into deeper layers of dirt, perhaps passing rocks and tree roots and insects and even underground rivers. Eventually, find a place to anchor your cord—you may find a giant crystal, or a boulder, or just a nice spot of dirt that feels stable and inviting. The deeper into the earth your grounding cord goes, the more solidly you will feel yourself connected to the earth. Once this cord is solidly anchored, imagine any energies that are bothering you (the stress of your workday, the upset you feel over your relationships or money, your physical symptoms) draining out through this cord into the earth. You can release anything you like from your mind, heart, body and spirit down this cord, to be transmuted by the earth back into pure energy. And then, you can welcome pure earth energy—see it as whatever color or form comes to you as nurturing—rising back up the cord, into your body, where it will renew and restore you. This exercise can be done as quickly or as slowly as you like, and as often as you need it.

I check my grounding cord regularly throughout the day, with the goal of maintaining it at all times. After a while of practicing this, you will find that you notice when your connection to the earth has weakened, and you will feel uncomfortable unless it is solidly in place. Sometimes, when the connection becomes truly weak, we really must take the time to put ourselves physically in nature to reestablish a strong connection with the earth. Ideally, we will spend time every single day in nature, simply soaking in the healing, restorative energies there.

Connecting to Source

Once you have learned how to consistently deepen and center in your spiritual Self, to step from the past and future into the present moment, and to connect deeply to the earth, you can establish a much stronger connection with Spirit, Source or Godde. This greater ease of connecting with Spirit occurs when our spiritual 'plumbing' is prepared for a greater flow of divine energy by having a solid, stable internal structure to hold it, and a good grounding connection to the earth. Without these, we are less able to manage the intense energies of divine flow moving through us.

Because Source is eternal and infinite, our connections to it can take an almost infinite number of forms. One thing my partner and I do often to connect with Source is to read the poems of 14th century Persian poet Hafiz out loud to one another. Because Hafiz was a true mystic, who lived and wrote from a place a deep and abiding connection with what he called "the beloved," simply reading his words puts us right back in touch with that divine for ourselves. Other ways people connect with the divine include: prayer and direct conversation with the High Self, the divine presence, or with angels or other guides; meditation and visualization focused on a particular aspect of the Godde; ritual practices such as making devotional offerings or participating in group rituals; or simply quieting the mind and inviting the divine to enter in. Books, audios, videos, tarot cards, other people, the earth—all these and many other things can be access points to Godde within and without. This connection, above all else, is the source of well-being.

In addition to pure Source, we can also connect with those divine beings who abide outside the human realm. Angels, guides, and helpers in the form of animal spirits, elemental spirits, ancestors and ascended spiritual teachers, are all available to us for connection, support, and guidance.

It is best to connect with these when we are grounded and centered, in order to truly assimilate and understand the messages they bring to us, but they are always available, offering help in times of need and guidance in times of confusion. Even when we don't know they are there, when we can't feel or see or sense them, they are in fact guiding us gently in ways we are able to integrate, even unconsciously. *We are never alone!* These helpers are absolutely always with us, and it can be truly wonderful to open the channels of communication so that we can talk with them directly, and be more aware of their presence, their support, and their guiding wisdom.

We can open our minds and hearts in many ways to the spirit guides, but some common ways are remembrance of beloved ones, prayer, and shamanic journeying. Though there are actions that accompany each of these methods of invoking spiritual help, they are really simply states of mind. In remembrance, prayer, and journeying, we are turning our attention away from the material realms, at least to some degree, and towards the spiritual realms. We are asking our minds and hearts to open to the presence of that which may be beyond our third-dimensional awareness, and to allow us to connect with that which is beyond. When we pray, we intentionally speak words and open our hearts to the presence of those whom we are invoking. But prayer doesn't have to be in the form of specific words; we can pray with ritual actions or motions (dance, for example, can be a prayer), or prayer can be in the form of simple, heartfelt 'talking with' those we wish to invoke.

Rev. Carol Bodeau, PhD

Remembering Our Ancestors

When we remember those who have passed, our ancestors, we are in fact invoking their presence. Even looking at an old photo album, or replaying moments from the past in our minds, can bring the spirits of our loved ones present with us. When we have moments of sudden memory, and sense that they are near, we can be assured that they are, in fact, right there with us. That song that plays on the radio just when you were thinking of them, or the image that pops up on your computer or television reminding them of you, is indeed a message that they are with you. So how can we cultivate this relationship with our ancestors, once they have moved into another realm?

The most important thing to do is this: believe in your own impressions and senses. If you 'feel' like they were sending you a message, don't instantly mistrust it or put it off to 'my imagination.' Yes, longing for them and wishing for them *does* cause us to have experiences of them, but that doesn't make those experiences less real. Just as, in life, when we needed them we called upon them and they showed up, the same is true once they are no longer present in bodies. When we long for them, *they come*. Occasionally, of course, just as in life, they are sometimes busy, and don't show up right when we ask. Sometimes, they send someone else in their place, or send the help we need in a different form. But they do always respond somehow. We must trust our own impressions and intuitions about these experiences, so that we can strengthen our connection with them.

Exercise #23: Connecting with The Ancestors

If you wish to connect deeply with your loved ones who have passed on, you might try this technique, which is often used by psychics to make such a connection for others. Begin by holding an object that is associated with your loved one: a treasured family heirloom, or a simple photograph will do. It doesn't even have to be an object that they owned, or even touched; it can simply be an object that reminds you deeply of them, or that somehow matches the energy you associate with them. For example, a small model airplane might connect you with an ancestor who was once a pilot. As you hold this object, deepen, center and ground yourself, moving into your own spiritual space. Allow yourself to feel connected both with your body in this time and place, and with your transcendent Self. As you do this, call to mind the spirit—the essence, the best qualities—of your beloved ancestor. Allow yourself to open your mind and heart, and simply observe—listen, feel, sense, see—anything that comes to mind. The ancestors don't always speak in direct words or images. They often speak in sensations (felt impressions of meaning, that we may be aware of as words but that we don't actually hear, or as temperature, color, mood, etc.) and in symbols. You will often hear mediums saying things like "a red rose is my symbol for..." or "they are showing me a ladder, which is my symbol for..." As you practice making these connections, your own and your loved ones' symbols will become more easy to recognize. Simply observe and trust what you experience. You can ask questions, express feelings, and even share unresolved past hurts and confusion. Our ancestors, safely on the other side in the realm of clarity and love, will often be ready to clear old traumas with you. If they are not, if by some chance their souls are still working things out and they need more time, you can set boundaries with them by stating clearly how you want them to interact (or not) with you as you move forward.

We can receive support for our journeys both by invoking our ancestors, and by setting limits on the amount of influence they have on our lives. Through intentionally stepping into their realm, the realm of pure spirit, we can interact with them in much the same way we did when they were alive.

Praying to the Divine, to the Angels, and to our Master Guides

Prayer is similar to this communication with ancestors, except that the angelic, divine or spiritual beings we are connecting with exist at different levels than many of our ancestors. When we pray, we are usually either invoking divine assistance—this is described as prayer of *intercession*, in which we are asking the spirit to intercede for us on the human level—or giving thanks in a prayer of gratitude and praise. Either of these types of prayer (and there are many others, as well) can serve to open the channels between us and the many faces of Godde, the angels and archangels, our master teachers, and our non-corporeal support system. We all have at our sides, constantly, a cadre of spiritual helpers whose purpose is to assist us on our way. These helpers, like the team of family and friends who may be available to us in our physical lives, are just a phone call away. And, in fact, they're actually more readily accessible than even that, given that they aren't limited by time, space, and matter.

There are so many forms and types of prayer, it would be impossible to describe them all, but they all have one thing in common: they assume, as a basic truth, that the spiritual realm exists, that it is real, and that it is listening. Even if our faith is small, in this moment or in general, the act of praying says that we have some belief or hope that there is a larger reality and that we can connect with it. And so we pray to call upon whatever help may be available to us, in the hopes that our communication creates a real connection between ourselves and the divine presences around us. For some, it is easy to feel, hear, sense, or even see these divine beings. Sometimes, a prayer results in a direct, immediate contact with an angel, guide, or helper.

One area where my own experience of direct contact is strong is in my interactions with Jesus, whom I often refer to as Jesua. Raised Catholic, I have always had a deep sense of the significance of this great spiritual teacher, and Divine Presence, in our world. And yet, for many years, I didn't have what many would refer to as a personal relationship with him. Though I did, in fact, go down to the altar at an altar call in an evangelical church once, that impulse to be near to this great teacher wasn't fulfilled by any formal religion or religious teaching. Instead, I found my relationship with Jesua through a painting: Glenda Green's "The Lamb and The Lion." This amazing painting, the story of which is detailed in her book, *Love without End: Jesus Speaks,*[2] has transformed thousands of lives and put many into direct and immediate contact with Jesua. Painted in an amazing experience of direct contact, in which the master sat in Glenda Green's studio with her while she painted, the image itself brings Jesus directly into your spiritual space. Even looking at the picture now, on the internet, I can't help but weep with love and joy. The presence of the divine, so powerful and so utterly unchained by time, space, and matter, abides in the image itself and shows up personally and profoundly when you look at it. Through spending time with Jesua through this book, and this image, I have come to

---

[2] Glenda Greene, *Love Without End: Jesus Speaks. 2ⁿᵈ ed.* Spirits Publishing, 1999.

have a deep and personal, *immediate* relationship with him. He sits on the foot of my bed, literally, and talks to me. He comes into my spirit whenever I call, and I am filled with his presence.

There is no price to pay, no specific prayer to say, nothing magical needed to make such contact. Simply being open to it, and allowing it to happen, unfettered by beliefs in unworthiness or lack or distance, allows this great, loving presence to be fully with me, at any time. I encourage you to look at the image, perhaps read the book, and see for yourself the sort of magic it brings about. This, too, can be a powerful prayer of invocation: simply opening a book that you feel called to, and diving in.

An Aside on Divine Intervention

Sometimes, our divine helpers call on *us, to help them* with something. As I was writing that last paragraph, I felt a deep pull from the presence of Jesua to step away from the computer, and go to my living room. He urged me to go to the piano, and once there to pick up a small native flute sitting on the piano. I began to play a soft, lilting tune, and on the window across from me up flew a red wasp that had been trapped in our house last night. My partner had tried to kill the wasp; he hit it with a newspaper, and we knew it was stunned, but couldn't find it. I had the sense it had retreated under the sofa under the window, and we simply let it be. As I played this soft tune, the wasp, looking recovered from his jolt yesterday, rose up to the sill and then onto the window pane. As I played, he began to dance, moving his body in rhythm to the music. I felt that it was my call to release him; though part of me was yelling "kill it!" in fear, the deeper sense of divine presence was saying, "set him free." So I spoke to the wasp gently, asking if it would like to be released. When I got a silent 'yes' I went to the kitchen, got a clear glass and a piece of strong paper, and returned to the window. There, the wasp sat patiently as I gently covered it with the glass, slipped the paper underneath, and carried it outside to set it free. As I did so, I heard Jesua say, very clearly, "Whatsoever you do for the least of my brothers, this you do unto me."

What a powerful and moving affirmation that, not only do the divine helpers come to assist us, *they come to work through us!* We are all one—the human, the animal, the insect, and the spirit. And when we open ourselves to direct communication with the other realms, we can be so much more a part of that greater flow of life, serving it in unexpected and beautiful ways. Often, the animals and elementals come to assist us as voices of the divine speaking through the natural world. Our brothers and sisters in the plant, insect, animal, and mineral kingdoms are all aspects of the greater divine One, just as we are, and our connections to them enhance and support our spiritual, and material lives. Our pets, and often wild animals, frequently come bearing the messages we need at crucial times. More on this in a moment, as we talk about shamanic ways of invoking help, but first let's return to the realm of the angels.

On Angels and Master Teachers

Though sometimes direct contact with the spiritual realm can open a channel once and for all, that remains powerfully present to us, often times our connections to the divine wax and wane. At one moment we might feel a strong connection, only to have it fade from our awareness and even from our memory. This is what happened for me in my relationship with the angelic realms; it took many years, and many discrete experiences separated by gaps of time, for me to develop a more consistent connection with the angelic realms. When I was young, the angels were something I imagined as far off, distant, and not very real. They were in my imagination, but not my experience. As I got older, and began to study Native American traditions, the western idea of angels like those found in the Jewish and Christian sacred texts faded from my consciousness, and I focused on animal guides and other kinds of helpers. But, a few years ago, the angels began to insist that I pay attention to them again.

My first and most powerful reminder of the angels came in the car accident I described earlier, when an angelic presence surrounded my car and protected me and my family. Over the next few years, I had little encounters with the concept of angels: references in books, friends telling stories, etc. But then, all at once, the angels and I decided it was time to start a real relationship, where we could communicate directly. It was during a particularly difficult time in my life, during my divorce, and the angels began letting me know that I needed to see and hear them directly. They began to show themselves to me in amazing ways. For example, one day on a lunch break from my work as a hospital chaplain, I took a walk across the college campus where our hospital was located. Wandering through a section of the campus I didn't know very well, I felt myself pulled off the path towards an area in the arboretum I had never seen before. This part of the campus is very old, and not maintained in the same picture-perfect way as the rest of campus.

I found myself near an old cemetery, a very small one, with only one or two graves. And in the middle, there was a beautiful angel statue. I stood near her, both literally and symbolically off the beaten path and feeling significant grief, and was calmed by her presence. That presence stayed with me as I walked back to work. The next day, a co-worker wanted to walk with me at lunch and, without any prompting from me or any word of my previous day's experience, she began talking to me about angels. That weekend, I was reading a book by the author Paulo Coelho that suddenly drifted into a conversation about angels, and—if it hadn't been clear to me already it certainly was then—I knew there was no coincidence in all this.

Coelho described how to become acquainted with your own guardian angel simply by asking it to appear.[3] And so I did. I simply said, "Well, it seems my angels are trying to get my attention, so if I have a guardian angel, and if you are here, could you please show yourself to me." Holy Moly! The entire room filled with brilliant light, and I felt and 'saw' in my minds' eye an enormous angelic presence, which filled every available space around me. I was completely blown away! My guardian angel is amazing, and huge, and very kind, and gentle, and yet extremely powerful. Now, I see and feel him in my car when I'm driving, standing behind me (he 'has my back') and in all sorts of other circumstances. I know I am never without him, and that is profoundly reassuring.

And yet, even that amazing meeting with my guardian angel didn't prepare me for the next level of angelic help, which has been coming to me recently. Though I was pretty comfortable with my own guardian angel, and though many of my teachers had taught me to invoke the support and help of higher level angels, including Archangels Michael and Gabriel, I have only recently begun to experience these great, universal forces working directly with me. In recent

---

[3] Paulo Coelho, *Brida*. Harper Collins, 2009.

months, the presences of Archangel Michael, Archangel Gabriel, and Archangel Uriel have become very personal helpers to me, as I open my mind and heart to the expanded presence of this realm of light.

So we are constantly expanding, if we are willing, into the realm of spiritual 'community.' Like the angels, another group within this larger spiritual community is the Master Teachers, or Guides. Brian Weiss describes this level beautifully in his book *Many Lives, Many Masters,*[4] as he describes messages brought back specifically for him by a patient, who channeled them during hypnotic regression. This level of help and support exists beyond the realm of the ancestors—though some of these being may have, in fact, at one time inhabited human form—where those who have reached a certain ascendant state abide. They assist us with our greatest callings, help us to stick to our true paths, and guide us on our greater, many-lives spiritual journey. These masters and guides are the sort of 'managers' who oversee our spiritual tasks and tendencies, and help us to craft human lives that match the journey of our souls. Jesua is one such Master Guide and Teacher.

Master teachers, like the Archangels, hold a presence that, while it intersects with our day-to-day earthly lives, is much more about our infinite, eternal and universal souls. They are our direct connection to the One, to All That Is as we are part of it. I can tell the difference between my Master Teacher's presence and that of other guide and helpers by the *magnitude* and perhaps the *amplitude* of his presence. He simply feels bigger. And while I have a very

---

[4] Brian Weiss, *Many Lives Many Masters: The True Story of a Prominent Psychiatrist, His Young Patient, and the Past-Life Therapy That Changed Both Their Lives.* Simon and Schuster, 1988.

personal and direct relationship with Jesua, I know that I also have another, more personal Master Guide who has been with me through many lives and who holds a vision of my own spiritual progress. He knows, if you will, the map and course I have charted for myself, and is committed to helping me stay on that path. Sometimes, he embodies in human form with me, so that he can support me directly as a teacher or guide.

These Master Teachers abide in the realm of the Boddhisatvas, and may even have a human form somewhere, as well. My Master Teacher appears as both ancestor and great, transcendent spiritual presence. Once, he appeared in a dream to me as a gigantic Buddha statue, hundreds of feet high, speaking directly to me about my path and my needs. But sometimes he appears as a human teacher, from another time, who is learning right along with me. Still, like the angels, such master teachers have a qualitative feel that is quite different from our ancestors, and carries with it the sensation of much higher vibrations and realms.

Another realm that has become widely accepted as a great source of companionship and spiritual guidance is that of the nature spirits. So let's talk for a moment about the shamanic traditions which allow us to access these guides and teachers more directly.

Shamanic Drumming and Journeying as Spiritual Invocation

The word "shaman" has its origins in the Tungus-speaking tribes of North Asia, in what we call Siberia. The role of the shaman is to traverse the realms—from human to non-human, from earthly to celestial, from embodied to the spirit realms—in order to receive messages, healings, and guidance which serve the community. Other names for this role include medicine men and women, and curanderas/ curanderos. In the history of northern Europe, village midwives served this role, prior to the witch hunts of the Middle Ages. Counsellors, teachers, healers, mystical travelers—these spiritual leaders have served as bridges between the material and non-material realms since the dawn of human cultures.

Many of these shamanic traditions, which are characterized by close connections to the natural world, include mystical practices that involve trance states and often, though not always, entheogens or plant helpers that induce altered states. At the center of many of these traditional cultures is the drum, which brings us the heartbeat of mother earth and which allows us to synchronize our own hearts with her and with one another. Often, medicine people are able to shape-shift, or travel in spirit form, and they sometimes have close allies in the animal and plant kingdoms. There are literally thousands of historical traditions that include some of these patterns, and many have been lost to us through the spread of colonial cultures across the planet. And yet much of this wisdom is being shared, now, through our easy access to travel—both material and virtual—and through the generosity of tribal teachers who recognize our common destiny as earth-beings.

Many of the traditions and practices of indigenous communities have been adopted by non-indigenous persons, in the hope of finding ways to heal ourselves and our planet. Ultimately, we all have indigenous roots, no matter our ethnic heritage, for all communities on the earth have earth-centered histories and traditions. But before we explore some of these techniques, a word on appropriate use of cultural practices that don't come from our own ethnic or cultural heritage.

--A note on appropriate cultural sharing

Study of Native North American and other indigenous traditions has become widespread in the last 50 years, since the cultural revolution of the 1960's and especially since the rise of internet technology. We now have access to teachings that come from many world tribes, tribes that were for centuries very private and inaccessible to non-members. As the economic and cultural devastation of indigenous peoples washed over the planet at the hands of colonial cultures in the 17th, 18th and 19th centuries, many indigenous communities began to lose control over some of their own cultural traditions. Languages and ceremonies were banned; children were forced to learn invaders' ways; and generations of wise teachings and traditions were lost. And yet, indigenous peoples—because of their incredible cultural strength and wisdom—have maintained a great deal of cultural autonomy and integrity. And now, as the descendants of the colonists (in the Americas, in India, in Africa, and elsewhere) begin to recognize the great loss that *all* have suffered as a result of colonialism, there is an upsurge of interest in, and respect for, these traditions.

Many non-native peoples are striving to learn the wisdom of indigenous traditions, in hopes not only of saving themselves from the ills of the modern world, but also in hopes of saving the earth herself. Spurred on by this passion for reaffirming life, we often seek out ancient rituals, teachings, and practices to guide and support us. We must do this with great care, though. Too often, non-native people assume that it's 'okay' to simply adopt and adapt traditions 'borrowed' from native people, and often assert that, since 'we are all one, no harm is done.' But many native people don't see it this way. Often, first nations people see such cultural borrowing as theft; having taken the land, the economic resources, and the lifeways of the people, colonials now wish to steal the very center of their communities—the spiritual ways that are sacred and central to the identity and life of these peoples. So adopting indigenous rituals and practices is, to say the very least, an incredibly delicate thing.

As a minister and teacher, as well as someone who studied for years to earn a PhD in cultural studies focused on European colonial interactions with Native North Americans, I know firsthand how easy it is to carelessly step into sacred ground where I do not belong. It is easy to underestimate the complexity and depth of certain ritual objects and actions, and to use them without truly knowing what they mean. Like children discovering shiny objects or interesting, new toys, we can play carelessly with things that are incredibly powerful, and incredibly sacred for others. This is not to say that we should not learn from the wisdom of these ancient traditions, but rather that we must do so with deep respect for the complexity and integrity of the traditions as a whole. We must not take these traditions and practices out of context, and we must use only those practices that have been shared as gifts, rather than taken carelessly.

Each of us, as we travel on the spiritual journey, must trust our own instincts. We must listen to the voices of our guides and ancestors, and sometimes these voices will clearly tell us that we must reach outside of our own traditions in order to move forward. But this does not mean that we need to do so carelessly, or disrespectfully. In all cases, it is possible to find ways to be more, rather than less, respectful in learning from the traditions of other cultures. When we open our hearts to the incredible gift we are receiving in the form of these sacred teachings, we are more likely to show deep respect and generosity ourselves in returning fair exchange for the energy we have received. Hundreds or even thousands of years of cultural accumulation of wisdom simply can't be acquired in a weekend seminar, or through a bookstore purchase. Yes, we can begin to familiarize ourselves with other traditions, to great benefit, but let's do so with a good dose of humility.

One teacher of mine found this sort of cultural care-full-ness a bit unnecessary, saying that his own teachers—of many indigenous traditions—emphasized the unity of humanity, rather than 'ownership' of spiritual truths by any one community. What I felt then, and still feel today is this: at the highest spiritual level, no one owns spiritual truths. And yet, we are inhabiting a planet that is riddled with the devastation of past hurts. Current wars are the result of disrespect by one culture for another, and back and forth and back and forth. Though we may not need to feel *guilty* for our interest in, attraction to, and deep connection with traditions that we were not born into, we can nonetheless *proceed with deep reverence, respect and humility in our explorations there*. And perhaps most important of all, we can be allies to those whose traditions we respect.

Too often, non-native peoples adopt and adapt indigenous traditions and rituals without paying any attention whatsoever to the *actual lived experience of those contemporary tribes and communities*. We buy books and items at stores that carry the sacred lineage of a particular tribe or culture, but never take the time to read about the contemporary struggles of that tribe. What is its current economic situation? What about the political condition in that community? Payment for an object is often not enough, in fair exchange, for centuries of hard-earned spiritual wisdom.

Let's be better world citizens than that. Let's commit ourselves to actually being *good neighbors* to the peoples whose spiritual sacred ground we wish to traverse. Let's make a promise to our human family that we will honor these traditions not just by practicing their rituals, and speaking kindly about their teachers, but by actually doing whatever we can to support their communities. We often act as if a romanticized, but now long-lost 'ideal' community from the past handed down these pieces of wisdom, but can no longer be directly interacted with. This is almost never true. Whether you are interested in the traditions of Asia, Africa, North America, South America, Aboriginal New Zealand, or the British Isles, please take the time to honor the contemporary culture that arose from that tradition. We don't all need to become activists, but we can all be good allies—through our words, our attention, and our simple deeds of respect—to the great teachers and traditions who share their wisdom with us.

Exercise #24: Being A Good Neighbor

Take a moment to list—in your head or on a sheet of paper—all the cultures from which you have learned spiritual truths. As you reflect on these traditions, ask yourself what you have exchanged for that wisdom. Have you had any relationship with the contemporary community from which these teachings come? Pause for a moment to send deep gratitude and loving energy to those people who inhabit the community from which you have benefitted. If you have not ever done so, think of one way you could take action to serve that community, even in a very simple way, and commit to doing so.

Drumming for a Vision

Drums, whether they are large community drums or small personal drums; whether they are made with hide or plastic; whether they are played with a stick or with the hand; are access points to the great mystery. They allow us to alter our brainwaves in a way that makes it easier to journey across the realms, and to connect with spiritual guides, teachers and companions. They assist us in dropping our human, three-dimensional forms and moving into our spirit bodies. Used by cultures around the world for millennia, percussion instruments have been essential tools for the human spiritual journey. Often, new students ask me about identifying and meeting their animal guides, and usually associate this process with shamanic trance states induced through ritual drumming. This technique is indeed a very powerful one for shifting out of the human realm, into a greater awareness, and for connecting with spiritual guidance while remaining deeply rooted to earth energy. Often on these journeys, we connect and communicate with plants, animals, trees, rocks, elements, insects and the other beings with whom share this planet.

Often, particular animals will begin to appear to us in non-visioning times, as well, once we are on a spiritual journey, and will make themselves noticeable in a variety of ways. The same type of bird may appear over and over again in a short period of time, or you may have a particularly potent encounter with one animal that you can't ignore. Often, when we are seeking such animal companionship on the spiritual path, we idealize large, dramatic (and often endangered or rare) animals such as the bear, the wolf, the eagle, etc. These animals figure large in our collective metaphorical consciousness, for they represent a time on planet earth when humans were not dominant, and nature was more in balance. And yet, often as not, much smaller, more ordinary creatures serve as the most important spiritual teachers.

One of my most powerful experiences on a quest was to get over my own disdain for, and simple ignorance of, insects. Before that day, a beautiful spring day in the Smoky Mountains, I had the usual love of butterflies and pretty honey bees, and the usual dislike of mosquitos and flies. But, sitting by the side of a lovely river for hours on end, I began to melt into the wholeness of the ecosystem around me. As I did so, the insect people began to come calling. Flies landed on my arm, and rather than brush them away, I spoke gently with them as they walked, so quietly, across my skin. I began to call them 'brother' and 'sister' and they sent messages of incredible kindness, wisdom, and respect back to me. At one point in the day, a group of tiny lavender butterflies decided to play with me, sitting in crowds on my hands and legs, then leading me to a new sitting position, where I saw other beautiful butterflies that were yellow, and black, and red and blue. A festival of butterflies! And I had been invited by my new friends, who saw that I was willing to treat them as equals.

I have since that time had an amazing experience with thousands of ladybugs, mating and dancing and gathering together in sacred places for them. I have become friends with the local stinkbugs who visit my home every winter, and who always bring me great messages of patience and protection. Lately, it has been cockroaches—incredible survivors!—who have been telling me to adapt and be resilient.

The earth-plane guides who come to you need not be impressive in size, or reputation. A skunk can be an incredibly powerful messenger. One great medicine person, a teacher of one of my teachers, always comes in spirit in the form of this smell. The smell of skunk is profoundly sacred to me for this reason. Little bugs, ordinary pets, songbirds—all are just as majestic and powerful in the spiritual family as larger or rarer creatures.

And there are no absolutely 'right' or 'wrong' ways to connect with those creatures who want to support your journey. Your family pets are certainly powerful totems and companions, here to serve humanity with their love and compassion, their playfulness and their instinctive wisdom. You may contact your companions by accident on a hike, or intentionally through meditation, or even through drawing totem or divination cards for this purpose. If you choose to journey with the drum, you'll need an experienced drummer to play while you go into a trance state, who will guide you in deepening, travelling across the realms, and coming back safely.

And if you choose to participate in a vision quest of any sort, whether it be a more traditional quest or a modern adaptation of a quest, please be sure to find a qualified and highly trained teacher and guide to assist you in this very powerful process. Questing takes preparation and follow-up, and is best done in the context of a continuing relationship with a trusted mentor, preferably one who has significant experience in the field.

This last method of connecting with Source is perhaps the most advanced we've touched upon here. We've talked about some of the basics of energy hygiene: deepening and centering in ourselves, and various ways of connecting to source and divine guidance. Now let's dive into the last regular practice we can use to establish and maintain a healthy energy body: establishing clear boundaries and protecting ourselves from unwanted energies.

Rev. Carol Bodeau, PhD

Protection and Self-Differentiation

Deepening, centering, grounding and connecting to Source are all ways to establish and maintain a healthy, balanced, optimal flow of energy and well-being in our bodies and lives. One last helpful technique at this most basic level is to also establish clear boundaries between ourselves and others, so that we are more easily able to keep our field clear of others' negativity and upsets. Though it is definitely possible (and some would argue necessary) to eventually become so strong a conduit of divine energy that 'protecting' ourselves becomes unnecessary, I believe that—at least for most of us at some time or other—we need to know how to make clear energy boundaries between ourselves and other people, circumstances, and places. Because we are truly all one, and all connected, we are of course ultimately unable to completely separate from the life around us. And yet, being able to distinguish 'me, not me'—to identify what is energy within my own system, coming from me, and what is energy from outside of me—is a necessary step for anyone working to establish full energetic and spiritual health.

Most empathic people have, at one time or another, carried emotions, thoughts, or even physical symptoms that did not belong to them. The character of Deanna Troi, from "Star Trek: The Next Generation" gives us a great model of this pattern. As the official 'empath' on the starship, she frequently is overcome by physical, emotional, and mental symptoms that she picks up from those nearby. On the show, this is her function within the community, and is considered an ability worthy of respect. For most of us still here on earth, this ability has less positive associations. We find ourselves not being able to tell why we suddenly feel so upset, or overcome with symptoms such as nausea, headaches, or anxiety. We lack the training and wise, experienced teachers who might make it clear these are not *our* symptoms, but rather belong to other people. And so we spend enormous time and resources trying to 'cure' ourselves of diseases and imbalances that were never ours in the first place.

For empathic mystics and seekers, learning how to differentiate between our own energy and the energy of others is absolutely essential. And it's important to note that an increased flow of divine energy and light in your system will *increase* rather than decrease the number of others attracted to you for healing. As we consciously attempt to increase our flow of energy, we will become a brighter beacon to those seeking divine light, but not knowing how to find it within. Too often, unconscious empaths become magnets for injured and hurting lovers, for companions with chronic troubles, and for co-workers who need constant help. These folks are all seeking a connection to a greater flow, and you appear to be a good access point. If this has happened to you, then the self-differentiation portion of basic energy hygiene is an absolute 'must do.'

There are many ways you can begin to experience, and steady your own sense of Self as separate—truly separate—from others. Of course, for most of us empaths, even suggesting that we separate may bring up some fear and hesitation. We are so used to feeling deeply, almost inextricably connected to others—and to having this sort of empathy be a source of power, comfort and identity— that giving it up seems dangerous and unwise. But optimal well-being comes from connection to the living earth and to our divine Source, rather than from connection to other people or circumstances, which are fickle, changeable, and unpredictable. So how to self-differentiate?

To begin, it's important to be curious about your feelings,

both physical and emotional. When you have a sensation, particularly an uncomfortable emotion like anger, sadness, fear or anxiety, or a physical sensation of pain, constriction, nausea, vertigo/dizziness, etc. ask yourself, "Is it obvious where this came from?" In other words, if something has happened that clearly led you to this feeling, clearly identify the source of that sensation. If the source is *not* immediately obvious, then that's your cue to start exploring other possibilities. Specifically, begin to ask yourself, "Is this *my* emotion or symptom, or might it be coming from someone else?"

Often, empaths experience thoughts, emotions and physical sensations every day that belong to others, without even realizing these are not their own feelings. Disentangling ourselves from others at this most basic level is the first step to becoming separate in the management of your own, highest energies.

Exercise #25: Empathy Overload

Think back to a time when you felt utterly overwhelmed by emotion or physical pain, but could not clearly understand *why* you felt so bad. You may remember an event that was acute, sudden and particularly upsetting, or a more chronic pattern of just not feeling right in a certain phase of your life, or around certain people. Perhaps this is happening to you right now. Consider for a moment who else is part of this story—who else is playing (or played) a role in this experience? And what about the physical circumstances—lighting, fabrics/textures/colors, the presence or absence of nature, can all strongly affect an empath. What other sources of discomfort *outside of yourself* might be causing (or have caused) your feelings?

As you begin to ask questions about possible external sources for your feelings, and to identify what is coming from you and what is coming to you from others, it's also important to use some energetic tricks to separate yourself from other's energy. There are a few simple ways to do this. One of the most common is to visualize a bubble of light and/or energy around yourself. By setting the intention that only helpful, beneficial energies may pass through this barrier towards you, while all that you wish to release can easily pass *out* of it, you are able to manage what you accept into your energy field. Another layer of protection that many people add is to fill the bubble of surrounding light with either golden or crystalline light that comes directly from the divine.

Many people supplement this technique by invoking the support of guides, angels, allies or other spiritual helpers. The Archangel Michael is particularly popular for this purpose, as he is reputed to be an excellent protector. Michael's protection is often pictured as a sphere of cobalt blue flame, and my own experience with it suggests that he is indeed a very powerful and helpful guardian. You might also call on your personal Guardian Angel to support you in keeping out unwanted energies.

Another technique that works for separating your own energy field from that of others is to carry stones or other talismans that are 'imprinted' with the intention of creating a protective field around you. For many months, my partner carried a small, specially designed vial filled with metal shavings which had been designed to deflect EMF's. When I'm feeling particularly sensitive, or am going into an environment that might be highly charged energetically, I often wear copper and other metal bracelets, which are designed to establish beneficial energy fields and create balance for the wearer. In all circumstances, I choose the jewelry I wear each day for the energetic properties it carries—leather for connection to the animal helpers and the drum (through its hide or skin), semi-precious stones for their various healing and grounding qualities, and metals which enhance my own personal boundaries and intentions. You can also use clothing—textures, colors, fabrics—and scents from essential oils to establish a clear circle of energy that defines 'me' versus 'not me.' When I am in professional or even personal settings that require especially clear boundaries, I often wear scarves specifically to protect my throat chakra and my heart.

In all of these ways, and in whatever other creative ways you can imagine for yourself, you can begin to make a clear distinction between your own energy and the energies that surround you. As you do this, you will find it much easier to understand when symptoms (physical, emotional, mental and spiritual) are coming from others around you, and from unhealthy circumstances. This sort of protection and self-differentiation, combined with a strong connection to your true Self and your Source; a clear intention of being centered in the here, now; and a strong connection to the earth, immediately begin to shift any imbalances you may be experiencing in your life. Physical symptoms of all sorts will begin to dissipate; mental clarity will come in many areas of your life; and a greater sense of identity, purpose and direction will come naturally from these simple, basic practices. Maintain them throughout your life, whether you are in a time of crisis or a time of ease, and allow them to keep your human system well-tuned for flowing maximum divine energies.

Level II: Cleansing and Clearing of Unwanted Energies

In addition to maintaining a solid, strong energy field, it's important to cleanse and clear ourselves of the energetic debris and 'clutter' that we pick up in our daily lives. There are many different ways to do this, but just as we take regular showers and brush our teeth every day, we need to make a habit of keeping our energy bodies fresh and clean. You can even add this to your regular, physical hygiene routine. For example, one technique that I have used is to imagine cleaning each of my chakras as I shower. As the soap cleanses my skin, I imagine the water flowing like light through my energy body, washing away any darkness or unwanted energies from my spiritual system.

Other types of visualizations that can be used for this purpose include seeing golden light moving through your body from head to toe, allowing divine energy to wash away any unwanted residues. Using your grounding cord to drain these impurities out also helps. If you find that you sense a lot of unwanted energies—perhaps after an unpleasant encounter, or even after eating foods that may not be of the highest vibration—you can do more pointed and directed clearings of specific organs or body systems. You can imagine water, light, color, temperature, or even textures moving through you. Be creative, and use your imagination to allow your spiritual Self to direct these clearings.

Exercise #26: Rose Clearing

One technique that I have used to clear out patches of unwanted energetic debris involves visualizing roses used as a sort of feather-duster. If you have a particularly unsettling emotion, belief, thought or experience that is disrupting your energy flow, you can wipe it away with the flower head of the rose. Begin by centering and grounding yourself, and visualizing your own energy field. You may perceive your field visually, as images, colors, sensations, or temperatures. Or you may simply sense its presence kinesthetically or with inner knowing. Next, notice where the disruptions you are experiencing are located in your field. They may appear as dark splotches or geometric patterns, as cords, or simply as uncomfortable sensations in one or more areas of your body. They may be in your physical system, or located just outside your physical body, in your aura. Now imagine roses (whatever color feels best to you), being moved by your own or a divine hand, sweeping around the areas where you perceive imbalance. As the roses 'dust' the area, they collect all the energetic debris that needs to be removed. See the roses actually changing color as they collect this energetic 'gunk' and watch them fill up with it. As each rose becomes full of energy that you want to discard, throw the rose 'away' into a field of pure energy. You may imagine this pure energy as the ocean, where the roses are dissolved back into nature, or you may see it as the sun, a ball of fire and light which immediately transforms the energy. Often, I visualize the roses being thrown into the air, where they explode into starbursts and then cascade down as color and light into the ocean, on the far horizon, where they are taken into a rising or setting sun. Use whatever imagery works for you—choose a different

> flower, or a different landscape. The goal is to use a tool made of beauty, to physically sweep through your energy field, collecting debris. You then allow the tool and the unwanted energies to be completely transmuted by higher energies back into a more pure form.

In addition to using visual imagery to clear your energy field, you can also use more material means for this purpose. The most common tool used in contemporary, 'new age' culture is white sage. Used throughout history since ancient times by both Native North and South Americans, and by ancient peoples of Europe, including the Celts and Druids, members of the *salvia* or sage family produce a sweet and powerful smoke which clears the energy field much like soap cleans the skin. When plants such as sage are dried and bundled, they make 'smudge sticks' which can be burned so that smoke swept around the body showers and cleans the whole aura. Similarly, various forms of incense, and even perfumes and essential oils, can produce this cleansing effect.

So, we can use our sense of sight through visualizations, and our sense of smell through smudging, to cleanse our energy field. We can also use the other basic senses of touch, taste, and hearing to do the same. One very powerful clearing experience I had recently—that was quite unexpected— came as the result of listening to particular music. As I drove up the mountains of North Carolina one day, I intuitively put on a piece of music that I enjoyed listening too. I knew it had spiritual power for me, but only expected to find it comforting and soothing. Instead, I found myself sobbing uncontrollably as it began to play. Surprised, but actually pleased, I simply surrendered to the experience; I could feel the residue of tension, worries, and hurts that had been coming up in my life pouring out of me. It was as if the music had tapped into a deep well of unresolved energy, opened the tap, and was allowing the hurt to flow out of its own accord. I played the track over and over, until I could feel that my energy body was clear of unneeded pain, sorrow, and fear. And then I allowed myself to listen to a few more soothing pieces of music, to steady my energy after such a huge release.

As many of us have experienced in our lives, music can serve as a beautiful tool for healing and cleansing our minds and hearts. We can also consciously use the sounds of bells, crystal and Himalayan bowls, chanting, and other sounds to clear ourselves of unneeded energies.

Words, too, can serve a healing and clearing purpose. Many mystical seekers use the language of the Hindu mystics, Sanskrit, for this purpose. Sanskrit is said to be the most vibrationally pure language available to us; it has the highest vibrational match between the sounds of the words and their energetic meanings. Using such words has the effect of re-balancing our energy fields simply through speaking them. For example, when we speak the mantra "Om" –the sound of pure creation in Hindu tradition—we are re-calibrating our own energy to its most pure, creative state. Or simply following the good advice offered by Don Miguel Ruiz, in his popular book *The Four Agreements*,[5] of speaking only words that are life affirming, and avoiding all words (about self and others) that are negative or critical, can be purifying to the energy field.

Using all the senses, we can find ways to remove the energetic 'debris' of our daily lives. Added to the regular practice of grounding, centering, and connecting to the

---

[5] Don Miguel Ruiz, *The Four Agreements*

divine, these techniques help to ensure not only spiritual health, but also physical, mental and emotional well-being. But what about healing from past or present traumas that hit us deeply? How can we respond energetically to heal the spiritual wounds caused by physical, emotional, mental and spiritual injury?

Level III: Healing Spiritual Trauma

Let's begin by getting a sense of just what might cause spiritual trauma, since we are not usually accustomed to thinking about injury to the spiritual self. Many of the experiences that cause trauma on other levels do harm at the spiritual level, as well: physical accidents and illnesses; emotional or physical abuse; traumatic natural events; or death of a loved one. Beyond these, and perhaps less commonly considered as having a direct personal impact, are events that occur beyond the boundaries of our own three-dimensional bodies: traumas in other (past, future, or parallel) lives or other realms; traumas experienced by our ancestors and familial or cultural lines; traumas to the collective unconscious (such as national or international tragedies); and traumas experienced by those we love and are deeply connected to. Finally, we can experience spiritual— and hence physical, emotional, and mental harm—from the harmful intentions of others. Referred to sometimes as spiritual attack, this is a less common sort of psychic assault that comes, either intentionally or unintentionally, from the projected negative emotions and thoughts of others.

Spiritual injuries can express themselves in many ways, as we have seen in a number of the exercises and stories described already in this book. More often than not, though, they appear as physical illnesses, emotional and mental imbalances, and as chronic limiting life patterns (for example, failed relationships, financial woes, etc). How, then, do we trace them back to their original causes? This is the level of energy management where good spiritual care-givers, folks trained in identifying and working to resolve such imbalances, can be incredibly helpful. Too often, it's impossible to recognize our own spiritual 'imprints' or wounds because so much of our energy is already tied up in dealing with them. We can be so habituated to managing the *symptoms* of spiritual or energetic imbalances that we are unable to sense their deeper causes.

By the time we reach adulthood, the vast majority of us have sustained a number of wounds on this level—many of them connected with wounds on the other three levels—and they have been festering for quite a long time. Some of these spiritual traumas will be small, and relatively easy to treat; others will be large and multifaceted, and take more significant commitment, time and resources to heal. For most of us in contemporary western culture, we have been given little training or treatment for the spiritual scars and painful energetic wounds that come with the traumatic experiences in our lives.

The place to begin with this level of energy hygiene is simply to assess our symptoms. We begin by asking, "What's out of balance?" And then we take a look at *all* our symptoms, without filtering anything. Rather than assume any symptom in our life 'must be' attributed to something more mundane, or more material, than a spiritual-level imprint, we begin by being willing to see the whole of our lives as utterly connected to, and sourced from, our spiritual Selves.

Note: give yourself anywhere from a full day to a week or even longer to complete this exercise, or simply let it percolate in your mind over time.

Exercise #27: Symptom and Wound Inventories

In this exercise, you will first make a list of all your physical, emotional, mental and spiritual symptoms. *Don't leave anything out!* Anything that has bothered you, from aching in your little toe to mental fogginess to grief in your marriage counts here. Anything in your life that feels less than wonderful gets put on this list. The goal is not to find a 'cure' for each and everything you write down, but rather to make sure you are including every possible material expression of non-material 'dents' in your energy field. This includes personal relationship patterns, financial woes, the condition of your home, your career, and anything else you care to add. You will likely fine patterns emerging from this inventory, categories of symptoms that are linked to one another and may really be multiple expressions of one deeper wound. And remember, even symptoms which have identifiable biological or material 'causes' are nonetheless sourced at a deeper level, and can therefore be helped by accessing that deeper level.

When you have finished listing all the symptoms you can think of, take a minute and take a breath. This can be an overwhelming experience. If you have never listed *all* of the things that are making you feel less than fantastic, seeing them all together can be either energizing or a bit depressing. So give yourself some credit for taking this big and important step towards real well-being. Then, begin another list, this one identifying all the traumatic events you can recall from your life. Again, *don't leave anything out*, even if your mind wants to insist 'Oh, that wasn't that big of a deal!' If it came to mind, it goes on the list. Include physical traumas like bike or car accidents, surgeries, and serious illnesses. Even a childhood flu can make a big dent in your energy field, depending on the emotional circumstances surrounding it, so list anything at all that comes to mind. Also include relationship traumas, difficult events in your work or professional life (including primary and secondary schools), and national or international events that you felt deeply. Finally, list events that you've heard stories about which happened in your family: parents or grandparents who went through wars; a cultural heritage of slavery or prejudice; economic hardships in your family line; and anything else that comes up as you reflect on the stories of hardship, pain, suffering or fear that have been part of your ancestral lineage. I know—this is a lot. But taking the time to name and draw out these deeper patterns will be well worth it in the long run.

This assessment may seem a little bit overwhelming, or perhaps it may even feel like over-kill—just too much mental analysis to be truly useful. But I assure you, if you take the time to really look at the whole picture of your own life, of all the things that aren't working as you would like them to, you will begin to see patterns that have been hidden from view. Because we are organic, wholistic beings—despite the western tendency to compartmentalize us into segments that seem discrete and unconnected—everything happening to us is affecting everything else that is happening with us.

Once you have a good overview of what's going on for you, you can begin to sense what areas have the most priority. Now, it may be that you have some very pressing, very urgent issues that need addressing. Physical illnesses or distressing symptoms; financial crises or relationship crises; mental or emotional imbalances and challenges that are limiting you—these are all high-level needs which must be addressed. If this is your experience, then your system is giving you a clear and helpful message about where to start; it's directing your attention to the area that needs healing the most immediately. Healing in this area will likely, in its turn, unlock healing in other areas. Try to consider that an urgent need might be a good thing, that your energy system is in fact working hard to help you identify causes of imbalance, and give you ample motivation to correct them. But even if there's no one clear starting place in your system, even if you have a number of mild symptoms of dis-ease (be they emotional, material, relational, spiritual, physical or other) you can still begin to directly address the energy imbalances that limit you and keep you from functioning to your greatest potential.

How We Heal

Let's begin with this: there is no one way, no 'right' or 'better' path, to healing and becoming whole. There are an infinite number of paths: innumerable healing systems, innumerable healers and modalities, and innumerable paths *just for you* that will serve you beautifully. You can't get this wrong. So don't fret too much about where to go next, or about how to do it the 'best' or the 'fastest' way, or the most efficiently. Whatever you choose will bring you just exactly what you most need, exactly when you need it. But it does help to have some basic information—some general understanding of the lay of the land—if you are seeking energetic healing for traumas.

As we have already been discovering, there are a few basic levels of the human system that interact with one another, and make up the 'whole' and the wholeness of our beings. And, there are healing modalities that can work through any one of these levels to affect the others. You may find that massage or another form of body work is exactly what you need to access traumas on the spiritual or emotional level, since these events may be stored energetically in your physical tissues. You may find that emotional therapies work best to unravel energy patterns that arose in response to mental illness or verbal abuse. You may decide that you really love prayer and meditation as a way to deal with chronic pain or fatigue, or that affirmations (a mind-based approach) are your best tool for dealing with relationship or professional difficulties. All of these approaches are perfect; you get to choose what works best for you.

But how do you choose? How do you know where to go next? The simplest answer is this: follow your heart. Let your own instincts and the 'coincidences' and synchronicities of life guide you. But set some intentions first. Decide *how you would like to feel* and imagine that coming true, then tell the universe—like Jean Luc Picard on the Starship Enterprise—"make it so!" Then see what happens. Healing is a mix of intention and surrender, action and being receptive, trusting and taking charge. You will be doing this dance consciously for the rest of your life/lives. There is no end to the healing journey; it is an ever-evolving balance of motion and stillness that takes us through layer after layer of awareness to greater and greater wholeness. And since we are infinite, eternal beings, our capacity for greater and greater wholeness, well-being, and even magical manifestation, is endless.

So far in this book, we've looked at a number of the kinds of traumas that can happen along the stages of the spiritual journey. And we've tried a few techniques for identifying, releasing and healing those traumas. But most of us need much more intensive healing for the deepest traumatic experiences that have touched us. We will likely need to find alternative healers of one sort or another to assist us along the way. *(Please note: this is only a very partial list of all the resources available to you, and in no way represents an endorsement of any particular school or modality. I present it merely as a place to start.)* You will need to take some time, if you haven't already done so, to explore what sorts of healing are available to you in your own geographic area.

One of the greatest advantages we have today as we embark on the deep healing portion of the spiritual journey is that we have access to an incredible array of resources, teachers, and even long-distance energy work. Through the internet, many of the best and most powerful new healers are doing work with thousands of people who live long distances from them. We no longer need to actually go to a physical office to receive the healing energies of great lightworkers and energy healers. Some of my most profound healings have come through on-line seminars, recorded talks, and audio-visual energy offerings provided on-line—many of them for free! Our global community is truly taking advantage of the newest technologies to make high-level healing available to everyone. Because energy isn't limited to space or time, you can receive healing from a piece of music played far away, or from a recording of a healing session that occurred days or even weeks prior.

This wide range of possibilities can seem overwhelming, though, and it requires of us a deep willingness to be our own best companions. While we are searching for outside healing resources, we also have to make time to do the simplest of things—eating meals slowly while sitting down, taking warm baths, walking in the woods, meditating or praying quietly, appreciating simple pleasures and simple beauty. We have to connect with our inner guidance system. If you spend *too* much time surfing the web for the latest, greatest healing techniques and tools, you may get lost in spiritual bypass—focusing so much on spiritual healing that you actually avoid doing the real work of it. It's better to devote quality time to the one or two things that would help you most, while practicing gentle self-care. Even I find myself spending too much time deleting emails from the many, many teachers and healers whose websites I have signed up for, and way too little time just sitting quietly with a cup of tea and the morning sunshine. We all need to find ways to balance reaching out and discovering new options, with slowing down enough to actually rest and do our inner healing.

This is especially true in the initial phase of healing. If you are someone who has already gone through the first big wave of healing in your life, you know that the initial burst can be very fast, very intense, and very transformative. Often, though, this initial wave settles over time into a slower, more steady routine of gentle awareness. But during the initial awakening of spiritual energies, during that first big release of pent up traumas and attachments, the rush of adrenaline and emotion and possibility and excitement can sweep us up and carry us along at a great speed. It is especially important during this early phase (and during later intense waves of healing or realization that may come up) to remember to ground and center ourselves often.

If you were sitting in my office right now, and we were having a session devoted specifically to your healing, here's what we'd do next: I'd ask you what you feel in your body, and then we'd begin to explore healing possibilities for you. So let's do that, over the distance of time and space represented by the pages of this book.

Exercise #28: A Healing Session

Take a moment to close your eyes—even before reading the rest of this exercise. Just close your eyes and breathe for a moment or two. Did you actually do it? Just a couple of breaths, there's plenty of time. Nowhere to go, nothing to do for just the next few moments. After you've taken a couple of breaths, allow yourself to feel your body. Simply become aware of the sensations you are feeling in your skin, your muscles, your bones, your organs, your blood, your breath. Allow yourself to become aware of all the subtle (and sometimes not so subtle) messages that your brilliant body is sending you about how you're doing. Do you feel well? Energized? Do you feel light, or dark/ heavy? Do you feel pain, or constriction, or do you feel expansiveness and freedom? Notice whatever most draws your attention, right in this moment. Whatever it is, that is where we start. If you allow yourself to really put your attention on the part of you that most wants your attention, and hold that attention with curiosity and receptivity, thoughts or emotions will start to rise up. Don't dismiss any of them! No matter how crazy or disconnected or random your thoughts or feelings may seem, I guarantee you that they are the breadcrumbs making a trail from outer sensations to your deeper energy body. Following this trail of thoughts, memories, emotions, impressions, we begin to unravel the energy patterns that hold you together, and that may or may not be serving you well. You can also do this exercise by focusing on a non-physical problem (like troubles in a relationship, or lack of purpose, or financial woes) and then ask your body to show you where that energy is stored. As you focus on the situation, allow yourself to notice any sensations you have in your body, and then follow them to deeper thoughts, emotions, or impressions. As you do this, you can use words, images, sounds, smells, or any of the other sorts of healing tools we've discussed to move the energies you encounter around. I will often invite clients to repeat the following phrases, adapted from my own teacher, Peter Calhoun: "I release you (fill in the blank—a person, a feeling, a situation) into the light. I forgive you and I forgive myself, and I release myself into the light." Of course, this process and others like it are often easier and more effective with the energetic help and support of a trained healer, but you can definitely do some of the work on your own. After you notice the sensations, thoughts, feelings, memories and anything else that arises, and after you intentionally release anything you wish to let go of, take time to simply sit quietly and feel your breath and the stillness of your body.

This basic technique of identifying symptoms in your body (perhaps associated with a troubling area in your life) and then opening up to the messages they might offer, can be used at any time to help you take another step forward. I have found that, with each little bit of clearing I do on myself, I am more able to find and receive the healing support that is available to me from outside myself. As I open myself up, I am more open to the help coming in. And this support can come in many forms, so keep an open mind. At one point in my own journey, when I was doing a lot of 'work' on making peace with the traumas my ancestors had experienced, some of my deepest healing came not from alternative healers or New Age techniques, but rather from working in a traditional church community. I had been working for quite a while on healing traumas associated with my father's lineage, and with the masculine energies in my life, and what showed up for me was a number of strong, healthy, wonderful older men who served as guides, teachers, and paternal figures for me in a completely neutral yet supportive way. The universe simply brought me a host of men who were whole, healthy and supportive just when I was ready to receive them. So be open to the magic of the universe, bringing you just what you need when and where you might not expect it.

Making Friends with Your Pain

As you enter into healing, you may experience significant physical, emotional, mental or spiritual pain. All of the techniques described here and in the index are meant to help alleviate some or all of that pain. But, unfortunately, some pain is inevitable whether we are spiritually engaged or not. We know that human life comes with many painful challenges, and most of our coping strategies are designed to numb or avert it, so that we can function more fully. When we undertake a spiritual journey—often precipitated by pain that can no longer be ignored—emotional pain especially can sometimes gets worse for a while. Perhaps a lot worse. When we take away the defenses and avoidance strategies that have been protecting us (and also limiting us), we are usually faced with feeling and acknowledging hurts that have been long-deferred.

As a friend once said to me, when I was feeling a lot of that sort of pain, "Healing hurts. It's afterwards that you feel better."

During the stages of crisis, awakening and reclaiming your life, it's important to make friends with your pain. Though you don't have to invite it to take up residence forever, it can be very helpful to give it a respected place in your home for a little while. What I mean by this is that your pain is trying to tell you something very important—about your life, about your energy patterns, about your relationships, about your self-esteem. And it's more likely to leave you in peace for good if you stop for a while, listen to it respectfully, and offer it some appreciation and respect for being a messenger carrying important wisdom which you need to move forward. If nothing else, don't waste energy trying to be aggressive *against* it; instead, allow yourself to be compassionate *with* it, as you take positive steps to release it.

We can never totally eliminate pain from our human experience. We can, however, understand it differently. We can treat it as an honorable guest, who is trying to share some important information with us. We can give ourselves time, patience, support, good food, abundant sleep, quiet environments, moments of fun and pleasure, and all the tools and resources available to support the pain as it completes its task and moves on. And as the pain begins to ebb, or leaves entirely, we may be left with feelings of incredible ease, joy, relief and liberation.

The Exhilaration
of Awakening

The crisis phase, and the need to deal directly with the imprints and traumas we have been carrying around, often leads to one of the most exciting and rewarding phases of the spiritual journey: awakening. The initial awakening phase of the spiritual journey is when we realize the extent of our own spiritual power. It's when we come to understand that everything really *is* energetic. We really *do* have the ability to create magic. We "wake up" to our own divine Selves, in a conscious and intentional way, and begin to take solid action to create a life of spiritual and material integrity. Although we may have had spiritual revelations or openings in the past, the awakening experience takes us to a whole new level of understanding about the true nature of reality, and our place in it. We may remember or re-claim psychic or intuitive abilities that have lain dormant, or we may turn fully towards a calling that we have been avoiding. In the awakening phase, we decide that our well-being depends on our own *willingness* to take charge of our energy. And we understand—sometimes for the first time—that we are indeed the creators of our own reality and co-creators with Godde in generating this whole experience we call life on earth.

It is a heady and exciting time. The awakening phase often involves intense and rapid-fire synchronicities, events that appear seemingly out of nowhere to deliver just the answer we were looking for, or the teachers we needed, or the opportunities we have been crying out for. Usually, we find ourselves connecting with all sorts of new people: teachers, companions, and communities that match us in ways we never imagined possible. And we find powers and potential in ourselves that we hadn't even considered before. For most of us, this time feels like a turning point in our lives, and almost always involves bringing up and dealing with old, unresolved hurts.

An awakening can be precipitated by seemingly external events, or just as easily arise from internal crises that have been building within us. For example, an awakening might be triggered by the death of a loved one, or by a spouse leaving you suddenly and unexpectedly. It can happen when we reach a certain age. Or it can appear seemingly out of the blue, with no apparent trigger. Perhaps an illness forces us to stop and reevaluate our lives, or we lose a job, or face a financial crisis. Sometimes, we simply read a book that changes our lives without warning. In all cases, we were simply ready for the healing to begin, ready to wake up to our divine Selves. It is as if a dark cover has been taken off our eyes, or the gates of an internal dam have been lifted to let the waters of wisdom and remembrance rush out.

Have you reached a turning point yet? Or perhaps a second or third turning point? Are you craving such a moment of revelation and transformation? There is no way to force these moments, no prescription for making them happen on command. But there are ways to prepare ourselves for them, to make the way ready for them. Simply reading this book, and other books like it, tills the soil to make you ready for awakening moments. They may not come immediately (while reading, for example) but they may come days, weeks or months after, as new ideas take root and begin to grow within you. Working with spiritual practices such as meditation also prepares us for awakening, as do new relationships, which can bring us to a new place where we are ready for revelation. You may also find that becoming physically active prepares you for spiritual awakening and transformation, especially if you practice an energy-based discipline such as Tai Chi or Yoga. Two of my greatest spiritual awakenings happened in yoga classes, and I was utterly surprised by both of them.

When I was in my early twenties, a PhD student struggling with PTSD on top of all the usual stresses of graduate school, I began practicing yoga at a local studio, as a way to deal with overwhelming symptoms of overwork. My crisis patterns included migraines, fatigue, odd neurological symptoms, and chronic digestive issues. I was also suffering from asthma and allergies, including a number of food sensitivities. Yoga seemed to offer a way to manage the stress I was under, and perhaps to help my body get a little stronger, and a little healthier. So I began attending weekly sessions, and I found myself experiencing subtle, odd responses to the practice. First, I found that my chronic irritable bladder symptoms went away whenever I practiced yoga. In fact, it was so effective at easing the tension in my bladder that I almost always had to leave class at least once in the middle to go to the restroom. I also found myself much more able to access deep emotions, and was experiencing a much greater sense of calm and peace than I have ever known. These physical benefits were enormous, and enough to keep me practicing, but then something much more profound happened.

One day, at the end of a yoga session, as we lay in the final pose of the class, *sivasana* or the corpse pose (in which the body is resting completely, arms and legs open and body sinking into the floor), I felt a strange sensation in my lower belly. At first, it felt like a gentle warmth, spreading through my middle, and then it began to grow and strengthen, until it felt like a powerful energy moving in my body. I literally saw, in my mind's eye, a huge serpent of rainbow colors, rise up from the base of my spine, swirl up through my body, along my spine, to the top of my head, and then spiral back down into the bowl of my pelvis. It was an incredibly intense sensation, and utterly overwhelmed me.

For those of you who know about the *kundalini*, you will recognize this rainbow serpent, but at the time I had never even heard of kundalini energy, the ball of internal fire that sits at the base of the spine, waiting to be awakened and harnessed. I had never heard of nor seen images of the rainbow serpent, and I certainly had absolutely no idea what this experience meant, or what it portended. From that moment on, though, a huge wave of undeniable, unavoidable healing began to sweep over me. Memories I had been avoiding, defense strategies that had been unconscious, and patterns that were no longer serving me became painfully obvious. In the weeks following the event, I found myself feeling profoundly emotional. I was swept by waves of grief, terror, rage, and physical symptoms that *demanded* I get down to the serious, committed business of healing myself. The kundalini energy is said to be the most powerful creative, healing force in our systems, and it has the capacity to create massive transformation, as well as to wreak a bit of havoc, when it is released. Because I had so much pent up psychic and spiritual energy locked in my system, and because I had set an intention of healing the symptoms this blockage created, my yoga practice released my kundalini to assist in my transformation.

It was a powerful, if challenging, situation. It took over a year for me to begin to get my balance, and that was only the beginning. When I learned, a few months after that yoga class, what kundalini is and how it works, I was truly stunned to realize that I had experienced exactly what the teachers and sages of many ages have said about this rainbow serpent. And it served as an initiation into an amazing journey of discovery and healing.

Years later, well into my healing process, I had another awakening experience in a yoga class. This time, I had some warning about what might happen, but was again surprised by its intensity. I had been practicing yoga for about 5 or 6 years by this point, and was studying with a teacher who had also been ordained as a Buddhist nun. Our yoga practice was both therapeutic and spiritual, and I had been enjoying the deeply healing, calming effects of a regular practice. During one class, my teacher suggested to me that a particular variation of a warrior pose, if practiced often, would bring me into direct contact with my high Self. I was a little intrigued by this idea, but felt (perhaps a little egotistically) that I already *knew* my high Self and that, well how could a yoga pose do that, anyway? (You'd think the kundalini experience would have made me a little wiser, but no such luck.)

I continued practicing for weeks and weeks, and almost entirely forgot about her suggestion. Until one day, in the middle of yoga class, as I held this particular pose, suddenly, without warning, I felt something indescribable. The best way I can imagine it is as a huge, immense, incredibly powerful presence, emanating both from me and within me. It was, in fact, my true Self. I was utterly stunned, and I burst into tears with recognition and amazement and overwhelming emotion. My teacher had been absolutely right; this was like nothing I had ever experienced before. Again, I was awakened to a whole new level of awareness, and that awareness transformed me deeply, profoundly, and permanently.

Once I actually felt, and knew in my mind, heart, and body, the presence of this larger Self, I could never go back. Awareness of it has grown and grown in me since that day, and has become more and more consistent and steady over time. With each passing year, I am able to maintain that connection for longer and longer periods of time, so that, now, I need only take a deep breath and shift my attention to be fully aware of it.

And yet, again, I had yet another re-awakening and deepening of this connection at a psychic fair I attended recently. I was there as a tarot reader, and on a break between readings, I listened to a speaker lead an exercise designed to help the audience connect with the high Self. Again I found myself called into more direct and sustainable connection with this true Self.

So you see, the awakenings can come in waves. The first wave of awakening often comes with surprise, even shock, and a sense of intense exhilaration. You feel as if a whole new world has opened up, and all sorts of new possibilities are available that you never imagined before. Even if your first awakening is more gentle, it always brings an increased sense of wholeness and well-being, despite obstacles and limitations you may still be facing in your life. You once again imagine that your dreams really *can* come true, and that there is support in the universe for you. Later waves of awakening may have a less surprising, more familiar feel to them, but can still be accompanied by feelings of euphoria, deep emotion, connection to a larger or transcendent reality, and intense physical sensations. At any awakening stage, you may experience sudden and amazing healings of chronic or acute illnesses. One client I knew, in a later awakening stage, was able to very suddenly and intentionally clear herself of all food allergies. Others suddenly find their money worries completely resolved, or new relationships entering their lives quite unexpectedly.

In short, the awakening phase is often the phase of *miracles*. These miraculous experiences in turn create new energy for further awareness, awakening and growth. For the duration of the period when they are happening— sometimes hours, sometimes days, sometimes weeks or month, or even years—such intense and ecstatic openings change our lives profoundly. And they are so addictive! Once you've experienced such an awakening, you will want to keep feeling it, over and over again.

And yet...

The awakening phase is also very difficult, challenging, and exhausting in many ways. For those who have gone through radical life changes as a result of this sort of awakening, you know exactly what I mean. Once you open the floodgates of your awareness to the divine wisdom that is within and all around you, you may be overwhelmed with information—and changes—that seem almost impossible to manage. When one man I know was going through his first big awakening, his spiritual guide came every night in his dreams to teach him, and barely let him get any sleep at all. Though this served to break down his defenses and make him more receptive to learning and growing, it was very tough on him physically and emotionally. Other people experience intensifications of physical symptoms (often allergies and sensitivities will intensify at such a time), or encounter very difficult relationship situations that must be addressed.

In one of my awakening phases—one of the later, seemingly less dramatic awakenings—I decided on the spur of the moment to quit a great job, move to a new state, and start fresh. I had been working as a minister in California. I was recently divorced, and had returned to studying with a teacher based near the Great Smoky Mountains. On a visit to the Smokies, driving from the airport to the mountains, I simply knew—without any doubt—that I had to quit my job and move East. I left behind two children, in their father's care, and went with no job, no savings, and no friends save one (who was himself going through a massive upheaval), to a completely new reality. I threw myself into the arms of destiny, and then waited to see what would happen.

Those first many months were excruciating! I had less than $500 in my bank account, and no job prospects. I was terrified. Challenges in my personal relationships compounded the problem, and I spent 3 months crying, meditating, praying and getting really—and I mean *really*—right with myself.

It was one of the greatest gifts I have ever been willing to receive. This was an awakening, and a transformation of the highest order. And I frankly didn't see it coming. I had already gone through my first, big "awakening" years earlier. I had been practicing yoga, meditating, studying with native teachers, vision questing, and doing spiritual work for over 20 years. I had awakened my kundalini and met my high Self. I had experienced innumerable visions, premonitions, past life memories, and spontaneous healings. And I had facilitated those things for other people. But that didn't mean I was in any way "done" with awakening. I expect that, as long as I am willing to be open and courageous, and to set intentions for being my fullest Self, I will continue to have such surprises creep up on me, jump upon me, and ease gently into my life.

So, wherever you are on the journey, please be gentle with yourself and aware of your needs. Inviting awakening is indeed an exciting, enlivening, exhilarating experience. And it is worth every single challenge it brings. But you will need to be ready to do a number of things to facilitate it, and these are true whether you are in your first awakening phase, or your second or fifth or tenth or more. You will need to be willing to:

- Practice radical self-care, including saying "no" to things that other people are used to expecting of you
- Sleep a lot more, and eat much higher quality foods (you cannot skimp on the material, vibrational resources you are feeding yourself during such a time)
- Cut back on activities, financial burdens, job responsibilities, and projects
- Ask for help, a LOT, and be willing to receive it—the universe cannot transform you if you are unwilling to accept new resources and support
- Let go, and let go, and let go—of your identity, of who you thought you were; of possessions, and places, and situations; of people; and of your stories about reality
- Be surprised, maybe a little or maybe an awful lot

- Redefine reality, in small and large ways—surrendering concepts of 'time,' 'space,' 'self/other' and similar concepts that have provided the scaffolding for your reality
- Step into the unknown, over and over again, relying on faith and intuitive guidance to see you to the next stage of the journey (remember, if you already knew how to get there, you'd already be there)
- Ask the mind, even command the mind, to take a backseat to the heart—your high Self works through the spirit and the deep, sacred heart; the mind is their servant
- Feel your feelings, fully, and surrender to the waves of repressed emotions that have been holding you back as you hold them in
- Cultivate deep patience, compassion, and forgiveness for yourself and others
- Make mistakes—you cannot learn a new way without trying and stumbling and trying again

If you are partway, or all the way into such an awakening, be assured that this is a wonderful, miraculous process and it will bring you gifts you cannot imagine. And you can also be sure that there will be more—perhaps many more—awakenings to come.

As the awakening phase moves over you, you come to know yourself in new ways, and find new possibilities available to you. Revel in the discovery, and be patient with the challenges. Welcome each awakening as it arrives. Ride the waves with as much joy, grace and gratitude as you can muster. And then, be willing to let go. Sooner or later, the intensity of each awakening experience will end. This may happen so quickly, that you doubt your own experience, asking "Did that really happen?" Or you may have an extended awakening, that leaves you thinking it will go on forever, before gently fading. But no matter how it ends, each awakening wave will likely leave us asking "What now? What next?"

CHAPTER

9

The Plateau

Integration

It is inevitable that the high of awakening must eventually give way to the lull of daily life. After the rush of change and growth, and the ecstasy of mystical experiences, we often go through a time of integration, when mystical awareness has to be merged with ordinary functioning. In this stage, we can find ourselves wondering where all that great momentum went. This slowing down process can involve a number of stages, which might go by completely unnoticed, or may be dramatic. Usually, immediately following the initial "aha!" of an awakening, there is a period of physical change that reflects our new awareness. We may start a new job, or a new relationship, or get down to the work of writing that book or completing that project. This first phase can involve a lot of material work, and physical shifting; it can take a lot of resources (money, time, emotion) and will often pretty much direct itself. The demands of starting a business, divorcing, going through a medical procedure, or relocating, come with their own prescribed set of activities. In this first post-awareness phase, we are often directed purely by the nature of the changes we are making.

Next, after the initial work of changing our lives is completed, we may enter a sort of 'honeymoon' phase, in which we enjoy the benefits of our new awareness and choices. This can be a blessed time of joy, peace and abundance. In this stage, we get to build new friendships, see new places, and experience new things with fresh eyes. Even if these new experiences are purely internal (perhaps after a more subtle, internal awakening process), they nonetheless give us a feeling of being in a new place. The intensity of the initial phases give way to gentler, often more enjoyable (if less ecstatic) experiences of well-being. If everything goes well during this early part of the integration process, we will find ourselves settling into a new 'normal.'

Eventually, though, we will begin to see this new place as 'status quo' and we will begin to crave even more health, more well-being, and more abundance for ourselves. This is natural; it is an essential quality of spirits living on earth. We are here to play with (as one psychic friend of my aunt puts it) "endless joyful creation." And that means a constant stream of new desires, new hopes, and new wishes. Staying put, letting things remain just as they are forever and ever, usually doesn't work well if we are truly letting our energy flow. Even for people who enjoy a slow-paced life, with very little external change, there is usually a desire to learn new things, to grow as beings, and to expand our understanding. And if we have the urge to stifle, or silence, this impulse towards new growth, it's usually because we are resisting the upheaval of the cycles of transformation.

As our new 'normal' becomes very familiar, we may begin to see the limitations of even this new place. We may hit a plateau, where we feel let down by the declining waves of intense energy. In other words, we miss the ecstasy of intense growth and transformation, and feel the urge to go even further into our true Selves. We may feel like we've hit a wall, or lost our magic. We may feel trapped in the minutiae of daily life and routines, or depressed by the ordinariness of our world. And we may be so caught up in craving forward motion, that we don't notice just how far we've already come.

The first time I consciously recognized this feeling in myself was shortly after the dramatic awakening that caused me to move from California to Tennessee. Only a couple of months after arriving at my new home, things seemed to take a steady turn for the worse. The initial excitement of reaching my beloved Smoky Mountains, of moving into a home I loved, and being closer to the seasons, real weather, and extended family—all of that faded as the challenges of my relocation hit me. All my big hopes and dreams were crashing into the reality of no job, no friends, difficulties with my partner, and a sense of despair at having just upended my whole life. I felt trapped and terrified. I decided to take a road trip to visit my aunt in Virginia, and set out on the 12 plus hour drive, armed with a pile of music cd's to keep me company. Of course, I spent much of the drive ruminating about the fix I'd gotten myself into, feeling like I was utterly lost and alone, and having no idea where to turn next. As night fell, and I drove through a dark evergreen forest, I put on a new John Denver CD. For the first time, I heard the song "Looking for Space" (from *Windsong* 1975).

The song describes exactly how I was feeling at that moment:

> *On the road of experience, I'm trying to find my own way.*

> *Sometimes I wish that I could fly away.*
>
> *When I think that I'm moving, suddenly things stand still.*
>
> *I'm afraid cause I think they always will.* [6]

For me, this song has become a post-awakening mantra. "Suddenly things stand still, and I'm afraid 'cause I think they always will." When the buzz of the initial awakening fades, and the process of integration brings me to moments of what seems like stagnant stillness, or even necessary loneliness, despair, and pain, I need to remind myself that this is just another phase of an on-going cycle. John Denver gave me a key to keep moving forward. The song goes on:

> *All alone in the universe, sometimes that how it seems.*
>
> *I get lost in the sadness and the screams.*
>
> *Then I look in the center and suddenly everything's clear.*
>
> *I find myself in the sunshine and my dreams...* 7

Now, I know to "look in the center" and find myself again.

This song, for me, is a reminder that this is a *journey* rather than a destination. It will always keep moving from desire to actualization to new desire. There will be ever-spinning waves of ecstasy and grief, hope and despair, excitement and boredom. When we're in the doldrums between awakenings,

---

[6] John Denver, "Looking for Space," *Windsong* Music Center of the World, 1975.

[7] ibid

on long, flat, uninterrupted plateaus of daily life stretching between peak experiences without any obvious relief, we can feel like it was all a trick, or a waste of time. At best, maybe it was just a pleasant diversion. At these moments, it's essential to recognize these times of integration and alignment for what they really are.

Let's take a moment to consider where you are on the awakening journey.

Exercise #29: Checking the Map

Where are you, right now, on your awakening journey? Are you entering your first big awakening, or maybe in the middle of a later repeat awakening experience? Perhaps you're coming out of one of these shifts in your life, making big changes or settling into a new normal. If you are currently integrating the effects of a big wave of new awareness, are you still in the 'crisis' phase, or have you entered the more subtle integration phases? Have you, now or in the past, felt a sense of despair or disillusionment, after a burst of new awareness?

Wherever you are, do you have a sense of the journey as being bigger than one temporary destination? For fun, consider drawing a map of your journey. You can imagine it as a virtual landscape, as a timeline, or as picture of where you would like to go next. Perhaps you want to rest for a good long while in a quiet place, or perhaps you're ready to charge off on some new adventure. Either way, remember this essential fact: the journey is always moving, always changing, with direction from your highest Self.

Usually when we are on a plateau, things are happening behind the scenes which are preparing us for the next big awakening. Though this preparation may be invisible to our personality self, we can actively participate in, rather than resist, full integration. Often, the frustration we can experience in the in-between phases gives us useful information about next steps. It can be helpful at these moments to do a few things: first, feel the stuckness or disappointment, and lean *into* rather than away from it. Allow yourself to gain clarity by recognizing what isn't quite as you had hoped. Second, step back and feel gratitude for all that *has* gone right, for all the new gifts and blessings available to you that weren't there before. Appreciate all that you *have* accomplished, and remind yourself that you are in fact a good creator. Finally, remind yourself that, just as you moved from your last 'normal' into this new phase, you can make the journey over and over again, bringing in more joy and more wholeness each time.

I often think of this as a honing process—we may have been awakened to the knowledge that it was time to change careers, only to find ourselves pretty upset when the new job isn't perfect, and doesn't hold the bliss we were expecting. Or perhaps we leave one relationship, with certainty that we're ready for the 'right' new relationship, only to find ourselves either alone or in another not-quite-right situation. Instead of judging these sorts of struggles as 'failures,' we can see them as simply another step on the journey to greater clarity about what we really want. We can remind ourselves that even if we feel stalled, or right back where we started, we are in fact in a new place, and not the same as we were before.

John Denver reminds us to 'look in the center.' In our center, we will find the calm stillness of patience, perspective and compassion. We will find some inner strength for looking just a little deeper, for a little bit longer, at those old patterns.

We will remember the importance of pacing. We will find compassion for the parts of ourselves that, while our spirits might be ready to move forward, just need a little more time, TLC, and rest. Please honor the part of yourself that wants some attention by asking, "what do I still need in this place?" During that first year after I moved to Tennessee, it turned out that I really needed 5 or 6 months of sitting very still with myself, crying, practicing radical honesty, and healing parts of myself that I simply had never given enough time or attention. Had I avoided that step, I would not have been ready for the wonderful things that came next. Starting a new business, being called to a new ministry with a congregation, deepening a new relationship—all of these absolutely required the work that came during those in-between months. My awakening was no failure; it just involved more steps and stages than I had initially expected.

During such a time, it's good to use some sort of internal reassurance that 'all will be well.' During those first months in Tennessee, I relied on one of Louise Hay's mantras: "All is well. Only good lies before me. I am completely guided, protected and taken care of on the journey." Even if I could not see where things were going, even if I didn't know how it was going to turn out, even if I felt stuck and trapped and terrified and disappointed, I clung to the faith that my previous choices had been guided, and that someone—some force, some presence, some part of myself that understands things better—was guiding me still. Honoring the importance of the in-between phase, and cultivating faith that more good things *will* come, is essential.

At this stage of the journey, it's important to avoid the dangers of what teacher Mastin Kipp calls "horizon thinking": looking only at where we're trying to get to, which—like the horizon—is always receding into the distance in front of us. Instead, we need to notice all the progress we're making as we move along the path. Sometimes spiritual seekers can be so busy planning the next adventure that they don't take time to really enjoy and appreciate the benefits of what they've already accomplished. But constantly looking ahead can be as big a hindrance to the spiritual journey as never moving at all. Imagine travelling to some wonderful exotic location—the Renaissance cathedrals of Europe or the majestic mountains of Asia; the jungles of South America or the beauties of Yellowstone National Park—only to take a couple of quick photos and rush on to the next scenic outlook.

Don't be a tourist on your own spiritual journey!

Take time to actually appreciate, to revel in and absorb, the wonders of each stopping place. Appreciation goes a long way to making those plateaus seem like beautiful vistas, where you can see both forward and backward, and observe equally where you have come from and where you want to go next. And you can get a little much needed rest in the meanwhile.

Finally, try to remember that confusion isn't a 'bad' thing. Sometimes, the spaces between mystical or spiritual awakenings offer us precious opportunities to discern subtle, small differences in our options. We get the chance to look at a wide range of possibilities, now open to us, that weren't even visible before the awakening shift. Sometimes, when we have an 'aha!' moment, we feel such clarity that we think we'll never have confusion or ambivalence again. But if you've gone through this process before, you know that ambiguity and ambivalence are a big part of the landscape. In fact, the bigger the awakening, the bigger the future confusions may be, since you've now widened the playing field considerably. If you've just entered a whole new world, with a whole new identity, chances are good it's gonna take you a while to get a feel for how things work, what your options are, and how you might want to proceed. It's one thing to say, "I'm going through that door!" and another thing entirely to know everything that will be on the other side. It's best if we can approach the new terrain with curiosity and as few expectations as possible.

My own ministry path has included a number of such moments of ambiguity and confusing new choices. My initial 'call' to ministry came through a revelatory dream, and changed my life forever. I quickly went from being a disillusioned college professor, to being a seminary student, and then a minister. After all those years of discernment—a decade as a college professor, a couple of years as a stay-at-home mom, a year or two of applying to and starting seminary, 5 years of school, and then a couple of years of working as an intern minister—I felt pretty sure that I was clear about what I wanted to do.

Not so.

I remember very clearly, during my first months in Tennessee, as I contemplated job opportunities and possibilities, feeling utterly unclear about what I really wanted to do. The door marked "minister" opened onto a *huge* field of possibilities! One day, I was certain I wanted to be a hospital chaplain; the next, a home hospice minister. The next day, it was working in children's ministry, and then I'd be sure I wanted to leave formal ministry entirely in favor of a private counselling practice. I was trying on professional roles like new outfits. I can even remember saying, explicitly, "Oh, but I *never* want to be the lead, solo minister of my own church!" (Of course, I have pretty much learned to stop saying "never" since the universe tends to hear this as "absolutely please bring me that.") Of course, I now find myself precisely there—solo, lead minister of a church. And yet, it is just a piece of who I am.

When we are integrating the new awareness and experience of an awakening, we need to take time to really explore options, consider possibilities, and make small distinctions. It's important to consider whether we want to own a boutique, or do our new business entirely on-line. We may need to spend a few months trying both out, to see what works best. And we may end up deciding we want neither, choosing to sell our wares through other vendors. We may write a complete first draft of that book, only to discover the first 200 pages were the preliminary, preparatory work for the actual book we needed to write (as was the case with this book). We may spend a few months or a year or two or three, in a transitional relationship, learning important things about ourselves that get us ready for the next, longer-lasting one. So take time to really absorb and complete all those intermediate steps, for they are essential preparation for fully embracing the next awakening, and the next step forward.

Disillusionment with Teachers, Companions and Spiritual Paths or Communities

A common experience that can follow a big awakening is finding ourselves disillusioned with, even in conflict with, the very people who helped us get there in the first place. Often, during the initial phases of a spiritual revelation or awakening, we are connected with spiritual teachers, companions, communities and traditions that provide us with life-saving wisdom, support and resources. These human allies to our spiritual big Selves often feel like coming home, like the 'real' family we've been waiting for. And yet, they aren't always meant to stick around for the rest of our lives. In fact, they usually don't. If you are moving consciously and intentionally along a spiritual path, chances are that you are changing fairly quickly. And this means that you will change teachers and companions fairly often, as well. To be sure, it is an incredible blessing when we find and connect with people who remain true spiritual family for the duration, but it's important not to expect it. Of the intense, deeply spiritual relationships I have enjoyed and fostered over the last few decades, only a very few have remained in my life long-term. For the most part, spiritual companions come and go at exactly the right moments, to support you, and be supported by you, when your paths cross. When you're together, it can feel ecstatic, eternal, and perfect…for a while. But even just as you're thinking, "This is it! These are my people!" you may begin to feel things shifting, changing and moving in a new direction.

Often, we rely on spiritual community to get us through the changes that come with spiritual awakening. But once the awakening has passed, we can be crushed when these companions disappear. And this can leave us feeling a desperate need or sadness. Often, they move on just as the next wave of awakening is about to hit, probably because they aren't the companions best equipped for the coming stages. We can miss them terribly as we face life with a new identity, or fear that we aren't able to face another awakening without their help. And yet how many times have you felt a deep connection with someone while immersed in an intense experience, only to find that you couldn't sustain the connection through daily life?

Even if companions stick around, we can be disappointed

by the fact that the 'high' of these relationships fades. Sometimes, the disappointment we feel with spiritual companions comes not when they leave us, but rather when they stay with us. If we build lasting relationships with people who were once central to our spiritual journeys, we may eventually find ourselves growing apart. Their journey may be taking them in a different direction, or we may be moving at different paces. Though we had a powerful moment together earlier on our paths, we may find that we are no longer a good match for one another. We might begin to feel angry, upset, or disappointed that they aren't 'there for us' like they used to be, or that they no longer understand us the way they used to. In either case, whether our disillusionment comes because they have left, or because they no longer feel like a good fit., it's important to let them go. And to let go of our expectations of them (and any future companions we may meet).

As I look back at all the amazing, wonderful people I have had the privilege to know and love, I am humbled by how deeply they allowed themselves to touch and be touched by me. They gave me spiritual tools, spiritual challenges, spiritual gifts, lessons, tests, and role models. They offered me love, and support, and sometimes brutal honesty. And sometimes they offered me disappointment, and disillusionment, as a way to help me move forward. One of these incredible people taught me a powerful lesson about letting go, after a deep and intense two weeks together at a retreat in the mountains of Montana. We were part of a group attending a spiritual workshop involving deep personal work, and we spent hours and hours together, connecting like sisters. We felt as if we had always known each other, and would always be connected.

When it was time to leave, this wonderful companion even took the time to travel to my home in California, to spend a day with my children (she had planned to come to California after the retreat, and added a visit with me to her plans).

We agreed that we were soul companions, reunited after who knew how long. And yet, we also knew that soul companions aren't bound by the rules of linear time and space; we knew from experience that such deep soul ties don't necessarily mean overlapping lives. Before we parted, we agreed that we would love each other as soul sisters forever, regardless of our material lives. We completely released one another from any sense of obligation or attachment about seeing each other again, or 'keeping in touch.' It was truly beautiful. We kept in touch by writing letters for a while, then went off on our separate journeys. And yet I feel the same love for her today that I felt so many years ago, and know that our souls are connected perfectly, just as they need to be. We gave each other the gift of total release from guilt, remorse, and obligation by allowing our time together to be just what it was, without any expectation of it lasting a minute longer than our souls (not our minds) said it should.

In the spirit of releasing all those companions who have touched us deeply, giving them and ourselves permission to move forward freely on the spiritual path, let's take a moment to call them to mind.

Exercise #30: Releasing Spiritual Companions

Think back to any powerful spiritual, emotional or physical experiences you have had. Consider who was there for you, really present with you, during these experiences. Are these people still a part of your life, or have they moved on? How do you feel about the present state of your connection (or lack of connection) to them? Are you at peace with these relationships, or do you feel any loss, disappointment, or disillusionment around them? If there are people who are still in your life from these experiences, are they truly a good match to you now, or have you perhaps continued the relationship out of a sense of obligation? Whether your spiritual companions are present in your daily life or not, you can release all bonds of obligation with them, freeing you both up for greater growth and opportunity. This does not mean kicking them out of your life; it simply means setting an intention of relating only from a place a deep spiritual presence and respect, being willing to be together when that is in your highest good, and letting each other go when it's time. Imagine yourself thanking them fully for the gifts they have shared with you, and letting them know that you will always treasure them, no matter where your journeys take you. You may even want to physically call or contact important people, just to say 'thank you' and encourage them on their journeys.

Sometimes, letting go of spiritual companions just means that, when they return, the reunion will be that much sweeter. One of my dearest spiritual sisters is someone who has moved in and out and back into my life again in surprising, exhilarating ways. Our first meeting occurred at another retreat in Montana. On the first night of that 10 day gathering, the 20 or so of us in attendance were asked to form two concentric circles, with the inner circle facing outward, and the outer circle facing inward. As we listened to music, we were to walk in opposite directions, so that we would meet the eyes of each person in the opposite circle. We would take a couple steps, pause and look into the eyes facing us, then move to the next person.

About halfway through the exercise, when the group had begun to sink into a more meditative, trancelike state, I found myself facing a woman whose eyes drew me in quite deeply. We didn't just look, we stared. Suddenly, and quite powerfully, we both burst into tears of joy. We absolutely recognized one another! Though we had never before met in this life, we knew without a doubt—both of us—that we were soul family.

"I'm so glad to see you again!" She cried out as she hugged me. And I hugged her back, crying and exclaiming over how much I had missed her, how long it had been since we had seen one another. We were, without a doubt for either of us, sisters. It was a wonderful ten days, as we got to know each other again (and some other long-lost soul family who were there with us, as well). We kept in touch for a few years, and even attended another retreat together at the same beautiful lodge near the base of the mountains in Montana. And then we simply drifted apart. There was no intention to separate, no disagreement, just the steady movement of time and demanding lives and separate situations. And, truly, I was perfectly okay with that. Though I thought of her sometimes, I knew that soul sisters like us operate on a timeframe of whole lifetimes, not brief years.

A few years after I had last heard from her, I found myself at a week-long training in up-state New York, at the Omega Institute. I was there to be certified in Past

Life Regression Therapy, by renowned teacher Brian Weiss, and was completely immersed in the beauty of the place, the intensity of the training, and my own journey. Imagine my shock when, on the third day, as I walked across the porch of the dining hall building, I looked up to see my dear soul sister walking across the other side of the porch. I was stunned for a moment, then I called out her name. She turned, looked blankly at me for a moment, and then yelled in recognition. We made what can only be described as an incredible scene. We screamed and yelled and hugged and cried, and every person anywhere near that building knew something powerful and exciting was happening. It was a wonderful and joyful reunion—again. We were able to spend some quality time together that week. I spent time practicing regression therapy with her and her partner, and she brought me to my first encounter with her spiritual teacher, Panache Desai. We brought one another things that week that were wonderful gifts for the journey, but that might not have happened had we not run into one another again.

It was pretty miraculous, really. But she and I have come to accept that this is the nature of soul companions. We stay in touch more easily now, thanks to email and Facebook, but we know that it's really divine soul intention that determines when we'll run into one another. And that is perfectly okay with us. There are friends who are with us for the daily journey, and friends who are with us for the big soul moments and movements.

So I encourage you to develop an attitude of non-attachment with your spiritual companions. The ones that show up, do so exactly when and where they need to. And they leave with exactly the same divine perfection. If we can release expectations and attachment, we can more fully enjoy the experience of unions and reunions, while freeing ourselves from the weight of obligation, guilt, remorse and a sense that we should 'hold back' and wait for others whose timing or pacing differs from ours. When we allow ourselves and each other this sort of freedom, we are actually making way for better and better relationships, built on mutual enthusiasm and joy.

✦ ✦ ✦

While letting go of spiritual companions can trigger some sadness and loneliness in us, letting go of spiritual teachers often brings feelings of anger, disappointment, and disillusionment. And they can make us feel disillusioned with the spiritual path itself. Of course, these feelings can arise if we have difficult separations from spiritual friends and family, but they are even more difficult when we separate from a teacher, healer, or mentor. And yet, this sort of letting go is one of the most essential stages on the spiritual path.

As I have said before, sometimes we find ourselves supported by the guidance of a spiritual mentor or teacher who remains with us for a very long time. But more often than not this isn't how things work. Often, as we move along the spiritual path, we will encounter many teachers and healers who help us for a while, then no longer meet our needs. Unfortunately, one of the core lessons at such a time is remembering that we hold our own teaching, our own healing, within ourselves. These people have just come as mirrors to show us where we are on the journey, to be outward guides for inward knowledge. But when we lack a sense of true confidence in our high Selves—which is often the case especially on the early stages of our journey—we may give to others more power than is really theirs.

Please note: there is a significant difference between *betrayal* by a spiritual teacher—when they take advantage of us for material gain of some sort, or when their ego needs are the driving force in the relationship—and the very necessary *growing up* process a spiritual seeker goes through. But it can be hard to tell where the line is, when you're in the thick of it.

When we are in the crisis phase of the journey, we often feel somewhat desperate for help along the way. And we truly do need support, encouragement and protection at these times. But, too often, we allow ourselves to believe that it is up to the teacher, healer or mentor to continue to provide that sort of on-going support when the crisis is over. Deep longing, that we may have for a parent or partner who will help 'make us whole' or guide us along the way, may lead us to see this person as *essential* to our spiritual growth and maturation. And we may also see them as somehow beyond the limits of human failure, confusion, and weakness. If they know so much that they helped us get past our traumas, then certainly they won't do anything stupid, selfish, or careless, right? And if they've been such great guides so far, how could they possibly fail to know the next step on the way? But of course these are unrealistic expectations that neither seeker nor guide can sustain for long.

I remember clearly my own disillusionment with the healer, described earlier, who failed to make the connection between my food sensitivities, my emotional traumas, and an eating disorder pattern. She had been a crucial support for me, in a really difficult stage of the journey, and yet I came to realize that she had completely missed a key insight for my struggle. Later, I came to realize that this was not really her responsibility. It was mine. Ultimately, it was up to me to face my relationship with my body, and food, squarely and clearly, not hers.

In another situation, I found myself disappointed with teachers who were unable to remain in relationship with me after I had moved beyond the initial phases of our relationship. When I encouraged some teachers to consider working more equally, more collaboratively with me, they were not interested in developing this new sort of connection with me. That hurt, and yet it was a great teaching for me. Perhaps it was one of the greatest gifts that these spiritual guides gave me: they showed me that *no one other person can be my all and my everything.* No one teacher can be your perfect guide at all times, any more than any one lover can provide for all your physical, emotional, mental and spiritual needs. They showed me that the only person who is constantly just where I am, who has just the right tools and just the right insights and just the right wisdom for my journey is me.

Everyone else shows up to match you, where you are. And you are growing, so it's important to understand that even the best of teachers, even the most powerful of healers, even the most steady and loving of mentors, is just a facilitator of a process that is happening *within* you, and that *you are in charge of it yourself.* At first, many of us don't want that kind of responsibility, and we will resist it. With anger, rage, grief, and judgment, we may tell ourselves and others that they 'should' be more reliable and more worthy of our dedication. We will sometimes demand that they improve themselves, to make our journey feel safer, and easier. And yet this usually isn't how it works at all.

If you find yourself at a crossroads with a teacher, then the message from your high Self is that you are ready for something else. And if you have felt abandoned by a spiritual guide in the past, or been disappointed that they let you down, consider forgiving them and yourself for needing to move on. This all might feel sad and upsetting and disappointing to the teacher or healer or mentor, too, of course. If you *are* a spiritual mentor, teacher, or healer, then you have as much responsibility for letting those you support know that you are *not* the one doing the work in their lives. You are not the one leading their journey—you are the facilitator. And if you are feeling a strong sense of attachment, then chances are good that they are showing you some work you need to do on yourself.

As spiritual lightworkers, we all have to address both sides of this dependency in our spiritual relationships. We have to let go of the idea that we can somehow heal, help, or awaken someone beyond what they have already chosen for themselves, just as we have to reclaim our own power over our own spiritual journeys. Often, those of us who take on roles as guides of some sort on the spiritual path fall prey to the ego's message that we 'should' be able to help anyone who comes to us. That's simply not true. We can only offer others what they have already set in motion for themselves. So let go of any guilt you may have about your own limitations as a spiritual guide or healer. Forgive yourself, just as you forgive those who may have disappointed you along the way, and embrace whatever learning or growth is available in each relationship, just as it is.

Please note, though, that this does *not* mean remaining in an abusive or destructive relationship, trying to wring some spiritual value out of it. If you find yourself in such a place, move on and embrace the knowledge that you can find new ways—more joyful, healthy ways—to experience spiritual growth and expansion.

Normal separation of spiritual companions is a little like graduating from high school, or moving away from home, or taking a new job. These all involve a lot of letting go, and forming new relationships. In fact, it seems likely that how we felt about those sorts of moments in our own formation—how the parents and teachers and other adults in our lives responded to us moving into adulthood, and how we felt about them at that time—may have a lot to do with the kinds of experiences we create (or repeat) with our spiritual mentors and supporters.

Just as a graduation is a turning point in our lives, that comes with both fear and excitement, this spiritual graduation is a turning point too. When we reach these sorts of letting-go moments on the spiritual path, we can feel either downhearted or exhilarated, or alternate between the two. Sometimes, the experience is so upsetting that we may lose our way for a while, and wander around in hopelessness, or bitterness, or self-pity. If this is the case, then surely the universe will provide opportunities to heal these traumas, as well as give us a chance to heal unresolved wounds from the past. Such a pivotal moment on the path is an opportunity to become more spiritually mature. It is a moment when we get to decide who's steering the ship, and what direction we would like to go.

The moment of disillusionment is often the moment to realize that, though others can be great fun as companions, and great support along the way, we are the masters of our own destiny. We are each in charge of where we go next, what we experience, and who we want to become. Once we take the step of letting go of asking others to shape our spiritual journeys, the path opens up wide in front of us.

CHAPTER

10

Commitment and Intention—From Reactive to Responsive to Proactive

In the earlier stages of the spiritual journey, we are often reactive. We make choices out of fear and pain, reacting to traumas instinctively. When we are in a reactive cycle, experiences give rise to sensations—physical or emotional—that in turn trigger defense patterns (behaviors, beliefs, and emotional expressions) that are largely unconscious. We may or may not recognize these defensive patterns, but if we do we will believe they are essential, necessary, and proper. These defenses are rooted in survival strategies that we developed early on (either in this lifetime or previous ones). And, often, they generate new experiences which require more of the same.

But as we progress on our path, we move into a more responsive mode, often during the crisis phase. As we begin

229

to heal, we may gain some perspective about our defensive behaviors, and begin to try out new options. We may be able to observe our old, reactive patterns and make conscious choices to step away from them, in favor of more healthy behaviors. We may try out a number of new techniques, teachings, and strategies that allow us to resolve old problems in new ways.

In this responsive mode, we become more conscious of our ability to direct the journey, and take charge to some extent of how we move forward. And yet we still feel obliged to act *in relationship to certain triggers.* For example, we may no longer let the sensations of anxiety dissuade us from taking the train, or the elevator, but we still have to take time to do the breathing or meditation exercises that calm our symptoms. Or we may no longer instinctively let our anger get the best of us, but we still need to do the journaling or talking with a therapist to 'process' what came up for us.

If we've been in the reactive phase for a very long time (and most of us are), then the responsive phase feels incredibly liberating. We finally feel as if we're no longer trapped by strong emotional or physical symptoms, or held back by unhealthy relationship patterns or people. This is an enormously healing, liberating stage of spiritual development.

But there is even more health and wholeness ahead, beyond the responsive stage, when we get to be true co-creators with the multiverse. To get there, we have to take the reins even more fully. We have to move from responding to consciously creating. Rather than just making choices when things happen *to us*, we start to create from *pure desire*.

For me, this is what the spiritual journey is all about.

It is about not just managing, but completely releasing, the limitations of my unawakened, small self and fully embracing, fully embodying my powerful, eternal Self. It is about really allowing myself to live my best life. Certainly, this part of the journey contains aspects of all the other stages; as we become more and more powerful manifestors, we will experience cycles of reactivity, awakening, new awareness, and back again to deeply unconscious material. We *grow into* manifestation, seeing it happen in small ways first, perhaps slowly, and then over time it becomes more and more common, with bigger and better results.

Unlike the earlier stages of the spiritual journey, which can often be marked into fairly distinct, separate moments, the later stages of the journey tend to be more subtle, cyclical, and interwoven. To be sure, there are peak moments and peak realizations, ecstatic experiences and dramatic shifts, but they circle back on themselves. We move from recognizing an old pattern, to healing it, to creating new patterns, only to see a deeper layer, or another block, that needs releasing. And this cycling, self-renewing process requires something different from us, usually, than the more crisis-oriented stages do. When we move into these more advanced stages of spiritual maturation, it is essential that we spiritual travelers develop solid intentions, supported by deep, persistent commitment and regular spiritual practices. As the major crises fade, we have to develop steady internal (rather than external) motivations and methods for moving forward and sustaining progress.

In the earlier stages of the journey, the forces propelling us along are urgent and insistent; in the later stages, it can be easy to lose that sort of drive, or to spend a lot of time meandering and wandering in spiritual exploration. To make true progress in the later stages of spiritual growth, we have to develop focus, and become practical masters of spiritual technology. This is where it becomes more about skill than surprise. We will have to cultivate our incredible revelations and unexpected new awareness. As children, we are moved largely by forces outside of ourselves: family, society, the physical and emotional maturation processes. And as adults in the crisis and awakening phases, our own physical and emotional needs and imperatives drive us. But as we mature spiritually, we must take a much more conscious, proactive role in the *creation* of our lives. This is the moment when, rather than insisting "I won't do that anymore!" we begin asking the question, "Wow, out of all these infinite possibilities, what would I really love to experience?" We begin to imagine, from a field of unlimited possibilities—and with no pressure in any given direction—what it might be *fun* to try out.

Don't we all long to have that kind of freedom and possibility? Don't we all wish we could take full control of the things that come into our lives?

Yes, of course we do. And yet that fully creative mode can seem elusive at best, and at worst pretty impossible. This is one of the most important forms of disillusionment we face as we 'grow up' spiritually: the disillusionment with our own spiritual process and potential. Too often, we imagine that our awakening will lead directly to powerful, sustainable manifesting. And we may certainly have bursts of proving to ourselves that we *can* manifest the things we desire. But the most important thing we have to learn, if we want to *sustain* the spiritual journey, is that it's never complete. That the learning and deepening and growing are never 'done' and that we never run out of old patterns, old material, to transform.

You will not be done with the human condition until you are no longer in a human body (and maybe not even then, perhaps). While you are here, you will never be guaranteed freedom from the challenges, nor liberated from the sorrow, loss and occasional fear and pain that come with being here in human form. The spiritual path doesn't lead to total freedom from what it feels like to be a person on planet earth. As the Buddha so powerfully demonstrated, it's not that we leave behind the experiences of human life, but rather that we develop a completely different attitude towards, and relationship with, them.

Exercise #31: Reactive, Responsive and Creative Assessment

Using the following chart, identify in which areas of your life you are reactive and responsive, and in which areas you have become more fully creative. You might consider your relationships, your health, your work, your family and homelife, your sexuality, your leisure and fun time, your intellectual life, your spiritual development, or any other aspect of life that is important to you. The goal is not to judge yourself for where you are in each area, but rather to simply identify the areas where you've developed a lot of spiritual mastery, and others which you might want to prioritize for the future.

Areas where I am mostly reactive	Areas where I am mostly responsive	Areas where I am creative

Disillusionment with Life on the Earth-Plane

Interestingly, one common response to this stage of the spiritual journey is to decide that we would just rather be *fully* spiritual beings, making the best of the earth plane as long as we're here, but really focusing on heading off to some more evolved realm. I have heard any number of friends and spiritual colleagues express the sentiment that they 'don't really belong here.' They will do good work while here, but they see themselves as belonging to another planet, another dimension, another reality. I don't disagree that all of these may be true; I myself feel connections to all of these other places. And yet, for me, there is no 'other' time or place. My spiritual education and experiences tell me that it's all happening right here, right now—anything else is an illusion. So not being *here*, utterly, completely and fully, just deprives *all* of my selves (wherever they are) of having the fullest possible flow of life, love and energy.

Many spiritual people feel utterly disillusioned with the earth, with the context we have created and chosen to participate in here. Often, when we wake up to our creative and spiritual potential, we can only wonder, "What in the world were we thinking?!" There is so much suffering, so much struggle. And so very many people still living, and suffering, in reactive, unconscious states. And we judge this all. We see it as their failure, or our failure, or a class we certainly should have graduated from by now. And we may very well just want out. Stop the planet, I'm getting off. Even many of the greatest teachers can slide into sending a message that somehow, focusing your attention somewhere or some-when else is 'more spiritual.'

I disagree. Though I respect each individual's journey— and thus have absolutely no attachment to where you are on your path—I personally want to be here, right here, as fully and as vitally as possible. To bring my absolutely fullest spiritual Self into this amazing, magical human realm. Into this miraculous body and form, and into this unspeakably beautiful world. There is simply no other place as beautiful, as rich with possibility, and as full of magic and contrast and wonders, as this place right here right now.

We are in it!

I remember having a conversation very early on, during one of my first awakening phases, with a spiritual companion who had given me a great deal of support, encouragement and guidance. I had learned a great deal from her. But there came a day when I recognized a huge difference between us. We were travelling in the Mojave desert with a group of companions, and sleeping out under the stars on the warm sandy ground. She began talking about star beings (which some people call aliens, or extra terrestrials), and how desperately she wished they would come and get her. She, and many others I have talked with since that night, longed to be removed from the earth plane to a more enlightened, evolved place in the multiverse.

"But," I asked her, "don't you want to be on earth?"

"Oh no!" she answered, "It's awful here! I want to leave as quickly as possible, and never come back to this planet! This is definitely my last life on earth!"

Once, a professional colleague at a university where I was working joked that "earth is the fifth hardest planet…. and I wouldn't want to be on planets 1 through 4!" There's no doubt that earth comes with a lot of challenges, a lot of contrast, and a lot of opportunities for both joy and suffering. Many spiritually focused people think that this means it is inferior. They see themselves as evolved 'beyond' it. This, I would gently suggest, is a variety of hubris and vanity that might require some spiritual exploration. I would suggest that there are some very highly awakened people who specifically come into this plane, even into the most difficult aspects of it, *to serve*—people who are in fact at the highest level of spiritual manifestation, so high that they need not be vocal or visible about it.

What I am suggesting is this: there's no 'good' or 'bad' place to be, spiritually speaking. There are perhaps easier or harder places to be, or lives that are more externally 'blessed' or challenged, but the very process of spiritual maturation teaches us that these are all illusion. So while the challenges of earth may be miserable sometimes, that doesn't make them inherently 'bad.' Their relative merit is determined *entirely* by the soul intentions of the one experiencing them.

So I don't judge anyone else's circumstances as 'good' or 'bad,' as 'right' or 'wrong' or as needing my intervention.

Instead, I respect that each person is exactly where they need to be. If someone is interested in transforming themselves and their situation, that's great. I am happy to be a presence of support, encouragement, companionship and guidance to whatever extent they might ask. But I will never see another's life experience as less valid or more 'awful' than any other. And I would never want to abandon earth because it's "too awful" here.

This is all to say that I believe earth, like any other place you can imagine or explore in the spiritual realms, is the best place there is. Now, it may have different foci than you are interested in right now. That's fabulous! If you are really excited and adventurous and want to explore other realms because you're curious, then by all means dive in with a full heart. But if you're focusing on other realms because you haven't yet made peace with where you are right now, you may find that the other realms don't offer as much relief as you would hope.

Where you are, spiritually speaking, is a matter of where you are in your own heart, in your spirit, and in your presence. It's not a matter of physical location. As your inner, spiritual being shifts, your location will shift to match. So, for me, letting myself just *be*, fully present, fully appreciative, of where I am, is the best next step in the journey.

Sometimes, once we get a feel for our own spiritual power and potential, we want to escape all the yet-unresolved material that we are still carrying. We want a shortcut. And the truth is, we can have as many shortcuts as we like! But they come from joy, not fear; from praising where we are, not criticizing it. As evangelical preacher Joel Osteen so articulately puts it, "Praise the Promise rather than Complaining about the Problem!"

If you have reached a point in your spiritual journey

where you are disillusioned with your own process, or with earth-life itself, then you may need to take a little vacation. You may need to just give yourself a chance to rest and enjoy yourself as much as possible. Rather than seeing this as failure—as being stuck or having 'gone as far as you can go'—you can see this as enjoying the fruits of your labor. So long as you know that the spiritual journey never actually ends, so long as you know that when things stand still, they do eventually start up again, you can give yourself time to appreciate and enjoy your life to the fullest.

And if you are still suffering—from an illness, from a chronic condition, from financial hardship, from loneliness—you can still practice appreciation and rest. You can still focus on appreciating and enjoying the gifts and blessings in your life, right here, right now. Perhaps you expected the awakening process to alleviate all your pain, to release you from all your struggles and suffering. And, when that didn't happen, you felt disappointed and disillusioned. Perhaps you left the initial crisis stage thinking things would be better than they are, and you need some comfort and reassurance that it wasn't all a waste of time and energy. This plateau, then, can be a gift. Take a rest; look around and see the beauty that surrounds you. Find the warm hearts that love you, the beautiful earth that holds you up every single day, the sweet promise of each new sunrise. And know that there is always infinite good just waiting to meet you. Engage in some vertical thinking: notice how far you've already come, and pat yourself on the back for the amazing progress you—and the community of life on planet earth—have already made.

At some point, it is really useful to make a solid commitment to *be here*. To just show up. Perhaps you made this commitment earlier in your journey, or perhaps *not* being here was never even a consideration for you. Perhaps you have always been committed to living this life as fully as possible. If so, then you are one step ahead, since presence is essential to any kind of spiritual growth or development. But if seeing earth as the best possible place to be is something you've never considered before, then the following exercise may be useful.

Exercise #32: Be Here, Now

Make a list of all the things you love about being a human and living on the earth. What do you really appreciate about life in a body? Ice cream? Sunsets? The feel of puppy fur? Competition? Building things? The sound of an orchestra playing Brahms? Make a good long list of all the wonderful things that exist in this reality, and that you appreciate. Then make another list of all the things you just really dislike about earth: poverty, sinus infections, taxes, winter, weight gain, the common cold, aging, pollution, global warming, and anything else you can think of that bothers you about this reality. When you've make both lists, ask yourself this question: even with all its imperfections, its troubles and trials, does the list of things you love feel juicy enough to make it worthwhile? Can you spend your energy focusing on the list of what you love, and direct some of that love to *a few* (not all! just pick one or two) of the things you're concerned about and want to see change about life on earth?

Can you make, or renew, a commitment to being fully present in this place, at this time? Can you commit to working with the materials of a human body, in a life on the earth, for your spiritual progress? If so, then things can start moving in a new way, more slowly perhaps, but more deeply, more consistently, and more sustainably. You can find a rhythm that is sustainable, making steady spiritual progress while living a 'normal' life and going about the business of being a human being on planet earth.

Disillusionment with Godde

Another form of disillusionment that most of experience at some time or another is what I would call disillusionment with Godde. If you don't have a belief in anything like a 'god' concept, then you may need to think of this as disillusionment with the force of the universe, or with the flow of life, or in some other terms. But whatever you name it, this stage involves feeling that the transcendent reality not only doesn't have your back, but that it may be actively out to get you. There have been many times along my path that I have felt utterly abandoned by the divine. Sometimes these periods lasted only for a few hours, or a few days; sometimes, they went on for weeks or months. When things get really rough, when you feel up against the almost impossible, you may find yourself doubting all together that we live in a benevolent multiverse.

This was true for me at the outset of my son's treatment for leukemia, which occurred when he was only a toddler. Faced with my child's life-threatening illness, and a minimum of 2 ½ years of intense, excrutiating treatment for him involving numerous spinal taps, horrifying drugs, and a host of physical and psychological side effects, I was—to say the least—pretty daunted. I remember very clearly one night, during those first weeks, simply feeling that I wasn't up to it. I was, to put a point on it, suicidal. Fortunately, that intense feeling of abandonment and hopelessness lasted only a couple of hours, and had given way to determination by daylight. But there were many moments during those years, and during other later challenges, where I felt that Godde had abandoned me.

At best, during some of my toughest times, I have felt that the universe was just standing by, watching and laughing, as I 'learned my lessons.' It has taken years of deep spiritual and psychological work for me to unpack the conditioning from family, church and society that had convinced me that the universe was at best neutral, if not downright punishing.

What do we do when we feel abandoned by the divine, transcendent presence that gives us life? How do we face the feeling that, rather than being here for us, our reality is trying to hurt us or undermine us? What steps can we take to get out of the bottomless pit that total loss of faith drags us into?

One simple answer is this: have a temper tantrum.

I remember when I first heard someone say, "Go ahead, get mad at Godde. Yell at her. She can take it." I tried it, and I can say that it felt fantastic. To really just let loose and scream and shout and rage at the divine—at whatever presence is controlling the whole, chaotic, painful, awful mess that human life can be, is incredibly liberating. And something magical often happens, when we really give full voice to our grief and terror and rage, in that way, to the source of all being: she listens. He hears us. They respond.

In those moments, whenever they have come to me, I have felt—after the waves of intense emotion began to subside—a deep, abiding *presence*. I felt Godde's presence, just there, with me, not judging, not condemning, not trying to change me or even to fix things. Just there. Peaceful, quiet, loving, compassionate. With me.

This presence is, after the storm, always abiding. It does

not leave us. It does not always give us quick or trite answers, either, but it does remain. Sometimes, the only thing that has restored my faith in this is to rail at the multiverse for *not* being there; enough yelling, enough sobbing, enough truthtelling, and I find that I am not alone, and that something is in fact holding me.

When you come to those places where your faith in things is utterly shattered; when you find yourself unable to believe in anything; those are the times for honesty, and letting go, and surrendering. If you can't surrender to something bigger, then surrender to the feelings, for they are the path. At the moment when you lose the path completely, let it rise out of you in your most honest expressions of whatever is happening inside. You will create it as you cry, as you express your bitterness, as you beg for mercy or plead for an answer. It may not look like what you're asking for, but that is not the point.

You can't always get what you want, but you will get what you need. And Godde doesn't need us to believe in her. The multiverse doesn't need us always to understand it, or make sense of how we are part of it. The divine order works whether we are able to see it or not.

Sometimes, the best we can do is just be truthful with ourselves about where we are *right now*, and the path will reappear eventually, in a day, or a week, or a month, or a year. When we lose faith in something bigger, we can still hold onto faith in our own truth *in the present moment*.

Commitment, Discipline, and Practice

In moments of disillusionment—with ourselves, with others, with our world, with the divine—it can be helpful to have spiritual practices that hold us steady despite internal earthquakes. Even if we're not experiencing such intense shake-ups on our journeys, we find ourselves feeling out of sync with the world around us. We may be unemployed, in the hospital, unable to function 'normally,' living in the wilderness or in an intentional community, couch-surfing, or traveling the world. Though both the shake-ups and the non-traditional ways of being can provide fertile ground for spiritual growth, they can make us long for more stable and predictable ground.

Of course, it's also possible that the *last* thing you want is 'normal' or 'routine.' But, even then, you will still need a life that is sustainable in one or more ways: financially, physically, emotionally, professionally. So regardless of whether you want to live an unconventional or very conventional life, whether you see yourself as finally having the chance to settle down into a normal routine, or as someone who is just now liberated to do as you please—either way, you still need to create a sustainable balance of spirituality and practicality. And this requires some clarity, some commitment, and some practical action.

Exercise #33: Balancing the Practical and the Spiritual

Buddhist teacher Thich Nhat Han teaches that the mundane, the practical, is also the most fully spiritual, so long as one is truly present. How is your balance of practicality and spirituality, right now? Do you wish you had more time for spiritual exploration? Or do you wish for a more settled, routine daily experience? Have you found ways to balance the requirements of this life, while still seeing it as a game or adventure that your spirit is traveling for a little while? If you could take one action to help balance these two parts of your life, what would it be?

I once heard a spiritual coach express the opinion that humans exist in a constant tension between the impulses of the body and the impulses of the spirit. He said that the spirit tends towards excesses of wanting too much, moving too fast, and being too adventurous, always looking towards the next experience. This is because the spirit doesn't really have to concern itself, in the big picture, with things like money, aging, death, and other practical matters. It is here for the *experience*! The body, on the other hand, is very concerned with maintaining basic physical stability, and so it is naturally interested in carefully weighing the risks versus the benefits of all those spiritual adventures. I find myself, often, having an internal debate between these two perspectives.

My spirit says, "Yes! Let's move across country or take that big vacation or leap out of this career into another!" And my body and mind say, "Hold your horses! We have bills to pay and people to consider and limited emotional, physical and financial resources!" On and on they debate, going back and forth. They also play this game after-the-fact: "You idiot," body/mind shouts, "Look how you messed up by taking *that* big risk!" And spirit calmly, but exuberantly answers, "But it was such fun! And look at all the cool people we met, and all the things we learned. Sure, we are still paying off the credit card bills, but it was worth it!"

Finding a balance between spirit's need to expand *beyond* our limitations and our body-mind's very real need for basic stability, can be a bit of a challenge at this stage of the journey. The good news is that, once we get into the true flow of our own energy, this balance will begin to take care of itself. In fact, when we really get into the flow, we won't even have to think about it at all. The multiverse will begin to do the work for us, and line things up with so much grace, ease and synchronicity that balance will come to us naturally. But at the beginning of being proactive, as we cycle through moments of reactivity, responsiveness, and glimpses of proactivity, we'll probably need a few tricks for keeping our flow going.

For me, nothing has been more helpful in this area than developing spiritual practices. The actual form of practice has changed repeatedly over the years, but I have always made a point of having some very regular—usually daily, but at least weekly—activities that keep me spiritually 'tuned up.' For years, I've kept journals. In them I record dreams and visions; ranting and raving about struggles; notes on realizations; exercises prompted by spiritual teachers and trainings; and anything else that I have felt like writing down. I also have a (fairly) regular yoga practice, which usually includes meditation. I hike as a spiritual discipline, and try to take a longer spiritual retreat of some sort (e.g. a workshop, a training, a spiritual vacation, etc.) at least once each year. I spend time with colleagues who help me keep my focus on what really matters, even when I 'don't have time' for the lunches, walks or extra gatherings these relationships require. I spend time alone, every day, in quiet reflection. And I try to learn about at least one new spiritual teacher or method every few months.

Another great spiritual discipline I practice is staying in touch with people much younger than me. I cultivate curiosity about the music, artwork, literature and technology that fascinates and engages the youth and young adults around me. This is an essential tool, for me, in keeping my spiritual channels open. These young people— the indigo and crystal energy children prophesied for many years—carry a very high vibration, and staying in touch with the things they love and that they create helps me raise my vibration towards their level. I am extra blessed in this area, because I have two amazing and spiritually advanced young adult children, who keep me aware and awake when I tend towards being an old fuddy-duddy, or get set in my ways. Frequently, they call my attention to habits of language or behavior that carry a lower vibration, and suggest new ways I might do things. Being open to this incredible wisdom has been one of the most powerful spiritual practices in my life.

It doesn't really matter what your spiritual practices are. What matters is that you consciously, proactively and consistently cultivate spiritual disciplines. Doing this is the way to keep your energy moving and flowing, and it is the way forward if you want to move out of reactivity, through responsiveness, and into a truly creative, and co-creative life.

How do you feel about the word "discipline"? I will readily admit that, for a long time, it felt uncomfortable, even downright yucky to me. I didn't want to be forced to do anything, and for a while I didn't understand that sometimes an unhealed part of myself will prefer—or 'feel good about'—behaviors that hold me back or limit me. It took years of steady spiritual focus, intention and action to develop a better sense of which part of myself was saying "yuck" and which part of myself was saying "yum" when I considered a practice or discipline. One of the best methods I have developed for understanding these differing perspectives involves imagining the voices in my head as a committee, trying to decide what action to take.

Exercise #34: An Internal Committee Meeting

When our defenses are triggered, we may have a number of conflicting, competing interests, goals and desire, all trying to get control of the situation. It can be useful to imagine all of these voices as characters sitting around a conference table, having a committee meeting in your mind. You will find that some of the participants in the conference will be *very loud*: fear, anger, and intense grief may speak up with a lot more intensity and urgency than patience, perspective and calm will. But who do we want to have making the final decision? In the reactive mode, it is the strongest, loudest, and most aggressive voices that make the decisions. In the responsive mode, it may be a calm, rational coping mechanism that gets the upper hand. In the proactive mode, it is the high Self, observing the meeting and yet able to keep all voices in perspective that facilitates the conversation. The High Self is able to recognize and meet the real needs of our many aspects, while holding out for the greatest good at all times. Imagine a situation in which you felt strong, intense emotions, which urged you to react or respond. Can you imagine whose voices you were hearing from then? Ask yourself these questions: How old is the voice of the anger? What made him so angry in the first place? Who else is at the meeting? What age is that voice speaking with terror, or intense grief? Has she ever met or talked directly with the anger? And who's currently leading the meeting? Are there any others at the table who haven't spoken yet? Give yourself time to really consider who is at the table when you are triggered, and think about who you might want to put in charge. Usually, when we're hoping for a real, lasting solution, we need to listen to all the voices, respond appropriately to the fear, grief, rage, etc. and yet still make choices that serve the *greater whole* rather than that one, individual, loud voice.

On the subject of discipline, I had an inner voice that said, "Discipline means being *forced* to do something, which means I'm not in control, which means I don't like it! I won't do it, you can't make me!" Until I spent some time healing that rebellious teenager, who saw 'discipline' as force, aggression, and repression of her natural inclinations, there was no way that conscious, disciplined action was going to feel natural or healthy. But once I recognized what she needed (rest, play, quiet time, fun, and a good dose of freedom), I was able to suggest to her that the larger *whole* of me needs to engage in some focused, intentional, consistent practice in order to achieve what 'we all' want.

Often, it is the unhealed, unappreciated parts of ourselves that try to run the committee meetings. But if we want to truly develop creative capacity, and live fully into our divine Selves, we have to let a more healed, whole part of ourselves facilitate the decision-making process. The physical, mental, emotional, and spiritual discipline involved in practices such as yoga, tai chi, meditation, regular prayer, and other forms of practice are meant to cultivate the detachment, perspective, and higher decision-making ability that these more mature parts of ourselves have.

What sorts of spiritual practices do you engage in? And how consistent are you with them? Frequently, after the rush and high of sudden awakenings, we can find ourselves disappointed that further spiritual development requires conscious discipline and practice. And yet this sort of discipline actually paves the way for future 'sudden' awakenings. In reality, long stretches of routine practice—daily meditation, consistent yoga, regular prayer or chanting, faithful hiking or fitness training—can give way to huge bursts of transformation. What may seem like a sudden, acute burst of awareness was probably being cultivated, silently and secretly, through those seemingly fruitless hours of practice that weren't giving any obvious results.

One way this became clear to me was when my hiking routine changed, after I moved from the temperate San Francisco area to the much more hot, humid, and weather-blessed region of the Smoky Mountains. In California, I could hike pretty much any time of day, any day of the week, year-round. In Tennessee, I have to deal with hot, humid days in the summer, and cold, snowy, icy and miserable rainy days in the winter. Where I could easily hike 10-15 miles per week in the San Francisco area, I've found I can barely get in 5 miles a week in my new East Coast home. The combination of limited good weather hours, and the much more difficult climate conditions, have conspired to severely limit my hiking habit. And it took me a few months to realize just how much this was stifling my spiritual development.

At first, I thought I was just experiencing a lull in my progress because of other circumstances: new relationships, a new job, a new business, a new community. But I found myself feeling more negative, more stuck, and more in struggle, than usual. I noticed that, as soon as I was on the hiking trail, I would begin grinning foolishly. I was profoundly happy the whole time I was on the trail, giddy over the smallest things: the movement of a butterfly's wings, the color of tree bark, the sound of the woodpeckers in the trees. I was absolutely elevated out of any troubles, any gloom, just by stepping into the woods. And that raised my vibration. I had not truly realized just how much hiking was an essential, necessary spiritual activity for me. Sure, I knew it made me fitter, and made me feel good, and gave me spiritual awareness and a sense of well-being and belonging. But I hadn't understood just how much that practice effected my overall spiritual state, and my ability to progress spiritually when I wasn't on the trail.

Ultimately, this realization was a blessing in disguise, because it taught me—with all those voices of resistance against discipline—that I actually need to embrace spiritual practices with a certain kind of conscious intent. Kept away from my habitual hiking practice by new circumstances, I found myself needing to cultivate other practices more consciously. So I set a greater intention for my yoga practice, and hired a physical trainer to help me hone and strengthen my body. I learned new meditation techniques, and began working regularly with a life coach. In other words, when I found myself deprived of a somewhat unconscious spiritual discipline, I discovered the value of such disciplines and became more proactive about cultivating them in my life.

> ### Exercise #35: Your Spiritual Disciplines
>
> What regular practices do you engage in that help you maintain a spiritual, energetic flow? These may be classes, or spiritual gatherings in community; they may be private or public, individual or communal. You may have practices that are daily, weekly, monthly, or yearly—in fact, it's a good idea to have practices that you cultivate within all these time frames. Take a moment to list all the things you do regularly that either are, or could become, spiritual practices. And then take a moment to consider any other disciplines or practices you have considered, or would like to cultivate. What is stopping you? If there are any voices at the conference table trying to prevent you from becoming more proactive, focused and intentional in your spiritual growth, identify them and their real needs.

Setting Intentions

My partner likes to say that all spiritual practices, all rituals, all forms of spiritual engagement, are just different ways of setting intention. When we pray for something, we are clearly setting an intention for a particular outcome. When we create a vision board, or repeat affirmations, we are clearly setting an intention. But we must also consider the possibility that every action, every breath, every unconscious and repetitive thought, is also an intention. When we engage in complaining or collective negativity, we are setting an intention. When we insist on speaking with integrity, or avoiding gossip or other destructive uses of words, we are setting an intention. When we breathe deeply, we are setting an intention.

So, just what exactly is intention, anyway? And what does setting an intention really *do*, energetically? We can compare intentions to emotions, in that both are like bows, shooting energy outward into the universe, and inevitably triggering a reply that comes back to us. When we send energy out—in the form of words, feelings, thoughts, or actions—energy comes back that matches what we have emitted. This is why everything that we send out can be considered an intention; what we send out tells the universe exactly what we intend or expect to receive in return. For the most part, humans run around sending out intention after intention, without any conscious awareness that they are asking, *directly and clearly*, for certain kinds of experiences in return.

Wherever our attention goes, there goes our intention, as well.

When we send out road rage, we shouldn't be surprised that we encounter bad traffic regularly, because putting our *attention* on negative driving experiences tells the universe, "Hey, I really am aware of negative driving! This is what matters to me!" If we focus on the horrors of the nightly news, we need to not be surprised when we feel depressed, hopeless, and more and more aware of all the things that *aren't* working around us. By the same token, when we put our attention on things that please us, we are sending the intention out that we would like more of such things. The universe, being an excellent manifestor of whatever we focus on, will gladly give us more of whatever we pay attention to.

In my experience, Abraham/Esther Hicks and the teachings generated by them are some of the best resources available on this subject. Many students of Abraham have created courses, trainings, books, and other materials that use this information in excellent and helpful ways. But you can find the same essential truths in the wisdom traditions of human history, from all over the world. And it is one of the hardest things for us humans to master!

I know that, for me, getting into the vibration of "what is possible" rather than staying all tangled up in what's going wrong, can be incredibly challenging. And there's another complication: while we need to put our attention on positive possibilities, that doesn't mean ignoring or avoiding difficult emotions or situations. Too often, we can use 'staying positive' as an excuse to avoid important, unpleasant feelings, memories and blocks in your system. It's important, even essential, to balance recognizing, admitting, and *releasing* old pain and old patterns, with keeping your eye of what's going well, and noticing how much progress you're making towards your dreams. This balance is at the center of spiritual practice: appreciating what is, and being excited about what could be.

11

I am Godde:
Finding Worthiness

If you have reached this proactive stage of the spiritual journey, or even had glimpses of it while working through the other stages, then you may have come across what may be the hardest, most slippery of all spiritual roadblocks: a deep sense of unworthiness. Most of us have this little monster hiding somewhere in our being—perhaps in your bank account, or your romantic relationships, or your professional career. And it can be so elusive! We think we've got the feeling that "I'm not good enough" licked, only to discover it lurking underneath another goal, another dream, or another prospect for expansion. If you were raised in western culture, then you almost certainly have some felings of unworthiness hiding out somewhere in your energy field.

Western culture, regardless of our personal religious or cultural backgrounds, is built on a core mythology that sets us up to feel bad about ourselves. While we are encouraged to have big ego defenses—to defend ourselves as good and powerful individuals—we are nonetheless programmed to think that this power is *external* rather than internal. The concept of 'original sin' has been around for a very long time, and it is embedded in our educational system, our economy, and our cultural mythos about identity and relationship. (And if you happen to self-identify as a woman, the residue from that particular set of stories, especially the "Garden of Eden" story, can be especially troubling.)

In Western culture, we have a deep belief that we are, by merit of being human beings on planet earth, inherently 'broken' or inadequate. If you compound this cultural baseline with specific experiences, lessons, or traumas that reinforced the belief that you're not good enough, you may find this particularly challenging to overcome. The feeling of unworthiness sits there, quietly acting as the secret saboteur, under the surface of a lot of dreaming, hoping, and striving for expansion and growth. While there is certainly value in almost all cultural stories and myths, they nonetheless can burden us with the legacy of some really problematic unconscious beliefs. Thinking of ourselves as inherently broken or corrupt, even very unconsciously, can slow down or even stop the spiritual process once we've gotten past the initial burst of awakenings.

What does it mean to think of ourselves as "worthy"? First, we have to ask: worthy of what? From whom? The concept of worthiness implies some sort of receiving, which requires a giver. Who is the giver in this model? Who has the power to give or withhold the good you are seeking?

Exercise #36: Giver of the Goods

Consider for a moment what the 'good things' are that you wish to receive. Do you wish for more money, or more free time? A more loving relationship, or more opportunities to do public speaking? What are you wishing you could *receive* from the universe? Now consider who you believe has the power to *give* these things to you? Do you believe, all the way deep down in every level of your being, that you can give them to yourself? Or do you have a feeling that someone or something else is going to have to at least cooperate if you are to get what you want? In the past, who had the power to give or withhold things you needed or desired? And were they generous or miserly with those things? Take a moment to inventory your experiences of desiring, requesting, and receiving or not receiving, the things you wished for.

It's one thing to wish to be healed from a serious illness, or to be freed from a very serious financial crisis. These are things that almost always seem reasonable and justified for us to request. But what about asking for *more*? What about asking not just for enough money to get out of debt, but enough to buy your own jet? What about desiring not just a career you love, but a career that requires almost no work, while allowing you to travel whenever and wherever you like? What about inviting not just a solid, loving, great partner, but asking for someone who is amazing, out-of-the-ordinary awesome?

How many of us hear these things and think "well that's selfish! And not very realistic, either!"

We each have our own 'set point' or internal glass ceiling for what we believe we are worthy of. Depending on our experiences and training, we may have a high set point in one area, while having low set points in other areas. These upper limits of what we deem to be "good" desires or levels of success and happiness, determine what is possible for us. Often, we have upper limits that match the upper limits our parents or family members achieved; we may unconsciously want to do our best, live the best life possible, *so long as we don't go too far beyond what our parents managed.* We may feel that, if we go too far in the direction of an amazing life, it will hurt and alienate others—whom we love—who have not yet achieved that kind of happiness or success.

Usually, there is some cost-benefit trade off going on when we don't allow ourselves to feel fully worthy. Sometimes, worthiness implies too much comparison or competition with others. Just as we can imagine there's not enough money, or resources, or time to go around, we can also imagine that our higher self-worth actually diminishes the self-worth of others. But this is only true if worthiness is given by an external, rather than an internal, source. If my self-worth and your self-worth are completely innate in us; if we each have an infinite reservoir of feeling good about ourselves, then there's no problem. It's only when my self-worth depends on being 'better' than someone else, or 'more' than someone else (more fit, more beautiful, more successful, more competent, more cheerful, etc) that there is a limit to how much self-worth can go around. In fact, this sort of external self-worth is pretty darned limited: the less internal self-worth I have, the less I'm likely to be generous with 'giving' it to others, or seeing it in them.

In order for us to truly believe, and act as if, we are worthy of the infinite good that is our divine birthright, we have to let go of thinking that our worth comes from anywhere other than our own hearts. And that can take some doing. Because we have likely internalized many of those committee voices first spoken by teachers, parents, television ads, and others, we might not be able to hear when we are devaluing ourselves. We will just hear those messages as "truth." We may actually believe that we are inherently weak, flawed, or impaired in the ways they told us. Uncovering all the places where we are minimizing ourselves because we were told to, is an important step in freeing up our creative power.

So how do you find your hidden feelings of unworthiness?

For most of us, there are some obvious places to look for low self-worth: all the places you simply won't make changes you know you need to make, and really *want* to make, are the first hiding places to explore. Second, look in the places where you most loudly *proclaim* your worth. More often than not, the 'self-worth' that needs to shout about itself, is probably hiding some much deeper feelings of inadequacy and failure. True self-worth doesn't need to be heard, or affirmed; it simply is. Third, look to the things you simply avoid consistently: books you say you want to read, classes you say you want to take, jobs you want to consider, people you want to connect with. All of these are likely hiding places for a belief that you're not good enough, not ready, not worthy. Finally, look to the places where you feel despair, hopelessness, or apathy. If you've given up on something that you once really wanted or believed in, chances are good that somewhere deep down you've decided it's "just not for you."

There are certainly other places where low self-worth can hide, including places where you settle for less than you desire, where you don't follow your own advice, or where you criticize others for their lack of self-worth. Take a few minutes to consider which of these possible areas might be places where unconscious feelings unworthiness could be hiding.

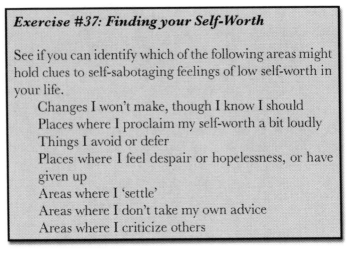

Exercise #37: Finding your Self-Worth

See if you can identify which of the following areas might hold clues to self-sabotaging feelings of low self-worth in your life.

Changes I won't make, though I know I should
Places where I proclaim my self-worth a bit loudly
Things I avoid or defer
Places where I feel despair or hopelessness, or have given up
Areas where I 'settle'
Areas where I don't take my own advice
Areas where I criticize others

Wanting to Stay Down

After you've mastered, or at least tamed, your feeling of unworthiness, you may still find yourself struggling to make progress in certain areas of spiritual and material development. Why would that be so? If you've figured out how much magic and potential you have, and you've decided you *deserve* to have the life of your dreams; if you've equipped yourself with the tools you need to move forward, and released tons of baggage and limiting beliefs, why would you still feel stuck?

The answer may be wishing to stay small. Caroline Myss describes this aspect of ourselves as the "victim" archetype, and says that we all have it, to some degree or another. [8] I know that, on my own journey, coming to terms with my inner victim—learning about her determination to practice self-pity, and her fierce commitment to remaining small—has been essential to forward motion. She shows up when

---

[8] Caroline Myss, *Sacred Archetypes.*

I need more rest, or more support; she yells loudest when I am violating my own boundaries, and tries to blame others (rather than me) for making harmful choices.

There are, after all, some seeming 'drawbacks' to claiming our own full power, and it's wise to acknowledge them before going any further. Of course, they aren't real drawbacks, but our egos can perceive them as such.

Being willing to have total agency in our own lives is a risky and dangerous business. It usually means giving up some comforts that we've gotten used to, including blame, guilt, and settling for less. Even though claiming full power in our lives might sound great at first, the truth is that most of us kind of like being victims, to one extent or another. This is one reason we find ourselves holding back, and sabotaging our best intentions. We're not so sure, deep down, that we want to have to take full credit—and responsibility—for absolutely everything that shows up in our lives. The ego, especially, isn't fond of this situation, because it means letting the heart and the high Self take the driver's seat.

So long as we remain in the 'responsive' mode, we can brush off part of the responsibility for our lives to outside forces. We can blame the imprint of parental failures, or the toxins of a troubled society, or the restrictions of economic forces outside our control. All of these and so much more provide handy reasons why we can't have the reality we say we want. And, so long as we believe in these external limits, they do control us. But after a while, after we've started to see the potential of our own creative Selves, we may have to face the possibility the we are a little addicted to our limitations. We can probably attribute a lot of this hesitation to fear of the unknown. We may wish for a new home, or new career, or new partner, but of course we know deep down that these things come with some unpredictable details. We can't possibly imagine or predict *everything* that will come with fulfilled desires; we have to give some of the details over to the multiverse. And that is a little frightening.

What will it actually be like if I get all I want? What will I have to give up, or lose, along the way? What will change that I didn't imagine changing? And will I really like it as much as I think I will? What if I've been imaging something that turns out to be awful?

I would have to say that this is the stage I find myself at in my own journey. I have had innumerable experiences of manifesting amazing things: jobs, relationships, money, health, and material comforts. And yet I persist in clinging to occasional dissatisfaction, and a feeling that somehow someone or something out there is 'stopping me' from creating the life that I truly want. Or do I?

What would happen if I got everything I dream of, all of it, and found myself experiencing all of it at the same time? Frankly, that thought frightens me a little bit. What would that mean? What would I find myself having to let go of? What if I succeeded in all those areas of my life? Could I really manage that much money/joy/success? Lately, this has been the area of spiritual awakening that has had my attention. And I've been discovering some fascinating beliefs that hold my limitations in place.

For example, the other day it occurred to me for the first time that I associate greater light, greater well-being, and greater success with *much* greater responsibility to others. In other words, the more filled with light I become, and the more this shows outwardly, the more people who will show up 'needing' me to take care of them. I feel this belief kinesthetically as if there are 'hangers-on' clinging to my actual body, like leaches draining my energy and resources.

Now where in the world did I get that idea? Somehow, I took in a belief that my greater good requires my greater service *in volume, rather than just in quality.* I have been holding back from growing more successful, financially, artistically, and spiritually, because I believed that I would have to increase my actual *work load* to match the uptake in vibration. But that's not true at all.

Underneath my desire to grow and expand, I was holding myself back because I held a limiting belief about growth and expansion itself. I assumed that one of the consequences of taking full responsibility for my well-being, and choosing a fabulous life that I loved, would be having to take on a *penalty* of greater work, exhaustion and depletion. Hence, staying a victim, to some extent, served me well because it kept me within a 'safe' zone of self-care, rest and not over-giving. This is a complex tangle of desire and self-sabotage, and it's just these very sorts of beliefs that we get to untangle at the more advanced levels of spiritual maturation.

As I go through this phase of the journey, I am continuously surprised by the stories, beliefs, patterns, and identities I have been embodying and claiming. My own life coach, an incredible woman trained in Christy Whitman's Quantum Success Coaching model, knows just the right questions to ask me when I'm grappling with places of limitation. "What," she frequently asks, "do you like about having that belief or experience?" It must have some really great value to me, or I wouldn't be hanging onto it. Often, when I really let myself enjoy explaining all the *great* things about a limiting belief, I am thrilled by the new awareness and the new possibilities that arise. And I am learning that this is actually the whole point:

You have to enjoy never being done with it!

When we reach this stage of the spiritual journey, the whole point is never to 'get it all right' or 'have it all done.' The point is to realize that there's 'endless joyful creation' as long as we choose to be here, and that means (as Abraham puts it) constant contrast. Without contrast—without seeing limits that can be transcended—we would probably just be bored. The trick, then, is to shift from seeing our 'limits' as problems, and instead to see them as fun opportunities. The trick is to see that I'll never create it 'all' because there is no actual end to the 'all' I might discover I want to create!

When we reach the truly proactive, creative state of being, where we are ready to truly and consistently co-create with this magical multiverse, we are ready to release all ideas of right and wrong, good and bad, success and failure. We develop a kind of equanimity, so that everyday synchronicities, minor daily miracles, and a pervasive sense of our own eternal soul become as sublime as the ecstatic peaks we will still sometimes experience. I believe this is the stage we are trying to achieve as an earth community. Enough of us have done the hard work of the crisis phase that, as a collective, we are ready to move away from our victimhood to our true creativity. We are on the verge, as a soul family of earth beings, to let go just a little bit more of our perpetual attachment to struggle. And the step many of us need to take at this time is just letting ourselves have fun no matter what's happening, rather than working so hard to 'fix' ourselves and everything around us.

If contrast is essential to the earth experience—and it seems to be so—then what we need to do at this stage is not figure out what else we need to "work on," but instead enjoy the fact there's nothing to learn, nothing to do, and nothing to fix. As Tony Robbins puts it, "our problem is thinking that we shouldn't have any." (*I Am Not Your Guru*)[9]

Human beings are storytellers and meaning makers; we rely on narratives to help us make sense of our world, and our place in it. What if we began to tell stories that weren't about our brokenness, as individuals, as societies, and as a global community, but rather were about how amazing, creative, interesting, and diverse we are? What if we re-narrated the 'problems' into creative opportunities, and storied the 'challenges' as fascinating learning experiences? This might seem impossible, but it's easier if we simply remember one thing:

I am Godde. You are Godde. There is nothing but Godde, and nothing but love, anywhere, ever. It's just us manifesting ourSelf in incredibly infinite, contrasting and perplexing but miraculous ways. Distance from this awareness—that we are each all Divine—certainly creates painful, challenging experiences. But it doesn't change the essential truth of who we are. If we are indeed eternal, infinite, divine beings, then there's nothing wrong, there never was anything wrong. There are just lots and lots of opportunities to explore, imagine, reimagine, create, and explore again, and infinite opportunities to recall our divinity.

I said much earlier in this book that there are, at advanced levels of spiritual awareness, ways to 'protect' ourselves that don't require defining ourselves as separate. This is the place where that happens. When we are able to truly experience ourselves as one with all life, when we are able to fully experience that everything is divine, the way we keep ourselves 'safe' changes. Rather than needing to

---

[9] Tony Robbins, "I Am Not Your Guru" HBO documentary 2016

put up energetic boundaries between ourselves and others, we simply choose to only connect with the divine in all that we encounter. We simply choose to be unrelated to, unaffected by, anything that is *not* divine. Many teachers are now advocating this method over the more familiar techniques of creating energy boundaries around ourselves. Only you can decide what feels better to you, but try this method out, if you are so inclined. See what it's like to simply see the Godde in everything you encounter. Perhaps, if you do so with enough commitment, clarity and love, even those in your presence who *can't* see their own divinity will be able to get the first glance of its hidden sweetness in themselves. Perhaps some of our 'problems' are just opportunities to show others that, despite their behavior or limitations, they too are divine beings waiting to be recognized.

Union with the Beloved

The everyday self gets very caught up in the struggles of daily, physical existence. I have to deal with a kitten who wakes me up in the night, financial worries that slow down my creative juices, a car that needs an oil change, and the ten thousand other things that the Taoists urge us to not be distracted by. And yet, it is these very ten thousand things that are my gateway to nirvana, to bliss, to infinity. In the Buddhist tradition, the *Vajrayana* path is one that I hope to embrace fully. For me, it is full presence, with full awareness of my divine Self and the oneness of all things, that makes daily life rich, rather than exhausting. And that feeling of richness, that sense of well-being, is simply one thought away, at any time. It is up to *me*, and no one else, to see the Godde in all things I encounter.

No one else can see, for me, the divine blessing in every illusory challenge. No one but me can see each difficulty as the doorway to my next great desire, the gateway to another experience of ecstasy. No one but me can know, for me, that I am utterly one with Godde.

Union with the Beloved is not somewhere 'out there' to be achieved or accomplished, but rather something to simply be remembered. If I put my attention there, then that's where my intention goes. If I choose to, I can experience my divine Self at any time simply by recognizing the divinity in each moment.

I know, I know—easier said than done. So practice, and enjoy yourself while you do it.

When my daughter turned 18, she purposefully went to a tattoo artist and got a tattoo of a compass on the inside of her left arm. The symbolic significance of this act was clear and powerful for her: the compass represents her own 'true north' which, from that moment on, was no longer *external to her,* but rather a part of her very body. In this way, she made a clear statement to her own psyche, and to all others, that her own inner Self would be her guide. On the spiritual journey, we all encounter the same landmarks that others have encountered before us. The spiritual terrain, because it is a *truth* throughout time and space, has been traveled by all who walk through this life hoping to wake up. And yet we each must be our own compass, our own guide. Each of us must chart our own course across the landscape of mystical experiences, of integrating body, mind, heart and soul. As you travel forward, let your own inner compass be your guide. Let the wisdom and experiences of others inform and influence you, but trust your own deepest Self to know the way that is right for you.

Take time to really, truly enjoy whatever you have available to enjoy, even the smallest and most simple of pleasures. Joy is the true pathway. Each of our journeys is unique, but the travel guide is the same for all of us:

Follow what brings you peace. Trust what gives you joy. Allow what shows you your heart's true desire. The road map is within you.

May your journey be blessed.

Printed in the United States
By Bookmasters